The Star Shiner

The Star Shiner

Memoir of a Celebrity Make-Up Artist

EVAN RICHARDSON

McFarland & Company, Inc., Publishers

Jefferson, North Carolina, and London

LIBRARY OF CONGRESS CATALOGUING-IN-PUBLICATION DATA

Richardson, Evan
  The star shiner : memoir of a celebrity make-up artist / Evan
Richardson.
      p.   cm.
  Includes index.

  ISBN 978-0-7864-7096-9
  softcover : acid free paper ∞

  1. Richardson, Evan, 1946– 2. Makeup artists—United
States—Biography.   3. Film makeup.   4. Theatrical makeup.
I. Title.
  TT955.R53.A3 2013
  646.7'2092—dc23   2013012991

BRITISH LIBRARY CATALOGUING DATA ARE AVAILABLE

On the cover: Portrait of Evan Richardson, June 2012
(photograph by Steve Ladner)

Manufactured in the United States of America

McFarland & Company, Inc., Publishers
  Box 611, Jefferson, North Carolina 28640
    www.mcfarlandpub.com

To those who dream
and dare to travel the road
to the end of the rainbow.

Table of Contents

Acknowledgments

The publishing of this book I must credit mostly to people that few, other than a small group, have ever heard of, but without whom this book would not exist.

I had been sending out query letter to agents for a couple of years after the final draft of the book was completed, and had had some success getting interest, but for one reason or another the agents were unsuccessful getting the book through the right doors. I had tried to convey from the beginning that my book was not a celebrity memoir of my work with celebrities but rather the story of my life as a young artist starting out in the big city of New York and the pitfalls I ran into—not the least being my own careless behavior—as many young artists no doubt still experience today.

But the agents kept pushing the celebrity angle. I was even told that no one cared about my life and the celebrities were the meat of the book and would be the success of it, which, in one respect, may be true. I began to feel like a nobody with some credentials that no one wanted to hear about. But I felt that I had a compelling story to tell, and some might want to hear it.

Then, a miracle! A man from a church I had begun to attend heard that I had written a book, and since he was about to publish a book (*Lillian Lorraine: The Life and Times of a Ziegfeld Diva*), he asked to see portions of my book. He liked what he read and immediately referred me to his publisher, McFarland, into whose performing arts line my book fit. McFarland read my book and liked it, and that is why the first person that I need to thank is Nils Hanson, a wonderful writer and a kind, generous human being who is responsible for bringing my book to life. Thank you, Nils, from the bottom of my heart for the kindness in your heart. Bless you always.

In my book I guess I do a bit of Mother-bashing. This is not to imply that my follies are to be blamed on my mother. For those I blame myself. I loved my mother deeply, and therein lay our problems. She loved me dearly, as I loved her. We were intertwined like two vines, and it was hard to tell which was which at times. My conflict with my mother came from my trying to untwist what we had twisted together so that I could be my own vine. I never achieved it in her lifetime. Our twisting was so strong that if she were alive today, I doubt I could have achieved my own success separate from her. I've often wondered if I even would have been able to write a book. The untwining that became possible after she was gone allowed me to breathe freely for the first time after a life of nearly suffocating.

Still, without my mother my book might not have been possible. When I was a child, she read to me all the wonderful children's stories that transported me to many enchanting places. Her voice reading those stories to me is the voice of the muse that I still hear today when I write. She taught me right from wrong—that I value most. And from her I learned to stick with things no matter the course, which is why this book is a reality today. Her absence will always leave a vacant, unfulfillable space in my heart.

So, thank you, Mother. I loved you as dearly as I know you loved me, and I always will. And I know that we never intentionally meant to hurt one another. Sometimes in anger things slip out, and in this we were both at fault.

Then there is my sister, Kitty, whom I need to thank. Many times she may have felt left out or taken a back seat because of Mother's and my intertwining, and for that I apologize. My sister was adopted and recently found her family of origin with my encouragement, but she will always be my sister. This is not to say there have not been difficult times as siblings sometimes have, perhaps aggravated by the situation with my mother and me—but my sister and I persevered and remain brother and sister. She has helped me financially when I have come to the end of my resources; she has encouraged me when I have come to the end of my understanding, and she has helped me remain strong when I have been about to crumble. Thank you, Kitty. I will always be grateful for your presence in my life and in the life of our family. Without you there would be another vacant space in my heart.

I want to acknowledge Steve Ladner, who has come to my rescue many times. He's a wonderful photographer in his own right and a wonderful artist in general. He kindly retouched images for me for this book and even took the photograph that appears on the cover. Several years ago he and I tried to begin a portrait business together with him doing the photography and me doing the make-up. It failed but we learned from it—perhaps never to do it again since everyone today, it seems, has a camera and doesn't need a portrait. He has been a trustworthy, personal and professional friend, and I am lucky to know him.

Without Stella Benakis at the Francesco Scavullo Foundation, I don't know how I would have put this book together. She has made phone calls on my behalf, given me dates for Scavullo's photos when I was clueless, and always been there when I needed her. Thank you, Stella, for all of your thoughtful help.

Then there is the New York Public Library, to which I owe a big debt of gratitude. Whenever I had a word of whose usage I was unsure, or needed information like dates, or needed incidents to be clarified, *Ask NYPL* was there five days a week until 6 PM to help me. Their staff tirelessly looked up information, usage of words, and any matter that I needed to make me look literate. Thank you, *Ask NYPL*.

I want to thank a group of people who are unknown, except to those who love them, as I do, but who have stuck with me throughout my many ordeals in life and remained there, in spite of our differences at times, and helped me through troubles I wasn't sure I'd survive, or even wanted to: Thank you, Marsha, my godchildren Jamie and Stephanie, Ellen Lee, Phyllis, Michael P., and Celeste and Karen, newer friends, but treasures, and all the wonderful friends I have been blessed to know at the Central Presbyterian Church on Park Ave. in New York City. And thank you New York City, and also Pratt Institute, for making my dreams in life possible.

Lastly, and perhaps most important of all, I want to thank Michael K., my loving friend and partner, who died 30 years ago of AIDS when the scourge first swept the country, when there was no hope or choice but to die. We were innocent then, foolish, yes, which doesn't excuse our careless behavior, but we knew no better than to take avenues that were destructive. His loving memory will always be a living presence in my life.

Thanks to everyone for your contribution to my book and to my life. Without any one of you I wouldn't have been able to write a book. It is with your love and support that I am now a published author.

Blessings to all of you always,
Evan

Preface

In 1997 I was delighted to receive an invitation from fashion photographer Francesco Scavullo to attend a party that Helen Gurley Brown was giving him at the Pierre Hotel on Fifth Avenue to celebrate his new book, *Scavullo: Photographs 50 Years*. Though it had been several years since we had worked together, I knew Scavullo and his crowd well. I had designed make-up for the fashion industry for more than twenty-five years.

When I arrived in the exquisite marbled interior, I immediately spotted Francesco standing alongside Helen greeting the guests. Pasting on my best smile, I joined the receiving line. Though I had done Helen's make-up several years before at Francesco's studio, she still had to be reminded who I was. Perhaps too many *Cosmo* deadlines and face patch-ups had dimmed her memory.

After the introduction, I glided into a lushly carpeted living room with wrap-around windows overlooking the city where guests in expensive evening attire—signifying a function to be reckoned with—mingled about sipping champagne served by white-uniformed waiters and waitresses dressed as upstairs French maids. Other guests were in the wood-paneled library, chatting in the hallway, or seated at white linen–covered tables, scanning the room to see who was there and encountering other eyes scanning back. Pale noodle-shaped models with heavily-mascaraed eyes languished at the sides of handsome, imperious-looking young men and peered out from dark corners as if there to suck blood.

At one of the tables I glimpsed a well-known, glamorous older model, one of Richard Avedon's cast-off favorites, her snow-white hair pristinely sculpted atop her head, chatting with a group of gay men while her peripheral vision checked the attendance for more promising game.

In the center of the room, as if placed there by divine authority, was

1

Ivana Trump, eyes darting about, making sure she was being observed and fleeing her perch when her ex, the Donald, slumped in looking more like a mussed-up shoe salesman than a billionaire tycoon. Also there were Martha Stewart (photographed by Scavullo at seventeen), the ex–jean queen Gloria Vanderbilt, Geraldo Rivera, Joel Grey, Tommy Tune, and the enormously tall transvestite RuPaul, who would stand out in any crowd.

I stationed myself by the dining room doorway and queued up for the elaborate buffet complete with an ice-sculptured swan when a hairdresser who had done Elizabeth Taylor's hair when I made her up for a *Good House-keeping* cover trundled over. Looking somewhat prematurely embalmed, from too much booze, he declared we were the only living artists who had started with Francesco back in the seventies.

I glanced around the room and it suddenly looked as though Madame Tussaud's wax museum had come alive, or a taxidermist had gone berserk and this was the results. The majority there had had their heyday in the seventies—and so had we.

As if we didn't get the message, when we gathered later on the small dance floor dancing to the music selections of Lady Bunny, an infamous downtown Manhattan transvestite, another transvestite got up and lip-synched Alicia Bridges' seventies disco anthem: "I Love the Night Life."

When I was danced out and sufficiently sloshed from champagne, I searched for Francesco and found him in a downstairs living room reviewing his years of work on a TV monitor with some familiar hangers-on from the "old days," still hanging on. I thanked him for the party, turned to the hangers-on and acknowledged them, and as I stepped into the nearly vacant street below, Bridges' anthem still echoed in my ears.

On my walk home, only a short distance from the Pierre, I reflected on the party, the nostalgia, the memories, the old relics that were still there—decades past their prime—and I was glad I wasn't part of that anymore when at one time it had all seemed so important.

"It was the best of times, it was the worst of times," Charles Dickens' immortal *A Tale of Two Cities* begins. In this case, it was the Rip-Roaring Seventies, and everyone scrambled for an invitation to the party.

Like the Roaring Twenties that followed the First World War and ended with the Depression, the seventies paralleled the Jazz Age in its excess, decadence, social upheaval, and re-evaluation that culminated this time with one of the cruellest, most deadly diseases ever inflicted on humankind: AIDS.

After a prim-and-proper, wholesome-and-homespun fifties, America was tired of acting a part and got real in the sixties with race riots, student revolts, leaders gunned down, psychedelic drugs and free love, and the country began one of its bloodiest wars in Vietnam.

It was a time when men grew moustaches and long hair and women emulated little girls in mini skirts and boots. Andy Warhol gave the art world Campbell soup cans, and pop icons Janis Joplin, Jim Morrison, and Jimi Hendrix burned up their young lives with excess as the Seventies began—pointing to the dangers that lay ahead.

While there was a kind of innocence about the Sixties, the promiscuous sex and excessive drug use they introduced defined the Seventies and turned those years into the most hedonistic decade America had ever known. It was the era of wife swapping at Plato's Retreat, dizzy, druggy nights at New York's notorious disco Studio 54, and dangerous, downtown homosexual sex-dungeons like the Mine Shaft and the Anvil.

Into this mix I arrived from Kentucky, totally unprepared for the turn my life was about to take, but willing to explore it all. I became a prominent make-up artist, one of the first to do make-up for American fashion magazines, and I was swept, like many, into this decadent lifestyle, glorified and promoted by the fashion industry that profited from it.

During the course of 25 years, I did make-up on over 130 stars from every walk of professional life: the film and theatre worlds, dancers, pop and opera singers, TV personalities, politicians, heads of industries, writers, artists, and supermodels. I did their make-up for magazines, TV, publicity, and personal appearances.

As the frenzy whirling around us grew to a creeching crescendo, it was only a matter of time before the dominos of the game came tumbling down. The fall for me was cruel and painful. My partner, my best friend for ten years and someone I loved dearly, was diagnosed with AIDS and died—a young man only 31 years old. The party was over. It was time to get real. We had all believed a lie.

This is the story of my struggle to overcome my own undoing and the torturous pull of my family and find a spiritual path back to life through the ashes of a decade of madness that can be likened to Fitzgerald's description of the twenties: "the most expensive orgy in history."

1

Coming to Town, Modeling in Paris

My mother suggested a poem by Henry Wadsworth Longfellow for me to say to my graduating class when I was salutatorian in my prep school:

> *Lives of great men all remind us*
> *We can make our lives sublime,*
> *And, departing, leave behind us*
> *Footprints on the sands of time....*
>
> *Let us, then, be up and doing,*
> *With a heart for any fate;*
> *Still achieving, still pursuing,*
> *Learn to labor and to wait.*

I had no idea what I was saying at the time or the sacrifice and difficulty that grand profundity entailed. And I wasn't even certain this was my sentiment or my mother's. I only knew that deep inside me I had a burning desire to succeed at something—but what that something was had so far eluded me.

So it was in the late 1950s, after a brief stint in the navy—an obligation every able-bodied young man then faced with the draft—I found myself on my first subway train heading to Pratt Institute in Brooklyn to study commercial art. I already had a B.F.A. degree from the University of Kentucky, but that had promised no more than a life of squalor in a little garret someplace with a bunch of paintings I couldn't sell—hardly my idea of the fame and fortune that I was seeking.

Like the Southern gentleman I was raised to be, I sat rigidly in my seat in my Sunday-best, dark-blue suit with the collar of my white shirt starched to a board and itching like hell and my red hair plastered down with Vitalis hair tonic. I clutched nervously onto my Samsonite bag, terrified that some-one might grab it or that when my stop came I wouldn't be able to make it out the doors in time before they slammed shut and hauled me off to some outback place like Timbuktu, never to be heard from again.

Planning my escape, I naively turned to a woman next to me and inquired which side of the train the doors opened at my stop. She had no idea and probably thought I was a mugger. The other passengers—recogniz-ing the hick I was—compassionately went into a conference and when they were finished it was determined which side the doors would open. When my stop came I grabbed my bag and leaped out the doors like a gazelle freed from captivity.

Lugging my heavy bag up the steep subway stairs to sunlight, I walked to DeKalb Avenue. As far as I could see down the hill in front of me were barren, dusty fields filled with bricks and rocks where houses had been torn down to make way for new construction. It was surreal, like the destruction after the Civil War in *Gone with the Wind*. Next to the dusty fields was a large red brick building that was Pratt Institute, built a little over 20 years after the Civil War in 1887.

Attending Pratt wasn't my heart's desire as it might have been for some other students. It was merely a means to get me out of that small, rural Ken-tucky town where I came from and get to New York where I'd always wanted to be. In my uncle's drugstore one afternoon I came across an ad for Pratt Institute in Brooklyn—not New York but close to it—and that's when my plan began. I had wanted to be an actor—that would have been my heart's desire—but being shy with low self-esteem would have made it painful to be in front of an audience, so I settled on art instead.

During my first year at Pratt, it became apparent that I excelled in the human figure. One of my instructors, Richard Lindner—whose paintings of grotesquely obese, dominatrix women clad in black leather hang in the MoMA—took a liking to me and suggested that I should be a fashion illus-trator. I had never heard of such a thing, but I was grateful someone had finally found something I could do with my art that I hoped would lead me to the fame and fortune I craved.

Rene Bouché—a famous fashion illustrator who drew for *Vogue*, and a friend of Lindner's—had an exhibit at Pratt that year. Lindner observed how I ogled Bouché's drawings in their glass encasement at the exhibit, and when it was over, he gave me as a reward the task of returning the drawings to Bouché personally at his apartment on Central Park South, right up the street from the world-renowned Plaza Hotel. For a poor student with my meager means, who rarely got farther into New York than Greenwich Village on weekends, this was a real treat.

I had read an article in *Vogue* about a painting Bouché was working on that had been commissioned by Tammy Grimes, a Broadway star who would appear in the 1960 musical *The Unsinkable Molly Brown* (which would be made into a film in '64 with Debbie Reynolds). Oh, how I yearned to be in *Vogue* like Bouché. How I yearned to be in anything.

Up in a small continental elevator I went to the top of Bouché's building and rang his doorbell. A small, balding man with a large nose answered—not at all the dashing figure I had envisioned who drew for *Vogue*. My tall frame towered over him, but soon his presence filled the hallway, and the surrounding buildings as well.

"Come in," he said, and like a teenager with a crush, I floated inside.

"Sit down," he commanded, and I did that too.

Everywhere on the walls and tables was his vast collection of fine art that reeked of world travel and success. In a corner of the room—with a large skylight overhead providing natural light for his work, as I had seen in many romantic movies depicting an artist's life—was the painting of Tammy Grimes still in progress.

"Gee," I mused to myself, "I could've had that finished in a day."

He took his drawings that I had treated with such reverence and unceremoniously tossed them onto a pile with others. As he pulled up a chair in front of me where I was rapidly disappearing into a plush, over-stuffed sofa, his dark eyes sized me up with the penetration of a needle.

"So," he began, like a conductor about to tune up a badly out-of-tune orchestra, "what do you want to do?"

"Do?" I repeated, startled that I had to do something.

"With your life."

"Oh, I want to be a fashion illustrator," I merrily chirped, thankful I had the answer.

"Why?"

I was suddenly speechless. I hadn't a clue. My newly discovered life's work was based solely on what Lindner had said, and I certainly couldn't say it was because he had told me to do it.

Soon I was back on the street looking up at Bouché's apartment building with that skylight crowning the top like a giant, pulsating Martian brain. My brush with fame was brief, but I now knew the answer to his question:

I wanted to be adored by *Vogue*, by the celebrities and the art world like him, living in that grand apartment with all that collected fine art—and that frigging skylight too. That was the real truth I had known all along. It didn't matter what the hell I did. I just wanted all of that.

My studies at Pratt completed, I moved into New York to an apartment building on the Lower East Side. Because it was being renovated, it was cheap and affordable; no one wanted to live there with the constant hammering and banging all day. But it was home and New York and—what the heck—I was young.

Armed with a portfolio of my best fashion drawings from Pratt, I began my push for fame and fortune. I envisioned myself making it big in the big city like Bouché. Each day I pounded the pavement, showing my portfolio until the ad agencies and fashion magazines closed.

"Thank you, Mr. Richardson. Your drawings are lovely. We'll put your name on file," I was constantly told.

Me as the boy next door (© Avery Willard).

Each time I left an office I was sure they would call me, but nothing ever came of it. I decided until things changed that maybe I could model. (I've discovered since then that a lot of disillusioned youth think this; why I'm not quite sure.) The model agencies disagreed. They were looking for the boy-next-door type, and I wasn't him.

I located a gym around the Macy's area—a no-nonsense place where truck drivers and construction workers worked out, nothing like the polished, corporate-managed gym chains today—and after several months of intensive daily workouts, I developed an impressive set of muscles that got me noticed on the street more than the front page of the *New York Times*. Back to the agencies I went, and this time one of them took me. All it took was that set of muscles to turn me into the boy next door—and the biggest whore in town.

The agency sent me for test shots from a photographer who worked for *Seventeen* magazine. New models need photos, and photographers test to try out new ideas. There's no pay, and when a real job comes along the better-known models usually get it, but testing still mutually benefits everyone.

The photographer agreed to test me, but when he gave me his portfolio to review, inside were only male nudes—some of the top models at that time. The deal was that I would get what I wanted when he got what he wanted—namely, me in the buff. I had no experience in these matters, but that was too progressive for me.

I got the shots I needed from less demanding photographers and began to work a bit, but not enough to support myself. Soon I was back making the rounds again—this time with both my modeling and fashion illustration portfolios.

One afternoon I stopped by B. Altman's department store on Fifth Avenue, intending to make an appointment to show my drawings. While I waited in the reception area for a secretary to finish her phone call, a tall, attractive man in a dark suit dashed out of his office and said, "Come in. We've been waiting for you."

Either he had mistaken me for someone else or he'd had too many martinis for lunch, but whomever he was expecting, he was getting me. I quickly followed him into his office, where he flipped through my portfolio, punctuating each flip with some sound of approval. When he finished, he buzzed some people on his intercom, and in marched his brainwashed staff. They, too, flipped through my portfolio and, coaxed by him, made similar sounds of approval.

When they completed their review, he slammed the portfolio shut and said, "You'll be making $50,000 this year and we'll increase it to $60,000 next year. Give my secretary your name and address, and we'll send you the clothes tomorrow."

That was it. And he didn't even know my name—and had the wrong person besides.

I went out in a daze. The amount he had quoted was equivalent to five times that amount today. I immediately called my mother to report the incident to her. She was as dumbfounded as I was.

Early the next morning the clothes arrived. Throughout the week, many more clothes arrived. Along with them came my old insecurities. With the noise in the building all day and sometimes into the evening and the difficulty of turning out that much work with no experience other than school, it was all too overwhelming. Soon the almost giddy success ended and I was back pushing the portfolios again.

At Saks Fifth Avenue there was a well-known fashion illustrator, Tod Draz, who did their ads and also drew for the fashion section of the *New York Times*. Along with Rene Bouché and Eric, who drew for *Vogue*, Tod was considered one of the best fashion artists in the business.

I concocted a plan to go to him as a model, but my real purpose was to snoop to see how he did his work. I thought that if I could just get some pointers, maybe I could improve my chances the next time. I was even hoping to convince B. Altman's to rehire me.

Tod was interested, but more in me than in imparting information. After a few sexual skirmishes with him that I managed to dodge, we became friends—at least that's what I thought at the time. What I did learn was that he was as insecure as I was and it took him many tries, as it did me, to get one decent drawing. The difference was that he had experience and could achieve results quicker than I could.

He introduced me to all his fashion pals, like Carrie Donovan, fashion editor of the *New York Times*, who, many years later, would appear in Old Navy TV commercials. With her huge, face-consuming, black-rimmed, owlish glasses, she was quite distinguished, if not frightening.

Then the unexpected happened: Tod called to say he was moving to Paris. He was as tired of the rat race in New York as I was becoming. With him leaving, all my chances of ever improving my art seemed to vanish. Then he asked me to go too. He promised to help me get started in modeling and said he'd introduce me to all of his Paris fashion friends.

He left and wrote encouraging letters from Paris, painting the life I could have there as a utopia. That fall I boarded the *Île de France* for a five-day voyage across the Atlantic to an unknown place where I hoped to find the elusive fame and fortune that I was still searching for.

My Atlantic crossing was an arduous one that confined me mostly to the bathroom recovering from seasickness. When the ship docked in Le Havre, I took the boat train into Gare St. Lazare in Paris. From there I took a taxi to Tod's apartment on the Avenue de Versailles.

It was early evening when, under clumps of cotton-candy clouds that rolled across the Parisian sky as in a Fragonard painting, my taxi passed in the distance the Arc de Triomphe and the Tour Eiffel, while, like a public offering of classical soft-porn, nude baroque statues were everywhere with massive drapery swirling around their bodies. Other than Canada and Mexico, this strange, wondrous place was as far away from my country as I had ever been.

After an overnight stay in a hotel close to Tod's apartment, I went with him the following morning to a cheaper hotel where a friend of Tod's had stayed on the Left Bank in the St. Germain-des-Prés area. The Hotel Béarn, owned by a Monsieur and Madame Lapalou, would be my home during my time in Paris.

Madame Lapalou was a tall, plump, rosy-cheeked woman with massive breasts that spilled out over the tops of her blouses. Her iodine-red hair was piled high in a pompadour in the front of her head while, in the back, she was practically bald. Her bright red lips were usually smeared across her face from too much wine and kissing everyone—particularly the men—who came in or went out of the hotel.

Monsieur Lapalou was a big, jolly Santa Claus–like man with rosy cheeks—like his wife from too much wine—baggy, unpressed pants, and bleary eyes from never sleeping. After a certain hour at night, it was his thankless task to ring everyone in and out of the hotel. From his bed he had a clear view of the front door and from the comings and goings of my hotel friends alone, it was no wonder the poor man's eyes were always red.

I settled into a room barely large enough to accommodate a big brass bed and an armoire—the only furniture—with a bathroom down the hall. The room being so small forced me and the neighbors in a hotel across a small courtyard to dress and undress daily in front of one another. The alternative was to pull across the heavy, cumbersome drapery that hung in each of our windows, and no one wanted to bother.

Adjusting to the French culture, with customs that were so different, wasn't easy for an American from the South. For instance, at the Lido, a Las Vegas–like show on the Champs-Elysées that Tod took me to, I was standing at the urinal in their only bathroom when a woman stepped out of a stall as a cleaning woman cleaned up around us. Then there were those pissoires on every sidewalk in Paris where men's pants legs could be seen behind a partition with a stream of urine between them. The toilet in a café might be a hole in the floor with a chain to pull to flush water into the hole.

Some of this seemed quite primitive to me—and certainly bohemian—but eventually the culture and I came to terms and grew to tolerate one another.

At a nearby café one evening, I ran into two dancers from the Lido that Tod had introduced me to, with a male companion I recognized as the actor Tony Perkins. He was in Paris for the opening of his new film, *Aimez-Vous Brahms?* (or *Goodbye Again* in America), which also starred Ingrid Bergman. He would also make a film with Orson Welles, who would direct and co-star in it, called *Le Procés* (*The Trial*), based on a Kafka story.

I had heard that Perkins was the current lover of Jean-Claude Brialy, a popular, handsome French actor, so I was confused and even put off by Perkins flirting with me. I was by no means as savvy as any of these people, but I had at least advanced up the worldly ladder enough by now to recognize a flirt when one came my way.

Perkins asked us all back to an apartment where he was staying. Once there, after a few more of his advances that had even the dancers winking at me in acknowledgment, he got so wasted on whatever he had consumed that he climbed out a window after a cat, which he threw back inside, and remained perched on the ledge, refusing to come back in no matter how we pleaded. Finally bored with the whole thing, I left. I have no idea what got him inside again unless he was bored with himself.

He would see a psychiatrist to try to make himself "straight" enough to marry, but I had another encounter with him years later back in New York when he didn't remember me). If that was the result of going "straight," the treatment had failed.

I found that stars like Perkins would use whomever they fancied for their momentary pleasure and discard them at will. Being on someone's casualty list didn't improve my life one bit, and I never regretted ignoring him.

To get me started modeling, Tod took me to the most renowned model agency in Paris, "Dorian," owned by Dorian Leigh, a famous American model and the sister of Suzy Parker, another famous American model, both Richard Avedon's favorites. Dorian was a small, fragile-looking woman—by then well past her prime, but still strikingly beautiful—with dark hair, pale skin, beautiful limbs, and a haunting presence—similar to actress Vivian Leigh whom Dorian resembled. For this reason I assumed she had taken the actress's last name for her modeling career. I later learned that Dorian's middle name was Leigh and she had used it as her last name when she began.

In many of my modeling shots I smoked to cover up my insecurity (© Les Editions Jalou "L'Officiel").

After seeing my portfolio the Dorian agency immediately signed me. American, German, Swedish, and English models were particularly sought by agencies. The French hated all these nationalities—and everyone else too, for that matter—but the leaner, more fluid lines of the Nordic races, as opposed to the more square, male Gallic figure, showed their clothes to their best advantage. The French could be stubborn and even arrogant, but when it was to their advantage, they could be quite flexible.

A job was coming up for *L'Homme* magazine, the French equivalent of America's *GQ*, and with me being a new face in town, the agency wanted me to do it. It was being shot by one of the best photographers in Paris, an American, Henry Clarke. He shot for many prestigious magazines, including French *Vogue*, and was considered the French equivalent of Richard Avedon. Both *L'Homme* and French *Vogue* were owned by the American publishing empire Conde Nast. Clarke would later shoot me for French *Vogue*, where I extended a diamond and emerald brooch—worth a sultan's fortune—to a coiffed, bejewelled Balenciaga-gowned model.

The shoot for *L'Homme* took place backstage at a Paris ballet, with the dancers in the background on stage in the lights and the male models in suits standing in semi-darkness in the wings. It was very Degas in concept, and when the photos appeared in the magazine, they were marvelous. Clarke had a way of painting with his camera that was perfect for the Degas approach.

When I first went to the Dorian agency, I didn't meet Dorian herself. Her bookers showed her my portfolio, and she approved it. Some time later, a French photographer, George Garcon, was having a party in his huge studio and I was invited, along with many Paris fashion elite. From the studio ceiling, Garcon had hung a series of swings and when I arrived, people were swinging in them, including a woman being pushed by a handsome dark-haired man. As I entered, the woman tumbled out of the swing from the thrust of the man's pushing and, at the same time, another man rushed up and slapped her across the face. As he raced past me, she fell into my arms. This was my introduction to the notorious Dorian Leigh, head of my modeling agency—drunk, disheveled, and severely slapped.

I never learned what provoked the attack, but from every indication Dorian was no stranger to drink, which may have somehow contributed to it. Like Vivian Leigh, she had the persona of a tragic figure—or at least one that courted self-destruction. Her bad judgment was illustrated by her several children by different men, and her many abortions. One of her lovers was killed in a racecar accident in the famous Mille Miglia in Italy, ending his life and the lives of numerous spectators, as well as the Mille Miglia, forever. And she was predeceased by two of her children, one by suicide.

I was on a shoot that Richard Avedon photographed for an ad for Air France where models posed as passengers in a mock-up of the inside of a plane. Being an old friend of Avedon's, Dorian was one of the primary passengers on whom his camera would focus. Before the shoot began, I was watching her nervously fidgeting with her make-up in a compact mirror.

When she saw my reflection in the mirror watching her, she snapped the compact shut and snarled, "What are you looking at?"

"I'm sorry," I said quietly, suspecting her fragile ego was wrapped up in this and it was by sheer will that she went on.

Time and debauchery had left her face ravaged and haunted by lost dreams. She eventually became a cook and managed to produce two cookbooks, but also managed to consume what she cooked and get fat. Her beauty gone, and time working against her, she and her agency would fade into fashion history, like many before and after her. She would die at 91 with Alzheimer's in a nursing home in 2008.

With Paris being the center of haute couture, Tod advised that I should have a tuxedo made for my work with a tailor he knew in London. I went there to be measured, and when the tuxedo arrived in Paris, it was the most splendid garment I had ever seen. I used it in many of my fashion assignments, appearing in it in *L'Officiel* magazine with more coiffed, bejewelled Balenciaga- and Dior-gowned models. In it again for French *Vogue*—shot by the great German photographer Helmut Newton—I was the young paramour pulling back the delicate window trimming of a secluded bistro on the Seine in search of my lady fair's husband, while she quietly sipped her champagne beside me in our private dining room, hoping she wouldn't be caught at her infidelity.

On a night shoot, I was booked with an American model from Chicago: Wilhelmina. While the photographer's assistants hosed down a small cobblestone street to make it appear that it had been raining, Wilhelmina and I sipped espressos at a nearby outdoor café. She confided that all it took in the morning to get her bowels moving was a cup of coffee and a cigarette— more information than I had solicited.

On the business side, she revealed that she was going to New York to try her luck at modeling. With my difficulty there, I advised her to stay where she was. She didn't take my advice, went to New York, and became a top model, one of Avedon's and Irving Penn's favorites. Later, she would start her own very successful agency called "Wilhelmina." Many times in my career I found that my opinions about the fashion industry couldn't be trusted. It was always an enigma to me.

Tod also introduced me to his rich Parisian fashion society. At a gathering in a woman's opulent apartment—where a staff of waiters served us a most lavish supper at small tables for four set up in her living room—I met the intriguing British actress Dame Judith Anderson, notable for such stylish films as Hitchcock's *Rebecca* and Preminger's *Laura*.

In my elegant dinner jacket again, I looked down at her sitting in a Louis XV wingback chair and coolly delivered a "Hi." My aloofness was intended to indicate that I wasn't impressed—which I was.

In her droll British way, she looked up and mimicked, "Hi," with as much enthusiasm as if I had been a statue.

It was she who was unimpressed. Shot down.

My modeling with French *Vogue* led to my doing fashion illustrations for their pattern section in the back of the magazine. Tod also drew for them, but for the editorial part, like Bouché and Eric in American *Vogue*, which he could never do in America because they were there. He also drew for Au Printemps, an upscale department store like Saks in New York. I got a small account with Belle Jardinière, a department store on par with Macy's, but I had to work much harder than Tod to make the cheap merchandise look good.

On hot summer afternoons, friends and I would go to the Piscine Deligny, a wooden swimming pool barge that floated along the banks of the Seine. There, everyone gathered to meet and exchange gossip, sitting in crowded packs on the uncomfortable wooden slats around the pool.

Nights we would spend in the St. Germain-des-Prés area, sipping café at the Café de Flore or the Café Aux Deux Magots next door. We would start at one and end up at the other. In pleasant weather we would sit for hours outside at the small tables under the awning and watch all of Paris go by. It was said that if you wanted to meet anyone in the world, they would eventually pass by here.

Throughout the night, the then famous of France would parade by: Johnny Hallyday, the popular singer; the unbelievably darkly handsome actor Alain Delon; Jeanne Moreau, one of France's greatest actresses; and the writer Françoise Segan, who, as a teenager, dazzled the world with her sensational first novel, *Bonjour Tristesse*.

Later in the evening, we would move across the Blvd. St. Germain to Chez Regine, a disco managed by Regine, a singer and sometime actress (and other assorted professions). She also had a nightclub in St. Tropez, which was doubtlessly backed by rich Riviera entrepreneurs.

When we grew bored with that, a few dark alleys away promised a notorious gay bar, where all of Paris came to party and twist to Chubby Checker's music. Jean Marais, the beast in the '40s French film classic *La Belle et la bête* (*Beauty and the Beast*), frequented there with his bevy of handsome young male hopefuls hungry for stardom.

After a night of carousing, in the early morning we would wind up in Les Halles, where fishermen brought in their fresh catch. In restaurants there we would consume the fresh oysters and wash them down with champagne.

A line that I will always remember was delivered there to a handsome male companion of mine by an enamoured but intoxicated and jealous male customer on the banquette next to us.

He turned to me and said, "You've got a cheap face," and then to my friend he said, "Ah, but my dear, you are Cartier."

What did he expect from me at six in the morning?

Tod had a deal with the *New York Times* that when he went on a vacation he would draw the locals and the fashions there, which paid for his vacation. I thought it was a great idea, and since I had wanted to attend the Cannes Film Festival in March, I made a trip to London to show my fashion drawings to Earnestine Carter, the fashion editor of the London *Sunday Times*, and proposed that I draw the fashions at the festival for her newspaper. She was quite enthusiastic about the idea and even asked me to immediately draw the fashions at several British fashion shows. She also offered to share the drawings with Eugenia Sheppard, the fashion editor of the *New York Herald-Tribune*, over some international hook-up before the age of the fax.

When I arrived in Cannes, it was a bustle of movie activity. I took a room in a cheap pension that Tod had suggested, which was clean and not far from the rich, upscale Carlton International Hotel on La Croisette where all the celebrities and movie higher-ups stayed. Afterwards, I went to the Carlton where Earnestine advised I would pick up my press pass.

The festival movies I saw with my press pass were dreary and boring. Like others at the event, I spent more time on the uncomfortable Riviera pebble beach that I despised in front of the Carlton. There I encountered Regine, the Paris disco queen. She asked one of my press companions who

I was—not remembering my nights at her Paris disco, or my dancing with her at her St. Tropez nightclub, or even the fact that afterwards, I had gone for a nude moonlight swim with other intoxicated night revelers.

When she was informed I was with the press, I was approved to sit with her. Mixing with the lower echelon of society hadn't gotten her where she was—perhaps too close to her own beginnings. The press she needed; me she didn't.

At a lavish luncheon—complete with caviar, champagne, and carved ice swans—I met Otto Preminger. He was at the festival to introduce his new film, *Exodus*, starring Paul Newman and Eva Marie Saint, and a new young starlet, Jill Haworth, who would be in *Cabaret* on Broadway in 1966.

Since I'd done only one noteworthy fashion drawing (of a woman in a one-shoulder halter-top bathing suit on the beach in front of the Carlton), I needed to quicken my pace. Preminger recognized that a drawing of his new starlet appearing in the London *Sunday Times* and the *New York Herald-Tribune* would be beneficial to his new film, and he readily agreed that Jill should pose for me after the luncheon.

At the same table with Preminger was Georges Cravenne, the husband of French starlet Françoise Arnoul, who appeared in the notable French film *Les Parisiennes* in '62. Being an actor himself, as well as a journalist and a publicist, Cravenne knew well the power of the press and wanted to get his wife in on this. He gave me the address where she was staying at the Colombe d'Or, a famous hotel secluded in the hills outside the tiny village of Saint-Paul-de-Vence, about a two-hour drive from Cannes. Not realizing the distance or the expense of getting there, I agreed to go.

Preminger constantly ridiculed Jill for the way she dressed and for her make-up, while I completed a drawing of her in a charming evening gown with a black velvet top and a flowing white chiffon skirt. She was 16 at the time, but I sensed in her a rebellious spirit that might one day break out. Years later, I would observe her at a trendy New York disco in her breakout period, slumped over the bar, feeling no pain—or maybe it was a lot of pain she was feeling, considering her condition.

After what seemed an eternity, my taxi arrived at the Colombe d'Or. Bathed in the bright Mediterranean sunlight, the hotel was set high in the hills above the Riviera, with a cobblestone courtyard in front and Picassos, Braques, Mirós, and Bonnards lining its rustic interior walls.

I was told that Françoise was sitting by the colorful mosaic-tiled pool that dominated the inside patio. There I found a lovely, tanned, auburn-haired young woman who revealed that the only fashion statement she had with her was the orange bikini she was wearing. People didn't come to Colombe d'Or to make fashion statements, but rather to get away from them. What was her husband thinking, sending me on this wild goose chase?

She asked me what I wanted to do now that I was there with nothing to draw. After my long, hot ride up there, I wanted a swim. She disappeared in search of a bathing suit and returned with something that barely fit my finger, which I managed to squeeze into. I plunged into the cool, refreshing water, and when I surfaced, Simone Signoret strolled by in a large straw hat and a black bathing suit ensemble, followed by Yves Montand.

Holy Arc de Triomphe, this place was hopping with French film royalty!

Simone took Françoise aside to inquire who I was, and when Françoise returned, she said that Simone was having a luncheon for a Japanese film company and had invited me to attend. It was that power of the press again.

Back in my clothes, I stood with Simone in the small dark bar watching the waiters outside in the cobblestone courtyard setting up her luncheon. All around the courtyard doing their mating dance were small, white fantail pigeons, or garden doves—presumably, where the hotel got its name meaning "Golden Dove"—though I don't know where the gold came from unless it was the intense Mediterranean sunlight that rendered everything a golden hue.

With nothing better to offer the great French film star, I said, "Look how the male pigeon puffs himself up and dances around the female and she goes about like she couldn't care less."

"Yes," she said, "but not so much that she fly away."

This was right after Montand's film with Marilyn Monroe, *Let's Make Love*, when they were reputed to have had an affair. Like the female pigeon, Simone would refuse to fly away.

Returning to Paris, I discovered that Madame Lapalou and her lover, Jean Louis, had been cavorting in my bed. To add to their effrontery, they had even neglectfully left behind their wadded-up, telltale, dirty sheets in my armoire. My next-door neighbor confirmed that she had seen them coming and going in and out of my room several times while I was away.

To compound the insult, Madame Lapalou had even reported me to the Prefecture de police for violating my carte de séjour, a card that allowed me to remain in France as long as I left the country every three months and had the card stamped upon my re-entry. I always felt this was a ploy by the French government to pilfer money and I ignored it. Not wanting to cause a rift between Monsieur and Madame Lapalou by disclosing the contents in my armoire, I went to court.

To my amazement, not only had Madame Lapalou reported me to the police, she now showed up in court like Madame Defarge in Dickens' *A Tale of Two Cities*, and even testified for me—at least that's what I think she did. The judge fined me the equivalent of $80, and then Madame took me out for a wine afterwards to show what a sport she was. Voilà, bien le Français.

In the air in Paris was the increasing rumble of war for America in a place called Vietnam, which I had never heard of but with which the French had been well acquainted for decades. I also had little knowledge of our new president, John F. Kennedy, who had come to office just as I left America. I knew he and his wife, Jacqueline, had come to Paris and she had reportedly charmed the French president, Charles de Gaulle, by speaking French— which would naturally charm the French, who liked things done their way.

I had also heard of the Bay of Pigs incident, which I barely understood, and the Cuban Missile Crisis would follow in '62, but these were distant drums from where I was. The French didn't interpret the news the same way Americans did, and things there had a different slant. I sensed that I was losing touch with my country.

The winter that followed was particularly brutal, raining constantly, and it was cold and damp most of the time. In Paris, the cold and damp is the bone-chilling kind from which you never quite warm up. With the weather came a series of colds that the doctor thought might be a return of pneumonia that I'd had when I was in school at Pratt, and part of the respiratory problems I'd suffered with most of my life.

The dark, gloomy days did nothing to improve my spirits, and both my professional and personal life suffered from all of it. All I wanted to do was stay in bed and sleep.

My relationship with Tod particularly concerned me. With as much work as he had, he was still jealous of what I had. He had been displeased that I used his idea and went to Cannes, though it certainly took nothing away from him. I suspected that he was more disturbed about my independence. Having been responsible for my being in Paris and depending on him for a time, he had presumed he had some kind of control—if not ownership.

When I first arrived, he had pushed me down on his bed and tried to have sex with me. I permitted it because I didn't want to lose this vital contact to my Paris life.

In the middle of his one-sided activity, he stopped and said, "You're not enjoying this, are you?"

I had remained stiff as a corpse throughout and couldn't have sent a stronger message had I been one.

"No," I said bluntly and to the point.

He withdrew and never approached it again, but it was obvious that his ego had been bruised. Naively perhaps, I thought he had asked me to Paris because we were friends. I certainly wasn't there to be his imported boy toy. Friends suggested that this was the real reason for his behavior now.

When my health returned in the spring, I was gaunt and had lost a lot of weight. Modeling was unthinkable, and I had no incentive for it, anyhow. My fashion illustration work, too, had dried up from my long absence. Tod had no more reason to be jealous.

America's involvement in Vietnam was worsening, and France's nearly ten-year war with Algeria dragged on. Regularly, radical Algerians bombed key places like Le Drugstore on the Champs-Elysées. Given such upheaval and my own situation, Europe didn't feel very secure or even appealing anymore. Everything indicated that it was time to return home.

I said goodbye to my Paris friends and booked a cheap eight-hour flight—by way of Anchorage, Alaska, with many stopovers—back to America.

There, on a sunny Friday afternoon in November 1963, my mother and I watched on TV as President Kennedy's motorcade moved through the streets of Dallas, Texas. Suddenly the screen in front of us showed pandemonium.

Walter Cronkite came on and said, "The president has been shot."

With Jacqueline Kennedy in her bloodstained pink suit standing by his side, Lyndon B. Johnson overnight became our next president.

Two days later, we watched Kennedy's assassin, Lee Harvey Oswald, shot on TV. The world had gone mad, and TV had become the monster that informed us of bad news.

I had already arranged to return to New York, and this was the world I was returning to: a world in turmoil, struggle, and change. Not only was the world changing, but I, too, had changed. I was no longer the impressionable young man who had once glibly asked for fame and fortune.

2

Back to New York, Montgomery Clift, Fabergé

When I arrived back in New York, everyone was asking: "Where were you when Kennedy was shot?" It was as if a defining line had been drawn in time, a line that was both an ending and a beginning, from which everything else would forever be measured.

The president's assassination had traumatized, even paralyzed, the country, when only months before the event the air had seemed so full of hope and excitement. In August that year, Martin Luther King, a black minister from Montgomery, Alabama, had given a rousing speech at the Lincoln Memorial in Washington, D.C.

"I have a dream," he had said.

It began the black movement for equality, but it also spoke eloquently for all oppressed people.

King himself would be gunned down five years later, followed by Bobby Kennedy two months after that. America appeared to have a lust for blood, and the killing of our leaders, coupled with the war in Vietnam, confirmed it. Nightly, the legalized murder and body count were reviewed on TV, and no one wanted to hear about it. For a diversion, the public attended James Bond spy movies and TV would offer *Laugh In* and *Sonny and Cher*.

Diana Vreeland had recently come to *Vogue* from *Harper's Bazaar*, bringing with her a staff of carbon copy fashion editors, and set about to change women's fashion based on the look of young girls. Flower children, or hippies as they were called, led the way, along with Twiggy and Mia Farrow with their chopped-off hair, flat chests, and little girl dresses. Rudi Gernreich designed the topless bathing suit in sync with women's liberation, and the mini-skirt was in. Every woman, regardless of age or figure, had to have one.

Sporting their minis along with long hair falls, false lashes, little girl pouty lips, compliments of Mary Quant make-up, they made the disco scene disguised as something they weren't.

Men copied the Beatles' mop-top haircut with long sideburns, bell-bottom pants, and the Edwardian look, and they too made the disco scene in their disguise. Timothy Leary introduced psychedelic drugs into the scene, and nothing ever appeared the same again.

I moved into a friend's Upper East Side apartment, but his constant parties—with my bed next to the bathroom that was frequented throughout the night—made it necessary to move. I found a small apartment on Irving Place where I set about to make a new portfolio of fashion drawings, using anyone who could fit into a dress as my model.

I took the portfolio around, but had little success. Even the art director at B. Altman's, who had once greeted me with open arms, now said, "We're not as adventuresome as we once were."

I avoided the model agencies altogether. Still vivid in my memory were the exhausting hours in Paris where I had stood around while garments were being pinned on me. I felt if they wanted a store dummy, they should get one. My mother doled out a pittance of money to help, but I was always close to starvation.

With little to do that summer, I accepted an invitation to look after a friend's house on Fire Island while he was away on business. The house was a large, grey wooden one on stilts—like so many Fire Island houses—with a spectacular view of the ocean.

On the beach one afternoon, I became aware of someone on the porch of the house next door looking through binoculars that seemed to be pointed at me. It was a little disconcerting having someone looking at me through binoculars, and it never stopped. Whenever I'd look up, there this person was.

At lunchtime, I got up to prepare something to eat, and as I approached the house, the man with the binoculars ran inside. I discounted him as some kook and gave it no more thought until I mentioned it to my host that evening on the phone. He said that the house next door belonged to Montgomery Clift, and it might have been him.

In bad health, Clift was being taken care of by a black man, I was told. The man who ran inside wasn't black, so I concluded it must have been Clift with the binoculars. What he was doing spying on me, I hadn't a clue, but it certainly got my attention. It's not often a big movie star spies on you.

The next morning, from the kitchen window that faced the walkway leading to the small Fire Island community of the Pines, I saw Clift hobbling along, helped by a black man. Clift looked old and worn and not at all like the handsome young man who appeared in *The Heiress* and *A Place in the Sun*.

The annoying binocular routine continued, and when my host arrived that weekend, we decided he would invite Clift and his caretaker to join us for a drink. He said he had an acquaintance with the caretaker, who he thought was quite nice and personable, but he didn't know Clift at all. The caretaker told him that Clift insisted on having his food in a bowl on the floor where he ate it like a dog.

The evening of our get-together, I was in my room doing some last-minute preparation when I heard voices outside. I could distinguish one voice as that of my friend, and one that may have belonged to Clift's caretaker, but nothing that sounded like Clift. I assumed he hadn't come, though I couldn't imagine the caretaker leaving him at home alone.

When I entered the living room, there was Clift with his caretaker and my friend. I was introduced, but Clift kept his head bowed and only grunted some barely audible response. The caretaker was indeed personable, and we all had a round of drinks, but he made sure Clift had only fruit juice.

Never speaking or looking in my direction, Clift finally left with the caretaker. The next day Clift was at his post with his binoculars, and he continued to run into his house each time I approached. This went on until I left the island some time later. What these shenanigans were about, I never found out.

I survived until Christmas and finally landed a temporary job at Bergdorf Goodman representing Revlon's Braggi line, a fragrance and skin care line for men. I was the first Braggi man.

Andrew Goodman, the owner of Bergdorf's, gave a Christmas party every year for all of his employees in his suite on the top floor of the store that he and his wife occupied, and I was invited. Halston was designing hats for Bergdorf's then, and he was sweeping around all over the place in his grand manner. He was yet to become a successful clothing designer. At the time, Joel Schumacher (now the director of two *Batman* movies and the recent *Phantom of the Opera*) was designing windows for Henri Bendel and ads for Revlon.

This was before conglomerates took over many privately owned American businesses. Andrew Goodman owned his business, as did Charles

Revson with Revlon. Estee Lauder, Helena Rubenstein, and Elizabeth Arden also owned their cosmetic companies.

Charles Revson, I was told, began by selling nail polish to stores with each of his nails painted a different color of polish as a demonstration. He'd say, "You like this one? What about this one? This one's nice," and so on. He sold a lot of nail polish that way, and it obviously paid off.

I got a few small fashion illustration jobs for catalogues, but I didn't seem to be getting anywhere. It had become apparent that I needed to reinvent myself—but as what? With my art experience, I decided that I should be able to do make-up. I had become fascinated with it in Paris—observing models changing themselves into something they weren't—and had experimented with it on female friends trying to create a more attractive look to improve the quality of their life. I had determined that whatever I did in life should have meaning, and if make-up could improve someone's life, that was even more of an incentive to do it.

I practiced on anyone who would allow me, and when I felt brave enough, I headed to the Revlon Salon on Fifth Avenue, where I approached the head of the salon and tried to convince her of my make-up ability. She couldn't stand her current make-up artist and agreed to try me out if I passed a preliminary make-up test on someone in the salon. Her artist, she said, would be going to lunch soon and while he was gone, I could use his make-up room to show what I could do.

When he left, I was scooted inside his room to await my victim. I looked around the room for make-up to apply, but there was very little except bottles of powder. I couldn't imagine what make-up he used for his work, but it seemed to me for a company the size of Revlon, with every conceivable product, there was a vast lack here. But since I wasn't familiar with their products—or products in general, at the time—they could have been staring me in the face and I wouldn't have known it.

Before I could get organized, the head of the salon rushed in and reported that the make-up man had returned and I would have to get out of the room immediately. She took me into the massage room—with even fewer products than the previous room—where I was told I would do the make-up on her while she lay on the massage table. I was so unskilled that I didn't realize that the perspective of the human face is quite different lying down than sitting up, the usual position we're seen in.

She lay on the massage table, and I began my work with what little make-up I could find. The rest I improvised with the painting skills I had learned at Pratt. However, this was not a painting, and thickness on the human face is not as desirable as on a canvas. Layers and layers of lavender eye shadow—the only color I could find—I painted around her eyes and over her eyelids. Then I decided to add false lashes—all the rage then—but I could only find a pair of fox-red ones. Whoever would wear those? On they went anyhow. To change their color, I coated them with gobs and gobs of black mascara until they stood out from her eyelids as if she had hoisted an awning over her eyes.

When she sat up, she looked like Vampira, queen of the night. If it had been Halloween, she would have been perfect, but as it was ... e-e-ek!

Before she could look in a mirror, I grabbed my coat and got out of there fast.

I met this woman years later—when I had far more understanding of make-up—and she pointed her finger at me and said, "You! I will never forget you!"

She told me that right after I left that night, a woman client had a seizure and had to be taken to a hospital and she had to go with her. All night, she said, she had to run around the corridors of the hospital with eyelids painted in three-dimensional layers of lavender and bushy, jet-black lashes coated like cardboard.

Well ... anyone can make a mistake.

After a bit of recovery and more practice, I ventured out again. This time it was the Georgette Klinger Salon on Madison Avenue.

Georgette was an attractive, blonde Hungarian woman who began by giving facials in a room the size of a closet on Madison Avenue. From there—with the help of her husband and her own shrewdness—she had built her business, which eventually expanded to Palm Beach, Los Angeles, and points beyond.

From behind her desk, she eyed me and asked, "Are you any good?"

"Yes," I answered, trying to sound convincing and hoping she wouldn't root out my past at Revlon.

"Okay," she said, and before I realized what had happened, my make-up career had begun.

The salon was primarily a facial salon and make-up was a courtesy, but the emphasis was to sell make-up products—the real goal of any cosmetic job, since there is a 500 percent mark-up that makes a hefty profit for the company. The outrageous prices are based on the psychology that a woman doesn't want to think she's putting something cheap on her face. The truth is that many drugstore items are equally fine and far less expensive than those sold in salons and department stores, where the customer pays for the packaging.

It's not hard to convince a customer of her need for something at a vulnerable moment when a product might possibly address her fragile ego. But I wasn't good at selling something unless I believed in it and felt the customer needed it, and I was, therefore—how shall I put it?—terminated at the Klinger Salon.

Following my exit from Georgette Klinger, I heard that Fabergé—who had previously been primarily a fragrance house—had come out with a line of make-up, and I suspected that they might need a make-up artist to go along with it. Whether they needed one or not, I intended to cram me down their throats.

In my best dark suit—my only suit—I arrived for my appointment with their products designer, Amelia Bassin, to whom I had been referred. This was the last time they saw me in a suit. With no other choices, I was lucky, the job didn't require one.

Amelia was highly creative and an original thinker, which was one reason Fabergé had hired her. However, the sales department didn't know where to go with many of her products that were ahead of their time. Like the world around us, the cosmetic and fashion industries were also in turmoil and transition.

Baby blue, mousey greys and browns, and pink were about all the eye shadows that were available then. Cosmetic companies routinely copied everything from their competitors and rarely demonstrated original thinking. An error in judgment could cost a product designer their job, which was why they preferred to let others bite the bullet before venturing out and claiming they had invented it. Amelia was one of the few rebels willing to risk, a trait that would eventually be her undoing.

With fire engine red hair and a voice that sounded like Carol Burnett in one of her nutty skits, Amelia wore Mondrian-print dresses, and her office resembled an Alice-in-Wonderland curiosity shop. Every knickknack imaginable—all collected for inspiration—was sprawled over every inch of space in the room. It was a trip to walk into her office and be transported into a fairyland—or a madhouse.

I think I got the job there because she sensed I was as crazy as she was. I, too, took risks; in fact, the greatest risk was passing myself off as a make-up artist. Even crazier, people were buying it. Or maybe they saw something that I wasn't yet sure of.

Also like Amelia, I was an original thinker and willing to throw it all on the craps table. Perhaps I was just too stupid to know better, but lucky enough to somehow pull it off. I hesitate to call it artistic flair, because it may have been arrogance, but for me there were an awful lot of happy accidents, as Rembrandt used to call some of his faux pas that he turned into triumphs. For my comeuppance, I had only to reflect on the woman at the Revlon Salon with eyelids caked in lavender and lashes that could have swept floors.

My first assignment when Amelia hired me was to meet the president of Fabergé, George Barrie. A wealthy man who had bought the company not only to further his wealth, but also to dabble in the cosmetic industry, Barrie had made the interior of the Fabergé West Fifties townhouse a warm, friendly, family-like atmosphere, which belied the turmoil upstairs between—feuding sales vs. creative departments. Not wishing to be involved in internal squabbles that he expected them to solve, Barrie kept his distance, but it was obvious that someone's head would have to go on the chopping block, and no one intended it to be their own.

I knocked at Barrie's door and heard a voice inside respond: "Come in."

I entered the dark wood-paneled office smiley, bright-eyed, and eager to make my mark.

Barrie—sporting a dark Florida tan that testified to his high-roller lifestyle—was putting golf balls across his grass-green carpet. He barely looked up when I told him I had been hired as the company's resident make-up artist.

Make-up artists, then, were a new breed. Several cosmetic houses like Elizabeth Arden, Revlon, and Helena Rubenstein were experimenting with what to do with them, but they were usually relegated to the company's salon—if they had one—and using them in department stores was a new territory. Amelia, too, had not yet mapped out her strategy and was just keeping me around until she did.

With as much interest as one of his golf balls might have had, Barrie putted one across the carpet into an overturned Dixie cup and said, "Welcome aboard." The introduction was over.

I returned back upstairs, thankful that part of my job was over with.

As I waited around until someone could decide how to use me, my daily routine consisted mostly of chatting with my co-worker, and products manager Barbara Lantz, a pretty blonde woman then in her mid-twenties who would one day be co-owner of the Zoli Model Agency after Zoli died. For the entire day, I would observe her putting on her false blonde hairpiece, false lashes, and make-up. By the end of the day, she would be fully coiffed and made up in time to go home and take it all off to go to bed. Unless she had some night job I didn't know about, where else could one go after all that work? It looked exhausting.

From Barbara's daily make-up ritual, I learned a lot about make-up, and I enjoyed my time chatting with her and my time with Amelia, too. Still, I yearned to be used. Finally, Amelia had a project for me doing the make-up for a TV commercial she was producing for the company. I was to make up a new model who had just come up from Florida named Lauren Hutton.

Lauren came to Fabergé one afternoon for me to try out some make-up on her and get acquainted. I thought she was pretty enough, but nothing special. I preferred a face that presented a challenge, where I could mold it and make something that wasn't there before. Lauren's face was what it was and needed little extra help. There was nothing for me to do but make it what it was, which was fine for her, but not exciting for me. Then, too, her nose was a bit crooked and bulbous on the end and there was this big gap between her two front teeth.

I thought Amelia was off her rocker this time for sure. Later, Diana Vreeland would "discover" Lauren and make her the "now" girl of the seventies and one of Richard Avedon's favorite models—and everyone else's too—with a million dollar contract from Revlon for ads. So much again for what I knew.

The commercial shoot was scheduled to begin at seven in the morning. To save time and money, and because the make-up I was required to do was quite intricate, it was decided that Lauren and I should begin two hours earlier, at five o'clock. Since there was no place for us to go to do make-up at that time of the morning, it was agreed that she would come to where I lived and had all the make-up. With my being between apartments, it was then the Pickwick Arms Hotel in the East Fifties.

At five in the morning, the hotel was less than cordial about allowing anyone up to my room, accustomed to only prostitutes arriving at that hour. When the hotel clerk rang me to say there was a girl down there raising hell to get up to my room, I knew it was Lauren. I could even hear her yelling in the background. Being a Scorpio, Lauren was no shy, retiring type.

When she arrived, I was glad she had been so forceful because there was no time to be hassled by hotel rules or any other nonsense; we had to immediately get to work. Since my room was small, there was little space to do the make-up, which involved painting a big blue flower around each of her eyes. We decided she should lie down on my bed and I would straddle her chest to have the best angle to paint.

It was the most bizarre procedure of my career, but we accomplished it, and she shot out of there to the studio with two big blue flowers painted around her eyes. God knows what the cab driver thought, picking up a woman in that condition at that time of the morning. Lauren was a game girl and deserved credit for enduring all that.

Weekly, I called *Vogue* or *Harper's Bazaar* to let them know I was alive and the new and happening make-up artist at Fabergé—with less emphasis on "happening" since nothing much had happened yet. My excuse for calling was usually that we had some new product they simply had to take a look at. Amelia liked that.

When an editor from some magazine arrived in our department, I sprang into action, charming and chatty as I could be, letting them know I was around, but, so far, there had been no takers. I was told each time by every editor: "The models do their own make-up," and from that they wouldn't budge. The magazines and the photographers, too, were convinced that no one could do a model's face better than the model herself.

"Who better knows their face?" I was told repeatedly.

But I saw horrendous make-up errors in every magazine and knew I could, at least, do better than that. Unknown to me, at *Vogue*, Diana Vreeland, the high priestess of 1960s fashion, was also appalled at what she saw. She hadn't yet solved the problem—but she would.

With not much more to do than schmooze with magazine editors and others who passed through Amelia's office, I became friends with Irene Satz, the president of Orbach's department store, whose moderate prices for Paris couture knockoffs had put them on the fashion map. A tall, slim, graceful woman with snow-white hair stylishly pulled back into a bun, Irene was the epitome of chic.

One night, Irene and I attended a fashion ball at the Park Avenue Armory. She wore a gauzy, see-through, sequined St. Laurent knock-off cocktail dress—the most talked about dress of his collection that season—and a make-up I had done with silver sparkles on her eyelids that I hoped wouldn't transfer into her eyes. Even in my elegant black dinner jacket, I was no match for my date.

Sammy Davis Jr. entertained at the ball. To a woman who requested that Davis sing "Mr. Wonderful," the title song from his 1956 Broadway hit by the same name, Davis replied, "I can't do that," and then crooned the last few bars of the song that said: "Mr. Wonderful, I love you."

"You see why I can't do that?" he said.

I also went by train to Philadelphia for a party with the president of the Fashion Group—an organization that promoted American fashion—and turned the president, a sweet but plain woman, into a glamorous presentation of herself. Everyone there was amazed and delighted at the transformation, including the woman herself. Already I was making a name for myself and people were becoming aware, but I was not yet through any significant door.

From the Pickwick Arms, I moved into an apartment in the East Sixties that I fantasized could accommodate both myself and a young man I had recently been involved with—but this was not to be.

I still believed in love. I felt that coupling was part of human existence, but all the men I met were at the party. Even the few I knew in relationships were having outside sex—so I wondered why they were together if they were going to cheat. And if that was the case, what was I saving myself for? Like Tod in Paris used to say, "You're a long time in the grave. Make hay while the sun shines." With love out of fashion, I decided to join the party with the rest.

I began going to a popular East Seventies gay bar called Harry's Back East, where every imaginable gadget, toy, doll, doodad, whatchamacallit, and thingamabob hung from every inch of the ceiling. The dust collected on these hanging objects over the years must have been prolific.

The sultry warm orange, red, and yellow lighting, contrasted by cool blues and greens, was reflected off the bar that ran the full length of the long room and created a seductive atmosphere that was ripe for a pickup.

In the back was a dance room with flickering disco lights and pumped-in disco music that continued until a big red light on the wall flashed on, alerting the customers that the police were entering the bar. Immediately, the music stopped and everyone mingled innocently about while the cops strolled through making sure no one was up to anything "lewd." By this was meant close male-to-male contact which, of course, there had been only seconds before they entered, and they knew it. If a bar had dutifully paid them off, nothing more was done; if not, somebody got hauled out, like the owner, and fined for something or other. In this way, the police bullied and harassed with their reign of terror until somebody paid up.

The moment the cops exited, the music resumed to its full, pumped-up volume and the writhing bodies slithered the night away before going to someone's apartment for the anticipated tryst. The mix of men in this bar from every lifestyle provided a virtual smorgasbord of male types for endless possibilities of sexual coupling. A whorehouse, by comparison, couldn't have achieved better results.

At Harry's, I met a young man who, after the obligatory sex, introduced me to a crowd that partied nightly at a popular Upper East Side straight bar called Mike Malcolm's. Oddly enough, Mike himself was gay. Later the group moved on to Arthur, a fashionable East Fifties disco owned by Sybil Burton, Richard Burton's ex-wife, and an assortment of other celebrities, including Roddy McDowall, the former MGM child actor, who I was told had the biggest penis in the disco—though I never confirmed it firsthand.

A young woman in the group called Super Chick, because of her height—who would one day reclaim her given name, Ann, and represent fashion photographer Francesco Scavullo—knew every bouncer in town. The line in front of Arthur was always huge, but with Super Chick on hand, we'd zip up the steps with merely a nod from the hefty bouncers at the door weeding out undesirables, while giving the peons left waiting outside their comeuppance. It was considered prestigious to enter unencumbered.

Down a long dark corridor, past the large disco room, to the bar room in the back, we'd stake out our territory close to the bartender, with whom we had purposely made friends, hoping to score free drinks or some dope.

Occasionally, some notable person like Liza Minnelli, a young star on the rise, would stop by our table to flirt with the handsome men who were on the lookout for one themselves. Even if you weren't interested in the same sex, or whatever sex you wanted and how many people you wanted to include, it was kinky and even chic to experiment. Psychedelic drugs like acid and mescaline, mushrooms brought back from the jungles of Colombia that contained psilocybin (a natural psychedelic), marijuana, Quaaludes, a "set-up" of uppers and downers that left you coming and going at the same time, poppers, angel dust, and, of course, cocaine and heroin were always available to help you accomplish anything you could imagine to "broaden your horizons" and get you out of your rut.

The world had turned unreal, and drugs enhanced the illusion that many didn't want to come down from. No one wanted reality, whatever that was, and if it meant returning to the uptight years that had preceded this, they weren't interested. Looking at dead bodies on TV and a war that accepted legalized killing as our right, many of draft age fled the country. Luckily, I had already donated my time in the armed forces before the whole mess began, so at least I was spared that decision. Those who were left just wanted to get high and stay that way until it all floated past and somehow disappeared.

The fashion and make-up worlds were also viewed through this haze, and creativity was presumed to be enhanced with a pill, puff, or pop of something. Fashion took on a wild look, as if viewed on an acid trip, which some designers might well have been on at the time of creation. Psychedelic designs were everywhere: in fashion, in movies, and on TV. Diversions to take our minds off the slaughter going on in some remote part of the world that few had ever even heard of, and most didn't want to hear about, were everywhere, and drugs contributed to the get-away. For that, they were therapeutic.

Flower children tried to nurture us with love, and, equipped with drugs, we thought we had accomplished it, but the Charles Manson murders showed us there was no truth to that. Drugs only helped us escape the cruelty and insanity going on around us, and doubtlessly triggered deranged minds that were prone to be that way. Nevertheless, drugs produced the party that few wanted to miss out on.

The friction between the two feuding departments at Fabergé was growing, and everyone knew it was only a matter of time until the axe fell somewhere. Barrie was becoming impatient, and either the children with their snits would solve their problems themselves or he would do it for them.

For me, without Fabergé I would be out on my own with whatever credentials I had so far—and from where I stood, it looked like slim pickings.

3

A Naked Tallulah Bankhead, Vogue Calls

Lonely, with time on my hands and little to do, I was led by my nightly prowls to a small gay bar in the East Fifties under the Queensboro Bridge. Upon entering, the bar area was quite narrow, but up some stairs, a large room in the back opened up for dancing, equipped with a banquette encircling the room with tables and chairs. The place was usually crowded, but it was raining that night and the group gathered there was pleasantly manageable.

While the music played and the mostly male couples—with a smattering of mixed couples—danced, a distinguished-looking man in his fifties with a thick head of greying hair at the table next to me began a conversation. He said his name was Jesse and that he took care of prominent women, usually socially prominent. I had no idea what "taking care of" meant until he explained that he was their companion, confidant, escort, and sometimes secretary. His job description sounded more like a gigolo to me, but I was curious and wondered if I could get such a position. After all, things weren't looking so good for me at Fabergé, and I could certainly have used a backup. But I could never have been as suave as Jesse, and if that's what it took, things didn't look so good for me there either.

Then he revealed that he was currently taking care of Tallulah Bankhead.

"Oh, sure," I thought to myself, "I take care of Minnie Mouse."

In bars, they tell you anything.

Suspecting that this was only a come-on, that he had mistaken my interest for something else, I turned my attention to the dancing couples.

"Come on," I heard him say, "I'll take you there."

Startled, I turned around.

"Take me where?"

"To Tallulah's apartment."

Either he thought I was a fool to believe such a line, or it was true. And if it was true and Bankhead was still up, God knows how she would receive someone coming in on her at this late hour. Still, it fascinated me. In bars you can also meet the most interesting strangers.

Tennessee Williams has a famous line in *A Streetcar Named Desire* that Tallulah gave him for Blanche DuBois to say: "I have always depended on the kindness of strangers." I reflected that in that respect, Tallulah and I had a lot in common.

The apartment building that Jesse took me to was in the East Fifties and close to Sutton Place, where one day I would also work with Gloria Vanderbilt. From the chartreuse and beige lobby, up we went in the elevator and into the apartment.

Directly in front of a small marble foyer was the living room where I immediately recognized this was indeed the great lady's apartment. An Augustus John painting of her from the 1920s (now in the Portrait Gallery of the Smithsonian Institution) hung over a fake fireplace mantel to the left of the room, while on the wall across the room behind a light blue velvet couch was a small painting of John Barrymore. (I later learned she'd had an affair with the actor as well as with Gary Cooper and James Cagney, to name a few). The other works of art and objects in the room and the furniture, mostly antique, were in exquisite taste with a feminine flair, unlikely to belong to Jesse.

I wondered why Bankhead would allow him to drag someone in here in the middle of the night, endangering herself, him, and her possessions. Perhaps he had a sixth sense about those he brought here, but it seemed an unreliable thing to do. If that's how he took care of someone, I was glad he wasn't taking care of me.

"Drink?" he said, going to a small bar table to the left of the living room entrance where every kind of liquor was displayed.

"Sure," I said, having every intention of having the drink and making a beeline for the door when it was finished.

I was curious and had come here for him to prove his claim, and so it was true, but that didn't include compromising amenities that he, undoubtedly, had in his game plan.

"Where is she?" I asked, sitting in a matching light blue velvet-covered, wingback chair next to the couch.

He spritzed some seltzer into the bourbons he had poured and saun-
tered over in a John Wayne way with two crystal glasses.

"She's asleep," he said, handing me a glass, "in the next room."

He sat down as close to me as he could, on the couch, which was why
I had taken the chair.

Putting down my glass, I said, "Where's the bathroom?"

He explained that it was down the hall, and I left the living room while
I pondered my next move. The hallway was short and accommodated a
mahogany dining table with four chairs and a crystal chandelier over them,
in front of a small kitchen. Across from that, next to the living room, was
a closed door behind which, I assumed, Bankhead slept. The bathroom was
at the end of the hall with another room next to that which, with no other
choices, had to be Jesse's. The overall apartment was moderate in size, but
adequately suited Bankhead's needs.

Coming out of the bathroom moments later, I saw down the hall a
small nude figure coming out of Bankhead's bedroom. I jumped back into
the bathroom, as much out of surprise at seeing a nude person entering
the hallway as just seeing anyone, and the figure jumped back into the bedroom.

We peered down the hallway at each other like two cats on a back alley
fence.

"Darling, do I know you?" her unmistakable voice boomed out.

"I don't think so," I said, meekly.

"Oh, well, that's all right then. Come on in," and she motioned for me
to join her as she returned to her bedroom.

Jesse had heard our exchange from the living room, and we entered
her bedroom together.

The only chair in the room was filled with clothing. Bankhead, now in
a dressing gown and back in bed, patted her pink satin bed comforter and
said, "Sit here."

Jesse and I sat on her bed, and she began some light-hearted conversation as if I were an old friend and not at all an intruder, but this was how
she got her information. A stranger in the middle of the night—who
wouldn't want information? Certainly Jesse asked for none, but then he had
another agenda.

The room was small and sparsely furnished with a large antique bureau
with a lamp, the one chair (fabric-quilted), and a queen-sized bed with a
bedside table and a small lamp on it. A large closet contained her clothing

and gowns she had pilfered from her Broadway shows. The one large window was heavily draped so that not a drop of light could enter.

Broadway was a late affair, and after a performance that wired her up, the party began and nobody slept until Tallulah said so, which was usually around four in the morning. Her hours of rest were from four in the morning until four in the afternoon, when she would arise and begin the whole thing all over again.

She had not been on Broadway in some time, but out of habit, her schedule stayed the same. I came to believe that her 12 hours of entombment were a kind of death wish: she never wanted to go to bed and she never wanted to get up.

Sitting on the bed, seduced by Bankhead's offhanded interrogation, I revealed that I was a make-up artist, which interested her, as I hoped it would. With my financial choices narrowing down again, and me not wanting to return to Mother's meager handouts that barely scraped me through, I used the occasion, regardless of how odd it was, to tout my wares. She was doing the same, seizing the opportunity to corral a make-up artist for less money than she would have to pay a union one. If it worked out, it could be beneficial for both of us. I was told to give my phone number to Jesse, and so he held all the cards.

When we exited the bedroom some time later, I made the decision. Hoping to strengthen my position here, I would go to bed with him. If not, he could say he lost the number or copied it down wrong, and the matter would be dropped. It was a compromise and a gamble, but I would make it.

He introduced poppers, amyl nitrite, into the sex that followed, and the smell like rotting decay nauseated me.

Falling on top of me when he was finished, he mumbled something like, "Was it as good for you as it was for me?"

My head throbbing from the poppers, I got out of bed and dressed.

"I'll see you," I said, implying that I had given him what he wanted and now I expected what I wanted.

Passing the doorman on my way out, I was sure he thought I was a male prostitute—which, with Bankhead as my payment, wasn't far from the truth. It was still raining, and I had spent all my money at the bar. With no umbrella or carfare, I turned up my coat collar and began my trudge home.

What was I becoming, doing something against my principles for a payoff?

"What principles?" I thought.

At the bar, I had been flattered by Jesse's attention. With little self-esteem, if a man wanted me, I felt that I had value. I had been so admonished by my parents, whom I never seemed to please, that I didn't feel I amounted to much. For those moments that a man wanted me, I felt appreciated, attractive—even loved. It was a short-lived aphrodisiac that needed constant refueling, an endless spiral downward into a void that could never be filled.

My mother had had me late in life and nearly died giving birth—something she never let me forget that signified to her an entitlement of ownership. Before me, she'd had two miscarriages and, afterwards, she was told she couldn't have children. That's when she adopted my sister. That was when she adopted my sister. For a time, I suppose, things were acceptable, but Mother's strong determination persisted and I arrived and immediately became her adored one—a position I had not solicited and an unpleasant one to be in since it fostered jealousy and resentment in my sister and father.

He had wanted to be an engineer, but his father forced him to become a lawyer like himself and take over his law practice. Then, marrying a domineering woman like my mother and taking care of his own mother after his father died made my father's life an unhappy one, and he drank because of it. Consequently our home was never a happy one.

Mother so indoctrinated me about my father's drinking that we had formed a pact against him, and he knew it. I especially hated him for his drinking because of how it made Mother suffer. I became for him a symbol of all he couldn't have, a scapegoat, literally a whipping boy. Drunk and enraged with jealousy, he beat me at the least provocation when Mother was away, knowing she would never permit it if she was there.

I wrote her once when she was visiting her father in Pennsylvania: "Please, Mother, come home. I'm being hurt here."

She didn't come home, and she didn't believe me anyhow.

Once he beat me so badly that I climbed into a bathtub and pulled the shower curtain across me to protect me from the blows of his fists. With my grandmother trying to pull him off me, I screamed repeatedly, "I wish I was dead! I wish I was dead!" It was as much a ploy to get him to stop as a preference for death over a life of abuse with him. But it only made him pound harder.

Inebriated, he attacked my mother one night. I heard them fighting and she tore into my bedroom, with him in pursuit, screaming: "Help me!" and pushed me between them. Summoning my courage, I said, "Don't you hit my mother!" and he slapped me across my face, sending me reeling backward onto my bed, knocking over a lamp. I crashed down on top of it, cutting my face badly. He then ran down the stairs to a guest bedroom to sleep it off. With my face and hands covered in blood, I loaded a .22 rifle I had been given as a Christmas present and positioned myself on the stairs with the barrel of the rifle pointed into the darkness where spooks of unmentionable horrors prowled. "If he comes back up the stairs," I vowed, "I'll kill him."

I was only 12.

Unwittingly, I was learning to deal with brutes, bullies, and predators that would come in handy in the life I was about to enter. If you can't reason or negotiate with them, you must destroy them before they destroy you.

A favorite uncle, my mother's brother, came into my bedroom late one night when I was a youth visiting him and drunkenly husked, "You wouldn't let me love you, would you?" Oddly, he put it in the negative as if expecting the rebuke. I looked up to see his shadowed face leering down at me in the darkness like a spectre. Then he added: "It won't hurt much," as if incestuous sodomy were a small pain that was quickly over and the scars that lasted a lifetime were equally small.

With my heart pounding, reminiscent of my father's fists, I again summoned my courage and said, "Go to bed, Uncle!" There was a pause as each of us considered what next to do, and then he slithered from the room like the predator that had entered.

I had thought of this uncle as a father when my own father betrayed me. I felt doubly betrayed by my uncle because I needed that father that was denied me and he took away the last vestiges of it.

With a stern voice I had protected myself from my uncle; I played dead to ward off Tod's advances in Paris; and I allowed Jesse his way to get what I wanted with Tallulah. Not an admirable thing to do, but when you're dealing with predators, what is admirable?

But there was no satisfaction here. The true reason for my nightly prowls, the real reason for sharing Jesse's bed, was not the lure of Tallulah but a constant search for a love that had been denied me, that endless spiral downward into a bottomless pit, an unquenchable thirst for which there was no panacea.

Several days after my late-night encounter with Tallulah, I was told that the creative department at Fabergé was being terminated and I was being transferred to the sales department to do whatever they wanted with me. Amelia and Barbara had both been let go, and after considering my situation without my creative buddies, I asked to be released, too, knowing that I could, at least, collect unemployment.

As I was collecting my belongings, I received a call from Jessica Canné, the beauty editor at *Vogue*.

"You've been telling us how you can do make-up better than our models," she said, "so come over and do it."

Bingo! It was the call I had been waiting for.

After an appointment with *Vogue* was arranged for the following week, I packed up and left Fabergé for good.

Soon after, Jesse called, too.

"The 'Living Legend,'" as he jokingly referred to Tallulah, "wants to see you." Then he added: "So do I."

Fat chance, I thought to myself.

With Tallulah on my side, I didn't have to compromise myself anymore. And with *Vogue*, it would be even more unlikely. I wasn't attracted to Jesse; I didn't know if I even liked him. I had gambled, and it had paid off. In that, he was the loser. I was on a roll and wanted to keep it that way to make up for all the time I had spent getting this far.

I was also heading down a dark road from which I might not return, and fracturing my heart in the process.

4

*Vreeland, Avedon
and Life with Tallulah*

Full of enthusiasm, I arrived for my *Vogue* appointment at their suite of offices in the Graybar building on Lexington Avenue. From a group of elevators, I selected the one going to *Vogue*'s floor, zipped up, and entered their softly lit, high-tech modern waiting area. A receptionist behind a large desk took my name, made a phone call, and reported back that I was to wait until someone came out for me. Nervously, I sat in a grey flannel-covered chrome chair thumbing through current Condé Nast publications, including *Vogue*, for last-minute inspiration. At last a young girl appeared and ushered me into *Vogue*'s inner sanctum. Through a maze of hallways, we arrived at the beauty department where several fashion editors were gathered, including Polly Mellen, one of Vreeland's most talented protégées.

Expecting some exciting face to make up, I was given the young girl who had come out for me, one of their secretaries. She was pretty in a plain way with dark hair, but by no means exciting and certainly not glamorous. For a magazine crammed with photos of exciting models like Jean Shrimpton, Twiggy, Verushka, and Marisa Berenson, how was I to show my stuff with Cinderella?

Determined to meet the challenge and make the most of what might be my only opportunity, I launched into it and created what I thought was a princess from a scullery maid. Polly Mellen and the other editors seemed impressed and immediately called in Diana Vreeland, the eccentric, egocentric editor-in-chief.

The editors stood at attention as the much-feared, flamboyant high priestess of questionable good taste, in a black cape get-up with her signature violent red lip color slashed across her mouth, swept through the door like a lion tamer about to lash some cats.

She stopped in her tracks and stepped back, studying the girl with the intensity of Rodin about to put his final thumbprint on a piece of sculpture. Suddenly, without provocation, she snatched up my box of powder and hurled all the powder in the box at the girl's face.

The editors gasped, and the girl nearly toppled off her stool. Her face had been instantly transformed as though she had been turned upside down and dumped head first into a batch of flour.

With the frightened girl on the verge of tears, Vreeland screamed, "I want the faces matte!"

The models had been using what was called "glimmer-sticks," greasy sticks of cheek color that made their faces shine and interfered with the photographers' lighting.

Vreeland had made her point, but she had outdone even herself.

"Now," she said erroneously, "you just take a brush and flick that off," and she roared like a freight train out of the room.

As unnerved as the girl and me, the editors apologized, and one of them took the girl to the bathroom to wash off her face. Mellen even stated that she thought Vreeland was losing it. I didn't know Vreeland, but her behavior certainly seemed to indicate that to me.

Indeed, others would feel the same, including Alexander Liberman, art director of Vogue and the future editorial director of all of Condé Nast. In 1971, Vreeland was replaced by Grace Mirabella, but she would continue her fashion work with magnificent period fashion exhibits at the Metropolitan Museum.

Not all was lost for me, however, and a week later Vogue called and booked me with Irving Penn and Richard Avedon, two of the most renowned photographers in the world.

Both men created books of their photography that were considered photographic art. Avedon's photographs of his dying father were riveting and a noble tribute. Penn's still lifes were breathtaking and showed his painting ability with the camera. For fashion photography, these men were the top, sought by every important client everywhere. For me with make-up, it was the chance of a lifetime.

Before the bookings, Polly Mellen and I scoured every theatrical make-up store in New York for make-up that was unavailable in retail cosmetic lines offered to the public. We bought eye shadow colors that were deep and mysterious, like jade and umber; foundations that paled in theatrical lights but gave a glorious tone to the skin in real life; and blushes and lip colors that were rich and vibrant. To get a bright red lip color, I had to have it made especially for me.

Vibrant lip colors had become practically obsolete. Gone were the deep and bright red lip colors that had been prevalent for decades, replaced in the '60s by bubble gum pink and the like.

Since the 1940s, Tallulah had been using a bright red lip color from Elizabeth Arden called "Victory Red." When the company stopped making it, she demanded they find it for her. They searched their basement, as they put it, and located a box of it that she immediately snapped up. That's how bleak the cosmetic industry had become. The public obviously didn't demand it—so why make it?

Like other magazine make-up artists, I eventually mixed my colors from a palette like a painter and created original colors, which was why Polly and I were going to theatrical stores. Theatre needed color to project from the stage, and we could make a magazine unique by displaying unusual colors there. The cosmetic companies, notoriously lacking in originality, searched the magazines continuously for these gems and copied them, making them standard today.

My first booking was with Irving Penn at his West Forties studio. Polly met me and led me into a large room with many windows and plenty of sunlight, where all sorts of what looked like hippie regalia or Indian tribal dress consisting of feathers, beads, and non-precious stones were laid out on a long table. This was to give me inspiration. I was then shown a small dressing room where a model was waiting. Penn was nowhere in sight.

Since the paraphernalia on the long table was an earthy collection of trinkets, beads, and such, I made the girl's face a bronze terra cotta like the clay earth of Arizona and streamed red, blue, yellow, and white streaks like feathers coming from her eyes and onto her cheeks, reminiscent of the feathers I had seen outside. I left the girl's face shiny and natural with no powder and beefed up the color of her cheeks with more terra cotta red. (Thank God for the theatrical store.) Polly then hung feather earrings from her ears and placed bands of multi-colored tribal beads around her neck, while the hairdresser wove more feathers into her hair. The result was perfect for the hippie-love-child look that was happening everywhere.

Penn then made his appearance to check what had been done and get an idea for his job ahead. A medium-height, chunky man in overalls with his hands dug casually into the pockets, he resembled more a midwestern farmer than one of the highest paid photographers in the world. He was very low key, to the point of saying nothing.

In a kind of reverence, the room remained quiet while he was there, and then he left without comment, followed shortly by the girl. That was the last I saw of either of them until the photograph appeared in *Vogue* some time later. It received a full page and was breathtakingly beautiful. Penn had responded gloriously to what he saw in front of him, and it showed. I had won this round.

My Avedon booking followed soon after Penn's. As laid back and low key as Penn had been, Avedon was the direct opposite—two horses of very different color. Avedon was short, slight, and wiry with dark hair and a tense disposition whose current never shut off. His electricity rippled the air, causing sparks to fly like steel off flint stone. It was an energy that grated on me like constant pricks from a pin and played negatively into my insecurities.

Immediately when I entered his East Fifties studio, the air virtually crackled with intensity. As comfortable as I had been in Penn's warm, sunny, conservative space, I sensed that here things would be difficult. Polly again met me and took me to a large dressing room, far larger than Penn's. Across from the dressing room was a narrow room with a refrigerator and a long, white Formica table. Behind a grey curtain was the main studio, large enough to play basketball in, where the photographs were taken. A model at one end would be totally swallowed up by the space.

This was not an atmosphere where I felt nurtured and supported, but rather challenged to a fight. Still, it was this challenge that jolted me to life like a Frankenstein monster and produced the most creative time of my career, bringing out all my artistic instincts and goading me to take chances.

The model was Loulou de la Falaise, whose mother, Maxine de la Falaise, and entire family were involved in the arts—always stylish and quite social. Then in her teens, Loulou would later go on to be a muse for Yves St. Laurent in Paris, inspiring some of his most memorable collections.

She had a face like a Botticelli painting: soft, pale pink skin, full sensuous lips that turned down at the corners, and pale blue eyes that seemed to dream dreams that only the brave, or perhaps the reckless, dare to dream. There were worlds behind those eyes as yet unexplored, and there was no doubt to me, with her curious, chance-taking, Taurus spirit, that they some day would be.

In some of these ways, we were the perfect match for the risky, surrealistic make-up I would create. With the world in the state it was in, where I was at, Avedon's restless nature, and this face—all the elements were here to lure me into it.

I began by removing Loulou's eyebrows. She had very few anyhow, and what there were were interfering with the design her face seemed to dictate. Being a valiant risk-taker like me, she was amicable. I then applied a pale ivory foundation base mixed with pearl white eye shadow all over her face and powdered it with baby powder. This gave her face a pale, fragile quality whose mysterious, luminous glow seemed to shine from within. I then mixed an unusual deep mauve color that went all around her eyes, replacing her eyebrows, and gave her eyes an outer world quality. A soft, pearlized pink went on her eyelids, lips, and cheeks; I applied this with my finger because a brush would have made it look more mechanical. Polly then placed a bib of luminous-green peacock feathers around her neck, and Suga, one of New York's most talented hairdressers, wove into her naturally auburn-blonde hair tiny, tight ringlets that encircled her face like a halo. It was breathtaking.

When the photo appeared in *Vogue*, it was given a full page like the one with Penn. Avedon had created a sensational photograph and helped me rank with Pablo, Elizabeth Arden's famous make-up artist. The price I paid, however—from the frenetic energy I felt in his studio—left my nerves severely jarred. (Regrettably, I am unable to display any of the Condé Nast photos for which I did the make-up. Months of negotiations with Condé Nast and the Avedon Foundation yielded only an offer to reduce their hefty fee while other publications graciously gave me photos of my work or waived their fee for me.)

I was told that I was a co-contributor to the photos, which was true, and that the photos belonged to the photographers, which was also true. But, as in the case of the Avedon and Penn photos, when a photo is a make-up photo—that is a photo for the sake of a make-up—the make-up artist is the co-contributor who starts the ball rolling from which all the other artists take their cue. So I wasn't just a co-contributor—I was a major contributor. Given that *Vogue* paid me only the $100 daily fee that was their standard at the time of the photos, I felt that for them to ask hundreds for work I had done for them was unfair.

However, anyone with access to the 1970s *Vogue* can see the photos. The Avedon photo of Loulou can be found in the Oct. 1, 1970, issue of *Vogue* on page 124, and the Penn photo can be found in the July 1, 1970, issue of *Vogue* on page 110. It is my understanding that *Vogue* is preparing their archives to present them in the near future on the Internet, and if that is so, interested readers can perhaps see them there.

Vogue never got my full name correct and credited my make-ups to "John Richardson." I allowed this for years in *Vogue* and other publications until I insisted on my full name: John Evan Richardson. Finally, I dropped the "John" altogether, having been named for my father, with whom I didn't want to be identified.

With the success of my make-ups with Penn and Avedon, *Vogue* quickly booked me again with Avedon, and this time it was with Lauren Hutton. She was to wear a red Indian sari that didn't seem to suit her, and her eyebrows were too dark and limiting for the eye make-up I had in mind. I bleached them, which caused her a great deal of distress and me a lot of grief.

I could have easily made up Lauren to look as beautiful as she was, but as an inspiration for fantasy—which this was about for me—her face had none of Loulou's qualities.

Loulou's face was what men fight wars over, while Lauren's strong presence would lead women into their 1970s liberation—two very distinct types, both beautiful in their own right. However, Lauren's face simply didn't inspire me further than what it was. Because of it, the make-up was by no means as exciting as the previous one, and neither was the photo. Avedon even had to do some retouching because the make-up I had created didn't lend itself to Lauren's face.

When I asked her at a follow-up booking how her eyebrows were, she replied, "Shitty!" and proceeded to tell Avedon that she didn't want me to do her make-up again.

This didn't exactly have a good effect in public relations for me with Avedon, since Lauren was becoming one of his favorite models and wielding that power. Then, too, Avedon was in the middle of a divorce and particularly on edge at the time, and before making a move he would consult with his most trusted hairdresser, Ara Gallant, the ex-husband of my old pal at Fabergé, Barbara Lantz. Perhaps the two had a divorce in common and could commiserate, but, for me, this seeming lack of security didn't buoy my shaky ego. Avedon even asked me for my opinions, and I had none and thought that if he didn't know, what could I add? It was a very uncomfortable position to be in.

Then I was asked for a return with Loulou, which was a relief. Avedon asked me to use the same luminous foundation on her as before, and this time I added tiny blue, fluffy feathers to her eyelashes with lots of sky-blue eye shadow around her eyes that seemed to pour from her naturally sky-blue eyes. The result was ethereal, fragile, and pastel. Everyone loved it until the negatives came out. Loulou's eyelids were half-mast in all the photos, suggesting that perhaps a mood altering substance had been added to the mix from the time of creation to the shoot. The photos were never used, and Loulou and I were never together again. I complained to Polly that Avedon's studio was getting on my creative nerves, and so I was relieved of the problem.

It was a good thing for me, on one hand, because I needed a rest from the pressure I felt building up. It was a bad thing, on the other hand, because I was broke.

Vogue paid very little and *Harper's Bazaar* paid nothing, as was the case with another Hearst publication, *Cosmopolitan*. They thought it was sufficient that artists received exposure in their magazines and could then take the tear sheets, the printed pages of our work, around to advertising agencies where we could get a good price for our services. The only hitch was that advertising jobs were hard to come by. Controlled by photographers who produced the ads, advertising, too, believed that the models applied their make-up best. In the meantime, we couldn't live from what we made with magazines.

Later, when things again broke for me, I refused to work for any magazine unless I was paid. This helped pave the way for artists to be paid $50 by *Cosmopolitan* and *Harper's Bazaar*, and $100 by *Vogue*. It gradually went up from there, but it was still the lowest of rates and not enough to support yourself if that was your only work. As photographers became more relaxed with make-up artists, advertising agencies changed, too.

On another note, whenever I did make-up for a magazine cover or for an inside story, the editorial department would call me—as they did all their make-up artists—to ask what colors I had used on the model's face that resembled some cosmetic company's colors which the magazine intended to credit to the company. Cosmetic companies were magazines' staple, their biggest advertisers, and the magazine was appeasing them by crediting the make-up to them. They were well aware that I had used my own products and not one of the colors they credited to the cosmetic company ever landed on the girl's face, which I'm sure is still the practice today.

The reason make-up artists use their own products is that they know what products work best for them and there is no time on a photo shoot to experiment with unfamiliar products from a cosmetic company. In this situation, every minute spent at anything is money and time is of the essence. Magazines knew all of this, but they wanted to keep their advertisers happy. Just other fraudulent things I discovered along my make-up way.

Besides working with magazines and advertising agencies, there was also TV advertising, but the make-up union controlled that and stood in the way of magazine make-up artists—inarguably better artists—from working there.

I had to take them to court to defend my right to do make-up for a TV ad, for which I had been hired, when they threatened to close down the set and walk all their technicians if their union make-up artist wasn't hired instead. Not wanting their entire shoot to shut down, the company that had hired me capitulated, and I sued the union. I obtained the right to work for TV ads, but each time I was considered, the union stepped in and the whole thing started again. Finally, I went to the head of the make-up union, Ed Callahan, and complained. He admitted that nearly every member of his family—his aunts, uncles, cousins, and even distant relatives—was in the union, and to guard their jobs, they intended to keep out everybody else.

The make-up artists with magazines would become a definite threat to the union. The TV companies, who wanted to hire us to get better results, knew the union make-up artists were untrained and inferior. The actors knew it too, and constantly complained about it and were forced to reapply their own make-up before the shoot began. Finally, the union agreed to allow outside make-up artists if their people were also hired and allowed to sit around for the day while the shoot took place. This cost everyone a fortune, but it was preferable to having the set shut down, or using a union make-up artist. For me, as the one who had raised the original ruckus, things remained difficult, as if I was on a permanent black list. But at least it opened the way for future artists and may even have improved the union ones.

My date with Tallulah took place soon after my first booking with Avedon. I was on a high, having done what I felt was an excellent job on Loulou. So it was with some credentials under my belt that I rang Tallulah's doorbell. A small, thin black woman, Emma, answered.

"Madame," she said, "is waiting for you in the living room."

I knew the direction to the living room, having been there just a couple of weeks before, though the circumstances of that visit now seemed a bit shabby.

Emma returned to the kitchen, and I went to the living room where Tallulah, in a pink silk dressing gown, was sitting cross-legged like a yogist on the light blue velvet couch—her territory and hers alone. A TV on a metal stand with wheels had been pulled in front of her. I stood in the doorway waiting for an acknowledgment. There was none.

Finally, she looked up from the TV news that was absorbing her and said, "Have a drink, darling," nodding in the direction of the bar table by the doorway.

It was early afternoon, and I didn't want anything and said so. She made no response but returned her full attention to the TV.

With no further invitation, I timidly ambled across the pale grey carpet and took a seat in the same blue velvet chair that I had taken the night I was there.

I looked around the room to make sure that I had seen it correctly. There was the Augustus John portrait of her staring wistfully down at me from above the fake fireplace mantel, and the John Barrymore portrait turned in profile as if there was no need to give its audience any more of itself on the wall behind the couch where "Madame" sat.

Conspicuously missing was Jesse, for which I was thankful. His presence might have taken attention away from why I was there—to interview for a job as Madame's make-up artist. It wasn't a social call to me.

Just as I thought we were alone, Jesse appeared in the doorway.

"Tallulah...," he started.

"Shut up!" Tallulah boomed out. "I want to hear what this fuck has to say!" She was referring, I assumed, to the commentator on TV.

Undaunted, Jesse continued, "I was just going to say I'm going out."

A bit annoyed, she waved him on, and he looked at me with an exasperated expression and left. It appeared that they had perhaps arranged it so she could be alone with me.

"Oh, God," I thought, "what will become of me with this crazy woman whose tongue could dissect me like an autopsy?"

I had placed one foot in the direction of the doorway in case I needed to run, when she switched off the TV, rolled it out of her way, and said, "Sit in front of me, darling."

I inched my chair in her direction like someone fearful of snakebite.

"I said in front!" she blasted like a trumpet, and my chair riveted pronto front row center with only a coffee table between us for protection. If there was to be a show, I could get no better seat. If I was to be dead, she had no better aim.

I reflected that this must have been what John Emery—the B-actor she had married in the 1930's—meant when at the time of their divorce, he had said, "A day away from Tallulah is like a month in the country." I would grow to know the wisdom of that.

Still cross-legged with her elbows resting on her knees, she scrutinized me as if examining my pores.

Then her head moved forward in my direction as if on a mechanical crane, and she said with the sincerity of an enlightened being, "Darling, do you believe in God?"

Caught off guard, I determined that if this was to be a philosophical discussion, I wasn't up for it.

I paused and then delivered, "About as much as you do, I suppose."

Her head craned back, and she looked at me with the eyes of a child whose balloon had just been pricked. I was sure Armageddon was about to rain down on me. Then she began to laugh.

"That's perfect, darling," she said. "You avoided the question beautifully. Let's have a drink."

I was in. The interview was over.

Why she had asked the question in the first place may not even have an explanation. Tallulah was prone to spontaneity with little thought to the consequences—like the time she had all her guests remove their shoes and later tossed them out the window. She didn't like shoes in her apartment that had been tracking up and down the street, and the next step just seemed to follow.

Even her wit was spontaneous. She said she never knew when these things would come out of her mouth. Of course, she had great mentors. Ethel Barrymore had introduced her to the famous "Round Table" at the Algonquin Hotel, a group of notable writers and wits of the '40s who had lunch there daily.

By now, I was ready for that drink she offered.

"Listen to me, darling," she instructed, as I started for the bar table, "I want...," and she demonstrated the amount with her fingers, "...this much bourbon..." (which amounted to about an inch), "...this much ginger ale..." (another inch), "...and one tiny ice cube."

If I mixed that drink for her once, I mixed it hundreds of times during the years I knew her.

The next day Jesse called to say that the "Living Legend" requested that I come over and do a make-up on her for a party she was going to. There was no mention this time of him and me. I concluded that Tallulah may have pointed out that if I was to now be her make-up artist, "him and me" were no longer appropriate. She was no fool; she knew the score—and she knew Jesse. This arrangement was fine by me because it got me permanently off a hook that I didn't want to be on in the first place.

A price for the make-ups was never discussed, and I decided to let it ride until either she or I brought it up. Obviously, there was to be some compensation, but I was delighted, for the time being, just to be in her presence.

It was later decided that I would buy myself a gift, paid by her, which would cost what I felt she owed me for make-ups, and we'd let it go at that. Even before I was about to bring it up, she would always suggest that it was time to buy myself a gift.

Of course, I could have used the money, living in my East Sixties apartment with only a bed and a TV, but this relationship was important to me and we bonded in a special way, not as client and artist, but as friends.

By the time I had done quite a few make-ups on her, we decided that the gift should be sizable, so I bought an overcoat and paraded it before her when I gave her the bill.

"Good God, darling!" she exclaimed upon examining the bill. "This is your gift for Easter, your birthday, Christmas, and every other holiday coming up for the next year."

EAST 57TH STREET
NEW YORK CITY 10022

My new coat, referred to in her note, was payment for Tallulah's many make-ups for a long time. The note reads: My Darling John John I know you have exquisite taste so I know your coat is divine Merry Christmas for several years All my love Bless you Tallulah.

"I'm not cheap, sweetie," I said, with a bit of irony.

"Don't call me sweetie!" she roared. Then she added, "Call me 'dear.'"

She thought "sweetie" sounded vulgar, which was why I had used it to goad her.

She had a good deal with me, and she knew it. A union make-up artist would have charged her union prices, and they would have had the union to back them up. With them, she couldn't have gotten away with a thing.

I shared with her that when I walked down the street in my new coat everyone looked at me.

"Well, don't they always, darling?" she replied.

She was charming that way.

Once when I was making her up and needed a certain angle of her eyes to apply eye shadow, I said, "Look at me, no matter how hard it may be."

"I love looking at you, darling," was her response.

She could also be a bitch on wheels, as well as reckless. I took a friend who wanted to meet her to her apartment one afternoon, and while we were there, she asked him to pass her a large jar that was close by him which she claimed contained aspirins. To our astonishment, she poured a handful into her hand and washed them down with bourbon. Later, he told me that the pills were amphetamines, and with him being a pill-freak, too, he knew.

Tallulah loved to do things to shock.

When I told her once that I couldn't have a drink because I was on anti-biotics, she asked for my doctor's name and called the operator for his number.

"Hello, darling," she said to the operator, "this is Tallulah Bankhead. What is Doctor so and so's number?"

Imagine the operator that got that call.

Then she called the startled doctor with the same, "Hello, darling, this is Tallulah Bankhead," and told him the situation.

After some "uh huhs" and "yeahs," she hung up and said, "It's okay. Go fix us a drink."

Who knows what the poor man really said. She was looking for a drinking buddy, and anyone around was it.

Besides our make-ups together, Jesse called weekly to invite me to dinner with Tallulah. She would invariably grab the phone from him to inquire if the menu was suitable.

"What about lamb chops, darling?" she'd ask. "Do you like lamb chops?"

"Yes," I'd answer—whatever she was having.

She never ate, but joined Jesse and me in the living room while we ate from small TV tables and she drank her meal. I knew this practice would one day catch up with her. She was already becoming frail, and her legs and ankles were no larger than my wrists.

My evenings there were frequent and sometimes outrageous, with Tallulah in her cups and hoping to startle Jesse and me, fluffing her hair and saying, "Darling, this is my natural hair color, never been touched."

We'd agree, knowing what was coming.

"Well, darling, if you don't believe me...," then she'd whip up her dressing gown, exposing her pubic hair as proof.

This act we'd seen hundreds of times, and it got no more than a yawn from us, which she had expected from two gay men.

Her next favorite routine was pulling out one of her breasts and saying, "Darling, have you seen this?"

Yes, we'd seen that, too.

Being claustrophobic, she disliked being bound by clothing, particularly underclothing. Because of it, her breasts had been reduced and made firm so she wouldn't have to wear a bra, and she delighted in showing them off.

Once when Jesse and I were sitting on the couch chatting before I went home, Tallulah, stark naked, raced into the hallway in front of us with her back turned and her hands covering her buttocks in a pretence of modesty and shouted, "Is anybody here?"

Truly, I don't think I've ever seen a flabbier, more unattractive buttocks, and certainly nothing to display.

The evenings when she wasn't drunk, she could be the most interesting and entertaining companion, regaling us with stories about herself.

One of them was about a time she was sitting next to a male pianist at a party with her dress hiked up, exposing her naked crotch. When he was unable to keep his mind on his playing, she bounced him back on track with, "Darling, have you ever been this close to an open grave?"

Another one was about a huge bouquet of roses that arrived every night in her dressing room while she was touring in a play that was coming to Broadway. The card on the roses always read: "From an ardent admirer."

When the play opened on Broadway, a man showed up and announced that he was the "ardent admirer," and said, "Tallulah, I want you for my wife."

EAST 57TH STREET
NEW YORK CITY 10022

She looked at him and responded, "Don't be silly, darling. I don't even know your wife."

True or not, I loved to hear her tell those stories.

She would read us scripts of sketches written for her that she had recorded and performed on radio and for her TV show in the '50s. They were very New York, putting her in the most unlikely and outrageous situations.

She showed me two diamond bracelets: one quoted in a five-digit figure and the other in a six-digit figure. One was given her by one of her many admirers, Jock Whitney, which she revealed was the most expensive, and the other she had inherited, from whom she never said. My job was to select which was the most expensive.

It was a test she continuously ran on those around her to be certain they knew quality. She intended to surround herself with only the best—though her actions were hardly the best at

Tallulah attempting a flowery birthday note while whacked on pills and bourbon. It reads: My darling John John I did not know it was your birthday until we spoke on the phone but I give you my love which is higher than Mt. Everest and deeper than the depth of sea Also I cannot spel Except I love you Tallulah times. She even went so far as to check on family backgrounds with other tests.

I placed the first bracelet over my wrist and the diamonds sparkled brilliantly. It was magnificent. Then I put the other bracelet over my wrist and it flowed like a waterfall of diamonds, caressing each curve in an exquisitely engineered work of art. It was unmistakably the one.

I will always be grateful to Tallulah for that test. After you've experienced the ultimate, you will forever remember what that is.

My father had died after suffering strokes for years, and Mother, having nursed him through it all, was now completely focused on me. She was making one of her many pilgrimages to New York and would be staying with me, which required that I get another bed for my sparsely furnished apartment. Tallulah pounced on the opportunity to conduct one of her tests. She particularly liked checking the credentials of mothers.

Before we left to see *Hair* one evening, Tallulah called to invite us for dinner and insisted on talking with Mother. Mother was so startled that she barely got a word in edgewise with, "Yes ... yes ... well, thank you, Miss Bankhead, I'm ... oh, of course, uh, Tallulah ... yes ... yes ... well, good ... yes ... yes ... well, good ... yes ... yes .... well, goodbye ... yes, good ... yes, goodbye."

Throughout the entire one-sided conversation, she was grabbing me to get me to take the phone, but I wouldn't. This was her test and not mine.

When Mother arrived in New York, she looked like a rag, worn out from years of my father's illness and frustrated by his continuous drinking, and then exhausted from dealing with the tangled business affairs he had left behind for her to sort out. Her future as a single woman was yet uncharted.

The day of our dinner with Tallulah, I scooted Mother into Kenneth's Salon where Kenneth, who had created hairdos for Jackie Kennedy Onassis, personally oversaw the richer auburn-red hue that was added to Mother's own red hair, which was fading. A hairpiece of the same color was then woven into her now sparse hair, and the result was spectacular.

Being family, she didn't allow me to do her make-up and went instead to Kenneth's very able make-up artist, who worked magic.

Before he began, he admonished her with, "Madame, you have eyebrows like *Rebecca of Sunnybrook Farm*,"—whatever that meant.

After her transformation, I saw Mother on the street in front of my apartment building, walking with a man I knew from my neighborhood.

She had gotten into a conversation with him at a local stationery store where she stopped to buy a newspaper. He was quite handsome and obviously intrigued with this beautiful woman.

When I approached them, Mother said to me in a coy, girlish voice, "He thinks I look like someone he knows."

"I certainly hope so," I said, "because you don't look like anyone I know." And with that, I left her to her own devices.

That evening when we arrived at Tallulah's, it was raining. I was so proud of Mother. She looked magnificent in her transformation and a new beige dress she had gotten at Bloomingdale's. Tallulah would not forget this.

With Jesse's help, Mother struggled in the marble foyer trying to get out of her rubber boots when Tallulah's impatient voice in the living room boomed out, "Kathryn!"

Nervous and realizing she was being summoned, Mother immediately sloshed into the living room—boots and all—to meet the "Living Legend." Tallulah was standing to greet her like one of the goddesses of grace and charm. To my surprise, she had even done a little make-up on herself and was in a lovely silk cream dressing gown with her hair combed. And the best part, thank God: she wasn't drunk.

"Oh, Miss Bankhead...," Mother started to gush.

"It's Tallulah, darling," Tallulah corrected her. "Tallulah."

"Yes, well, uh, Tallulah...," Mother started again.

"Won't you sit down, darling?" Tallulah interrupted her, sitting territorially on her blue velvet couch and motioning for Mother to sit in a chair strategically placed directly in front of the couch.

This was eerily reminiscent of my first "interview" there, and with Mother now front row center, I suspected that something was up.

"Make Kathryn a drink, Jesse," Tallulah commanded, while Mother removed her boots and handed them to Jesse. "Make us all one, darling."

Jesse put the boots in the hallway and went to the bar table as Mother settled into the chair in front of Tallulah that had apparently been reserved for her.

Tallulah was being far too gracious, and any extreme with her signaled trouble up ahead. I was waiting for act two as I took my seat in the familiar blue velvet chair next to the couch.

Mother thought she had died and gone to heaven, being treated like royalty by the great Bankhead.

Jesse came over with the drinks and sat by Mother, who nervously chattered away about everything from her recent trip to Paris to finding a live squirrel in her toilet bowl (which she tried to flush down). To this Tallulah listened with a bit of interest, but it was unusual that she should be so quiet for such a long period of time.

Sitting cross-legged like a yogist again on her couch, Tallulah contentedly sipped her drink while looking at a small alarm clock placed on the coffee table in front of her. I had never seen the clock before and recognized that she must have placed it there—but why?

Mother continued her chatter when suddenly Tallulah bellowed out, "All right, you Southern bitch! You've talked for half an hour, now it's my turn!"

The old Tallulah was back. Mother looked as if she had been shot out of a cannon at a circus. No one had ever been that rude to her before, but then, she had never met the "Living Legend" before. Now she knew why she was a legend and why she lived: to do what she had just done.

The evening was off and running, with the bourbon flowing like a spigot had been turned on. After Tallulah's style of greeting her, Mother was ready for a drink. The pretense was over, and she was facing the reality here: "Fasten your seat belts. It's going to be a bumpy ride," as Bette Davis described her upcoming evening in the film *All About Eve*, which Tallulah revised for radio.

"After all, darling," she said to me, "the part was written about me, and that bitch got it. She got all my plays"—an exaggeration referring to Davis' doing the film of Lillian Helmann's play *The Little Foxes*, in which Tallulah starred on Broadway, "—so why shouldn't I do her 'Eve' thing?"

After hors d'oeuvres of gefilte fish—which she insisted Mother try, suspecting a Southerner had never had them—Tallulah had Mother try on several of the costumes hanging in her closet from plays she had been in.

She'd say, "Jesse, put that black dressing gown I wore in *The Little Foxes* on Kathryn," and Mother would dutifully follow Jesse into Tallulah's bedroom and return to model the dressing gown for us.

We never got the meal promised us and had to make do with the gefilte fish, which we wolfed down like a school of them had swum down our throats, in a fruitless attempt to avoid the ill effects of the alcohol that constantly appeared in our glasses.

In spite of the outrageousness, the evening was Tallulah's way of honoring our friendship, which our relationship had grown to be. She never ate, and guests were expected to follow suit. Besides, with food she couldn't get them as drunk. Whether on a stage or in her living room, she was always a colossal show woman, and though the performance was never dull, it was not one that Mother ever cared to repeat.

When we returned to my apartment, she was still reeling from her experience. I had taken her to a crazy woman who had insulted her and made her run around in her clothes all night. She couldn't figure out how I knew Tallulah Bankhead and it appeared she felt that I was slipping out of her grasp. I could have told her that going to bed with Jesse and being able to do make-up were the reasons, but, of course, I didn't.

She never understood where I began and she ended, and she asked many times, "What do you know about make-up? You studied art," never putting together that make-up and art were the same, and that I could do it and she couldn't.

She couldn't accept that I had this artistic ability, believing that everything had to have come from her. It never occurred to her that I wasn't her. She assumed that by just giving birth and nearly dying, that sacrifice entitled her to everything. That was her reality, but it wasn't mine—a constant source of unpleasant friction between us.

After my father's funeral—before which I cried once, only once, in response to his death—Mother had grabbed my arm and said, "You don't have to go like him. You can be a success. Do it ... do it for me," as if she had a claim in it. And she wasn't even subtle about it; it wasn't for me that I was to do it, but for her.

She had wanted my father to be big in Kentucky politics like his father, who was judge of the court of appeals, but my father drank, so that washed that up, and she had turned her attention to me. I was to be her knight in shining armor, but I could never measure up because I was always trying to implement her ideas, not my own, and consequently I always felt inadequate.

I had been infatuated with Mother all of my life. From her own self-promotion, I believed that she was everything I wanted to be, or should want to be. Now it seemed the tables had turned and I was everything she wanted to be. In that, we were a perfect match. I mistook her abuse of my father for his drinking as strength, and she mistook my art as something she owned and could have. I never told her that she was the reason I was a make-up artist.

Mornings, as a child, I would sit mesmerized, watching her apply her make-up, transforming her pale, delicate, undefined features into a distinct beauty. With fox furs strewn around her neck, she'd daintily lift the veil of her hat with her index finger to take communion in church and carefully tuck the veil back under her chin while I observed. To me she rivaled every siren on the silver screen. She was often told she resembled Irene Dunn, my favorite movie star, and I was convinced that she, too, was a star, hidden by the remoteness of that stifling little Kentucky country town.

Even now I knew that I would do her bidding—like the surrogate husband I had become—even at the expense of my own life. In spite of it all, I was driven to please her, to seek her admiration that she never gave me. If she had, the game would have been over, I would have won, and she would have lost me. She couldn't allow that. No, the game had to go on, on her terms, or she would no longer be "Mother."

Once, I introduced her to a girl I was going with at Pratt, and afterwards I asked her what she thought of the girl. "Not much," she answered, which I knew meant that I was to get on with my career and with what really mattered: my relationship with Mother. I immediately dropped the girl. It was the same with Tod in Paris, or anyone close to me. She tolerated nothing less than total ownership, with no interference.

So, returning from Tallulah's in our inebriated state, it was not unusual that she should try to claim ownership of that relationship in a covetous, even jealous way.

"Everything you have," she declared, "and everything you are, you owe to me!"

She wanted it all, even my relationship with Tallulah, who respected me for the man and the artist I was, something Mother never could have done. No, I was to forfeit even that to Mother. This was the eternal price I was to pay for her nearly dying from my birth. This I would owe her forever.

As she went into the bathroom and punctuated her declaration to me with a slam of the door, I thought to myself: "You're right, lady. Everything I have I owe to you: someone who uses sex to get ahead, promiscuously sleeps around, drinks too much, smokes too much pot, and hates himself most of the time." Did she want to claim those too?

When my sister and I were children, we shared a bedroom together. One morning while my sister was getting dressed, I was standing on my bed stretching with only my pyjama top on that exposed my genitals. Mother saw this and darted into the room, dragged me from the bed, and into the next room.

I was always afraid of this room as a child because it was kept dark to keep the sunlight from fading the fabrics. Inside, she said, "You exposed yourself to your sister, now expose yourself to me."

Then she tore off my pyjama top and beat me with a belt she had brought with her.

Opening the closet door, she said, "Get in."

I crawled inside and she closed the door and locked it. Cowering on the floor of the closet, I was comforted by the darkness that soothed my stinging skin and became the friend I needed. Darkness would one day dictate a way of life for me.

In the sixth grade when we were all beginning to express our budding sexuality, I drew a naked woman and circulated the drawing around the room. The teacher snatched it up and threatened to take it to my father. Instead, she took it to a drugstore where all the town gossips congregated in the afternoon to report the latest news. I was the afternoon news.

Mother heard about it and confronted me. By then I was aware of her injustices: her accusations with no proof, her emotional blackmail about my birth, and even opening my sister's and my mail. To her, we were her property. She had bought my sister and nearly died for me.

"I didn't mean to draw a naked woman," I skillfully denied. "I just didn't have time to put the bathing suit on her."

She bought it and sat back relieved that she didn't have a pervert for a son, which would have reflected on her.

So expertly, so profoundly she had put women on pedestals and pronounced them off limits, that what else was left? Maybe it was always there, but it stands to reason when a woman stands over you wielding a belt while you crawl naked on the floor below her, that doesn't exactly build your manhood. Was she even responsible for my sexuality, in cahoots with my father and my uncle, to clandestinely drive me into the night, desperately trying to fill a void that was unfillable?

She left for Kentucky a few days later. We managed to squeak out a few civil moments during the rest of her visit, but our battles were beginning to tell on her, as well as wearing me down, too. I believe we both knew that our days together were numbered. There would be a couple more visits, each with progressively more disturbing results that drove me further away from her.

I believed that she made it impossible for me to have a personal relationship with anyone but her, and I hated her most for that. Ours was a complicated love/hate relationship. I loved her dearly but hated the insidious pull she had on me. I had been made to feel that if you loved someone, they had to hurt you, or vice versa. This would play out in all of my future intimate relationships, and would nearly destroy me.

5

Lucille Ball; Tallulah Dies

My work with *Vogue* was not over; it had just slowed down since my departure from Avedon's studio. I was routinely trotted out to do jobs, but they were usually on location, which meant that I was stuck doing make-up on models in trailers parked in front of some location, usually an apartment building, hotel, or some other outside place.

Every time anyone entered or left the trailer, where the clothes were also kept, it bounced up and down from the impact of their movement, and so would whatever line I was currently executing on a girl's face. If I was on her lips, a red line would streak straight up to her nose and I'd have to stop, wipe it off, reapply make-up, and begin again. It was frustrating, but I had no desire to return to the hectic conditions in Avedon's studio. I was far happier working in a trailer than there.

I didn't particularly like models either, and that was another downside. With my own modeling, I had had a lot of experience with them, and, to me, many were spoiled, pampered brats who were treated with kid gloves to get photos out of them and discarded when a newer crop of faces showed up. They were deluded that this pampering and preening would last forever, but I knew the truth. They were around as long as they were young and necessary, and disposed of at the appropriate time like tissue paper after a good nose blow. Many were foolish young girls who believed that they had found a dream, but I knew that one day this bubble would burst. That would be the hardest day of their lives, because everything they were about was riding on it.

I asked one of them once, "Who's your favorite actress?"

She answered, "Brooke Shields."

I then asked her, "Who's your favorite actor?"

She answered, "Pee-wee Herman," not realizing that this was a character created by Paul Reubens.

Of course, there were those who were quite smart and gifted and would go on to have substantial careers in film and TV and have their own businesses, but those were few compared to the many that traipsed to the camera with their perfect faces, smiles, and long-limbed bodies, and then disappeared into some model dumpster. Some wouldn't even survive to do that.

Polly Mellen's catch phrase for everything at Avedon's studio was "It's divine"—everything was "divine"—and it had gotten to me. I didn't think anything was divine about the fashion world. I was an artist and considered myself part of the art world. Fashion seemed so transient and superficial: here today, gone tomorrow.

What could be divine about being crammed into a mouse-sized trailer or a room the size of a closet with a gang of giggling, chattering girls—with hair blowers going, rock and roll music blaring in your ears, the fashion editor, her assistant, the hair stylist, and me all jammed in there together—along with masses of clothes hanging from racks that the girls kept trying on and pulling off while the photographer screamed, "Where's the model?"

What's divine about that? Hell by comparison would be divine.

Fashion was never my passion. I had ended up here because of modeling and my fashion illustration, which I hadn't even chosen for myself. Theatre and film was always my true passion—if I'd had the courage to have chosen that—and so this was my penalty.

Tallulah was my one connection to the world where I longed to be. She may have been vulgar at times, but she was real and gutsy, and you knew where she stood. Theatre dealt with universal truths that were lasting and important. What could be important about the placement of a button or the plunge of a neckline?

Then *Vogue* came through with a job that would change my destiny and find my place in all this. I was booked for a photo shoot with the biggest entertainer of them all: Lucille Ball. I was ecstatic, though I had no idea how I would create the exaggerated make-up for which she was known.

I had loved Lucy since she was in movies at MGM, but I had never seen her *I Love Lucy* show that ran from 1951 to 1961. I rarely watched TV and had little interest. This job offer, however, was years after the show ended when she was married to Borscht Belt stand-up comedian Gary Morton, whom, I was told, she had met in the Catskills.

A friend of mine, hearing about my working with Lucy, had jokingly written in chalk on the sidewalk outside my apartment building, "I Love Lucy." All of my friends were as excited as I was.

The morning of my scheduled appointment with her at the Plaza Hotel, I was nearly ready to walk out the door when *Vogue* called to say that the booking had been canceled because Lucy would do her own make-up.

Hanging up the phone, I stood motionless, feeling totally disappointed. I had so looked forward to this; in fact, everyone who knew me had. I felt I had let down a lot of people—not the least of whom was myself.

Then an idea dawned: I would go anyhow and pretend I hadn't gotten the call. The most they could do was tell me what I already knew, but by then maybe I'd have a chance to meet Lucille Ball. In fact, it was the kind of thing Lucy's character, Lucy MacGillicuddy Ricardo, would have done on the *I Love Lucy* show.

I was booked; I was going.

Arriving at her Plaza suite with my make-up case, I knocked at the door and a short blonde woman—who looked like a replica of Lucy herself—with a short, tossed-salad do, lots of make-up, and bright red lips, answered.

I told her who I was and that I had been booked by *Vogue*, and she, not knowing anything about it, let me in anyhow. I was as charming as I could be, having enough experience with these things to know that to get to the higher-ups, I needed to ingratiate myself with those who surrounded them.

The woman told me (even showed me pictures that didn't resemble her at all now) of a dance team she had once been part of in Hollywood called "Renita and Ramone." She said they had appeared in MGM movies where Lucy had met her. Now she was Lucy's dresser, and I wondered what had become of Ramone and their dance team. Perhaps they had split up, and this was the next best thing she could get. I found out later that she also drank, which may have been the problem.

While we chattered away, with me sitting in a chair by the door, in marched Lucy in sunglasses and a mink coat, with her hairdresser, Irma, a frumpy, frizzy dark- haired woman with gnarled, arthritic hands that worked miracles with Lucy's hair. She, too, had been with her since her MGM days. With a quick glance at me, Lucy shot straight into her bedroom and shut the door.

Irma stayed in the living room part of the suite with Renita and me, and again, without yet knowing who this new woman was, I made myself as charming as I could. I explained what I was doing there, but she made no mention of Lucy not needing me. I had no idea who made the call to *Vogue* canceling me, but it didn't seem to be these two.

Finally, the door to the bedroom opened, and Lucy motioned for Irma to come inside. The door was closed again, and Renita and I resumed our idle chitchat, which, by now, was becoming annoying. I hadn't come to spend the day chatting with this woman, who didn't particularly interest me. I had come to see the great Lucille Ball, whom I had hardly gotten a glimpse of behind sunglasses and a turned-up collar of her mink coat on her dash to the bedroom.

Moments later, the door again opened and the lady herself stepped out. I automatically sprang up as if the Pope had just entered the room.

"Irma tells me *Vogue* sent you to do my make-up," she said, with no mention of the canceled appointment.

"Yes," I said, observing her obvious, thickly plastered face of make-up that I assumed she had applied herself with the dexterity of the hands of a gorilla.

"Come in and touch me up," she said, and I wondered where on her face there was room for more.

I scooted inside, with Renita and Irma both seeming to cheer me on.

I later learned that her interest in me stemmed from a dispute she was having with her current make-up artist, a Westmore of the old Hollywood family of make-up artists, who, at one time, she had intended to marry.

Over to a large Southern-exposure window in the bedroom I pulled a chair. It was far too low for my tall frame to bend down to do anything about her make-up—whatever that might be—but I was determined to do something.

The make-up she had done looked like it had been applied with a trowel: inches thick of Max Factor panstick, blue eye shadow for days, false eyelashes that protruded two inches from her lids, eyebrows drawn well onto her forehead, blood-red lips that nearly touched her nostrils, cheeks rouged until they appeared to be bleeding, and all of it powdered like the dry Sahara Desert had hit it.

I did the best I could to calm down the intensity, soften it, and make her face humanly believable.

When I was finished, she looked in a hand mirror, got up, and said, "I'm doing the *Ed Sullivan Show* tomorrow night. Do you want to do my make-up?"

Did I? "Yes," I said immediately, before she changed her mind.

I was then asked to come along on the shoot for *Vogue*—still with no mention of the cancellation.

Triumphantly, I packed up my cosmetics and turned to join the two women in the next room as an official part of Lucy's entourage. Then I heard her behind me add, "And honey"—I turned around and met her cold, steely eyes—"you'd better know what you're doing."

Gulp. I didn't, but I sure got the hang of it fast.

While riding in the limousine to the photo shoot, I observed Lucy's beautifully swept up hairdo and its quite natural color, so different from the garish orange-red color I had seen her in. I complimented her on how beautiful it was.

"It's a wig," she said.

"Which part?" I asked, assuming Irma had used Lucy's own hair to sweep up and added false hair on the top.

"All of it."

The whole thing was glued onto her head. She never used her own hair, which was dyed red from her naturally brown hair to match her wigs, but, in fact, was short and not that attractive.

"Boy," I thought, "what they can do in Hollywood."

The shoot was quick and painless, and I returned home to prepare myself for the morning when I would return to the Plaza to make up Lucy from scratch for the *Ed Sullivan Show* that night. The show was a traditional Sunday night family extravaganza and had been CBS's top rated show since 1948.

I would make her up that morning so she could go to the Ed Sullivan Theatre to do a run-through of the title song from her current movie, *Yours, Mine, and Ours* (also starring Henry Fonda). The song had been staged in Hollywood with the 18 kids from the movie and would be repeated that night. The make-up had to last throughout the day and still look fresh that evening. I would be able to check it out with the director on the studio monitor and make whatever adjustments were necessary according to what we saw. I had never done anything like this, of course, but my risk-taking nature was like the voices of the Sirens beckoning me on.

To up the ante of the risk, I would be using some new products from Revlon's new Ultima II line that I had never tried before. One was a colored moisturizer that I hoped would give a vibrancy and moisture to Lucy's dry, lifeless, overworked skin from years of too much make-up applied too often. Her skin never got a rest. With the moisturizer, I would be using their cream foundation that promised to give her skin the coverage she needed but not the "build-up" she had been getting from the Max Factor panstick she was using. I was also using a new, sheer, translucent powder with a technique I had developed where I applied the powder with a damp sponge that left the skin soft, dewy, and lifelike, something Lucy's skin badly needed.

To top it off, I had bought new false lashes that I had trimmed in a special way to look real and, again, lifelike, not like those two-inch, phony-looking things she had on when we met.

I had also instructed her not to put a thing on her face before our meeting that morning.

She had said to me, "I have to put on my eyebrows, honey. My husband's never seen me without my eyebrows."

She explained that Samuel Goldwyn had had her eyebrows shaved off when she began in films in 1933, and they never grew back.

I agreed that her husband shouldn't see her without eyebrows, but I asked her to only pencil them in lightly. I wanted to control where they ended up this time, and it wasn't going to be on her forehead as they were previously. And her lips weren't going to be drawn up to her nostrils again, either. Whatever I was going to do, there would be no repeat of any of that.

From this point, it was a roll of the dice. Either Lucy would look spectacular that evening, or I could kiss any future plans for a Hollywood career goodbye forever.

The following morning was St. Patrick's Day, and getting across Fifth Avenue through the parade and crowd of people with my make-up case—which now weighed a ton with all the new products—was a chore.

I rang the bell of Lucy's Plaza suite, and Renita again answered. A moment of chatter with her, and I immediately went into Lucy's bedroom where I found her staring out of the window at the parade, whose thunderous roar below was only a dull, muffled sound from our height.

Without turning around, she mumbled, "I hate Pat O'Brien."

I pulled the big chair over to the window again, and she sat down. The work began. She had obeyed my instructions to the letter. Her eyebrows were lightly penciled in and easily removed. She didn't look like herself without the make-up, particularly without her eyebrows, but at least this time I wasn't dictated by a lot of bad choices that I had no option but to follow in an effort to soften them down; now I could make my own choices.

The Ultima II colored moisturizer and foundation worked perfectly together, giving her fragile, age-spotted skin the coverage it needed without looking like a mask. The sheer, translucent powder applied with a damp sponge kept the foundation in place and made her skin glow.

Blue eye shadow, which Tallulah hated on herself, was softly applied around Lucy's blue eyes to bring out their color.

(Tallulah always protested, "Don't put blue eye shadow on me like Lucille Ball," and so her shadow was always brown. She thought blue eye shadow on her made her look like a floozy, which she also thought it did to Lucy. The secret was not to plaster it on, as Lucy had been doing. However, after Lucy, I began using the same Ultima II colored moisturizer and foundation on Tallulah, whose skin was dry from age and drinking, and it produced the same youthful glow.)

The lashes I had specifically trimmed for Lucy were then added on top of her own lashes, which I mascaraed and blended into the false ones to give a real look.

We approached her eyebrows together, with me beginning by wiping off her design and replacing it with a lightly drawn version slightly below where she had drawn them for her husband's benefit that morning. My design gave her a less startled look and was a more natural placement—definitely not on her forehead. I asked her to go over my design and redraw them, which she did, and they came out perfectly.

All any of these women needed was guidance and support in their artwork because, after years of watching it applied by expert artists in Hollywood, they could do their own make-up. However, after a time, they had all gotten into bad habits, which needed to be controlled by another eye.

Like Tallulah, Lucy insisted on doing her own lips. I began, as I did with Tallulah, by again drawing a light line around her lips for her to follow so she wouldn't get carried away, and she followed it to perfection.

The lip design both these ladies used was designed for Joan Crawford in the '40s. It was a lip line well over the natural line that made lips larger, wider, and exaggerated. At one time, every woman in Hollywood used this design—whether it belonged on them or not—and influenced the public to do likewise. It took years to get these exaggerated lips out of vogue. These ladies, like a lot of others from the old school, never got over it, and it made them look quite clown-like at times, but certainly distinct.

When our work was complete, Irma was called in to take care of Lucy's hair, and I was scooted outside so the two women could do their collaborative thing, which I sensed they preferred to do in privacy.

When Lucy emerged from the bedroom, the creation was a sensational Lucille Ball. Lucy herself said she never looked better, and I was immediately asked to join their team in Los Angeles for her new TV show, *Here's Lucy.*

At the run-through at the Ed Sullivan Theatre, the only comment the director had when we observed Lucy on stage from the monitor was that I should increase her lip color. That was a first. Usually it was, "Tone her down." I had purposely kept her lips a softer color for day so she wouldn't look so made up running around that day and I had intended to increase the color that evening. It was an excellent experience that came in handy for the stage work I would later get into in my career.

After the run-through, I returned to the Plaza with the troops to pick up my make-up case. There we were met by Lucy's husband, Gary Morton, and "Little Luci," big Lucy's then 19-year-old daughter, Luci Arnez. I was asked to put "a very little make-up" on "Little Luci" before they went shopping.

As I did the make-up, Morton showed me seven watches from Cartier and Harry Winston that he had placed up and down his arm and asked which one I liked. Because of the nature of his question, I assumed he had brought them all back to the hotel to choose one to buy. I pointed out one that caught my eye and asked which he was buying.

"All of them," he answered, and looked at me like I had asked a stupid question.

Considering the multi-millionaires they were, I guess I had.

"It would sure get confusing to me which one to pick each day," I thought.

That evening in her assigned upstairs dressing room at the Ed Sullivan Theatre, with her freshly adjusted make-up, Lucy waited with Irma, Renita, and me to go on. To calm her nerves and take her attention away from the performance she was about to do on stage in front of millions of TV viewers, Lucy played a word game with Renita, something like "ticktacktoe" where words to questions were penciled into squares until someone had the right alignment to win. Lucy was such an avid player that, rather than hard-draw the squares each time, she had had pads of the squares printed.

While I sat on the dressing table next to Lucy observing what she was writing in her squares, and Renita and Irma sat in chairs across from us, George Hamilton, who was on the program that evening, popped in the open door with his usual deep tan, enhanced by more make-up than Lucy had.

She introduced me, and, unimpressed, he disappeared into his dressing room. Moments later, we heard chattering in the hallway and looked up to see three matronly women—who were obviously from out of town and had somehow gotten backstage—standing at the door.

"Look!" said one of them, standing about a yard away from Lucy's face and pointing at her. "There's Lucille Ball!"

Without looking up as she scribbled a word in one of her squares, Lucy kicked the open door and it slammed in the woman's face. Close to going on stage, this was an intrusion she did not intend to tolerate.

During her trip East, Lucy was also scheduled to appear on the *Mike Douglas Show*, an afternoon talk show that originated in Philadelphia, and she asked me to join them to again do her make-up. Before we left, however, she wanted me to arrange a visit for her with Tallulah, which I did.

Tallulah had done an episode of the *I Love Lucy* show in 1957, when the characters moved from Manhattan to Connecticut. In the show, Tallulah tells Lucy to get out of her house, to which Lucy replies, "I've been thrown out of better places."

"You've never been in better places!" Tallulah bellows.

During rehearsals for the show—which was originally planned to guest star Tallulah's old nemesis, Bette Davis, who had had an accident and couldn't do it—Lucy continually snapped her fingers at Tallulah to get her to read her lines faster, and it had infuriated Tallulah. In the end, Tallulah stole the show and revitalized her sagging career with many TV appearances after that, notably a recurring part on the *Batman* series in the '60s playing the Black Widow.

When a reporter asked her how she had come to California to do Batman after such an illustrious New York stage career, she answered, "By jet, darling."

Lucy was basically terrified of Tallulah, but she sensed that Tallulah might not be around much longer and she wanted to see her before she left New York. Her visit may also have been a kind of apology for her bad behavior while Tallulah was on her show.

For Tallulah, however, this was over a decade later when she didn't need anything from Lucy. She had no intention of putting up with her dictatorial ways again, as she previously had out of respect that it was Lucy's show and she had needed the exposure it gave her. She would grant this blue eye-shadowed, dyed red-headed floozy a visit, but it was on her territory now and it was Lucy who had requested it—not the other way around.

After turning down Tallulah's first few attempts at offering a drink, Lucy finally relented and had one—a whopper—which let her guard down.

When the time was ripe, Tallulah hauled out the big guns and spouted out, "How much did you have to pay Desi to get rid of him?"

Before she had time to think—and with the booze working on her—Lucy responded, "A million dollars."

The question was inappropriate and doubtlessly delivered impetuously as Tallulah was prone to do, but she got the answer she had wanted, and this time it was her treat. It was the last time the two women spoke, probably much to the relief of Lucy.

Many of the stars had some smattering of acquaintance with each other, having met somewhere along their career way. Katharine Hepburn called Tallulah to complain that all she did was work.

"At least you had some fun in your life," Hepburn lamented.

"You have millions, darling," Tallulah reminded her, knowing that was more important to Hepburn than fun.

Lucy, her two women companions, and I traveled to Philadelphia in a black stretch limousine that comfortably accommodated all of us and our belongings. The women chattered constantly, to which Lucy, more concerned with the condition of her bladder, barely listened. At a Howard Johnson's, she asked the driver to pull over. Wrapped securely in her long, expensive mink, she got out, aimed herself for the front entrance, and sailed into the ladies' room with a crowd of surprised onlookers on both sides of her path.

"That was Lucille Ball," people murmured, and the crowd began to grow around the ladies' room entrance. Women darted out of the bathroom and reported to their colleagues that Lucille Ball had been in one of the stalls.

Soon Lucy emerged—again wrapped snugly in her mink with her head held high—and marched back to the limousine without a word or an autograph for those who pursued her. Getting in, she slammed the door as deliberately as she had slammed it in those matrons' faces at the Ed Sullivan Theatre. Lucy may have been grateful for her public, but she gave every indication that she preferred them at a distance. In addition, she may have felt that going to the bathroom was a private matter, even if it was done in a public place.

The morning of the *Mike Douglas Show* taping, I found Lucy waiting for me in her bedroom at the hotel where we were all staying. Morton and "Little Luci" had returned to California, and Lucy would be returning the following day.

I did the same make-up on her that I had done for the *Ed Sullivan Show* a couple of days before, but this time she got up afterwards and I got a look at her face. It seemed to have dropped, and the make-up had traveled down with it. It looked nothing like it had when I applied it with her head tilted back.

I came out the door and encountered Irma on her way in to do her hair thing.

"I think I've made Lucy look horrible," I said, and then explained how the make-up wasn't where I'd put it.

"Don't worry," she said, "I'll take care of it." She disappeared inside.

Sure she would have to somehow start over, I anxiously waited in the living room of the suite for them to come out. When they did, Lucy looked like herself, and I couldn't imagine how the miracle had been performed.

Irma explained that from years of making those exaggerated faces, Lucy's facial muscles and skin were slack and her face had fallen—but she was a "bleeder," I was told, which I assumed meant she bled if she was cut and couldn't have a face lift because of it. To compensate, Irma had developed a technique of rolling Lucy's hair in a series of tight pin curls that pulled up her face and the make-up with it, like a Venetian blind going up. Her wig was then glued on top of it. It looked perfectly natural but, in reality, was excruciatingly painful. Throughout the day, Lucy would constantly push some long object like a pencil or the handle of one of my brushes under the foundation of her wig to relieve the tension of the relentless pull on her hair.

Backstage at the taping, a woman was standing there whom I didn't recognize. She smiled at me and I smiled back, still with no recognition because I never watched television. With a freshly lifted face for the *Here's Lucy* show premiering that September, she was Vivian Vance, Lucy's female sidekick in three of her TV shows. The *Mike Douglas* producers had arranged for Vivian to be there to surprise Lucy, who was there to surprise Mike Douglas. It was a double setup that everybody—especially the audience—thoroughly enjoyed.

(I was told Vivian complained that all Lucy did was work and made her work too. That was why Vivian finally quit TV after nearly two and a half decades of it to enjoy her remaining years with her husband until her death in 1979.)

After the taping, we were led downstairs to a long concrete tunnel that we were told was the back entrance of the theatre. When the double doors of the entrance were opened, a mob from outside poured in which startled all of us, particularly Lucy whom they went for.

She stood paralyzed, and a look of terror crossed her face.

I grabbed her arm and said, "Come on."

Pushing through the crowd and running interference in front of her, we parted the throng like Moses at the Red Sea and sped across the street where we walked briskly down the sidewalk with the rest of Lucy's troop following.

Realizing I was still holding her arm, Lucy abruptly snatched it away in a defiant gesture to reclaim her authority—now that we were a safe distance from the mob—and proceeded in front of us, nonchalantly observing the store windows as if out on a stroll.

Thou shalt have no other Goddess before Lucy.

Walking down the hall on Lucy's floor back at the hotel, Lucy and I passed an open room door where two maids were inside cleaning and making up the beds.

"Look!" said one of the maids. "There's Lucille Ball and Mr. Mooney," referring to the Theodore J. Mooney character Gale Gordon played on *The Lucy Show*.

Lucy turned to me and said, "If they think you're Mr. Mooney, all is lost."

That evening, Lucy and Vivian dined together in a dark, secluded corner of the hotel dining room, while Renita, Irma and I shared our dinner at another table a discreet distance away to give them privacy. Lucy had taken off her wig and Irma had released Lucy's hair, which made her look like a bulldog with her dropped face, not at all what a hungry, autograph-seeking public would recognize as the glamorous Lucille Ball.

The following morning before I left for New York, Lucy jotted down on a notepad that she'd pilfered from the Plaza Hotel her contact information to discuss my working with her. Then she reached in her purse and tipped me $20 for my time with her. A tip wasn't expected, required, or even wanted, but for two major TV appearances to introduce her new movie and her new fall show—and considering the time I had spent touching up and altering her make-up—$50 or $100 would have had more class, particularly since she wasn't personally paying for any of it, to say nothing of her status in the entertainment industry. Twenty dollars might be what one would tip at a beauty salon for an especially good hair job.

I mentioned this experience with Lucy to Tallulah, and she said, "She's notoriously cheap, darling. Everyone knows that."

She didn't elaborate further, but it gave me pause about working with Lucy. I consulted a lawyer recommended by Tallulah, and we drafted a letter to Lucy stating the salary I would require to transfer to Los Angeles, which included a car, unnecessary in New York but essential in Los Angeles. I never heard from her, but I would take it up with her at a later date.

While I was with Lucy in Philadelphia, Tallulah went to Chestertown, Maryland to visit her sister, Eugenia, and Eugenia's long-time friend and sometimes lover, Louisa Carpenter, a du Pont heir.

Tallulah and Jesse shared the guesthouse with its own pool that was usually reserved for Eugenia, who stayed with Carpenter in the large main house on her many- acre estate with Eugenia's adopted son, Billy Bankhead, a handsome young man whom Carpenter greatly loved and treated as her own.

Eugenia had a voice like Tallulah, but that's where the similarity ended. Nevertheless, Eugenia was a vixen with sufficient looks and coquettish charm to beguile men, having been married seven times as proof. One of the men she was believed to have beguiled was her own father, whom Tallulah thought favored Eugenia over herself, a never-ending source of sibling rivalry.

Over bridge one evening in Maryland, Tallulah, in her cups, said to Eugenia, "Sister, you've been so nice to me while I've been here, I want to give you a little present. Go into town tomorrow and charge something to me."

The next day Eugenia phoned to say that she had gotten herself a vacuum cleaner, but when she told Tallulah the exorbitant price it had cost, Tallulah screeched, "You could have bought your own vacuum cleaner if you hadn't squandered all your money on those seven husbands of yours!"

"Tallulah," Eugenia said calmly, "I had more fun with those seven husbands than I ever could with a vacuum cleaner."

In wit, Eugenia did rival Tallulah.

Tallulah and Jesse returned to New York with Eugenia, and Tallulah immediately planned a party for her. She invited me and several of her close friends, including Jesse's gay male friends, and her old chum, the actress Estelle Winwood, who was in town and always a delight, especially for the gay men.

Winwood lived to be 101 and appeared in, among many things, a 1976 movie, *Murder by Death*, with Truman Capote. She was a wise, spry old thing with a caustic British wit that Tallulah adored—as did everyone.

I naïvely said to her, "I bet you know a lot of things I should know."

With her wide-eyed, multi-lifted face that barely moved anymore from

Tallulah sunning with friend.

its constantly amazed Tweety Bird expression, she observed me like a bird pulling up a worm and delivered, "I don't doubt it."

My make-ups on Tallulah were now including events like her appearance on the *Merv Griffin* TV show, a BBC interview shot in her apartment, and a memorable party at Sardi's for the opening of the 1968 movie starring Patricia Neal, *The Subject Was Roses*.

Neal had appeared on Broadway in 1946 in Lillian Helmann's play *Another Part of the Forest*, for which she received a Tony and the Drama Critics Award for best new actress. She played Regina Hubbard, a character Tallulah originated in Helmann's acclaimed 1939 play, *The Little Foxes*.

I was coming off a mescaline trip that I had taken the night before with my "Arthur" crowd, and I was still seeing double and in no condition to do anything, much less a make-up. I was also expected to wear a dinner jacket and look reasonably presentable after an hour of Tallulah's make-up, an exhausting feat in itself. It was I who needed the make-up.

As I began my work, Tallulah, already inebriated—for which I was thankful considering my own state—related one of her amusing tales that she loved to tell where she would impersonate the people involved. This time it was about when she told Ethel Barrymore that John Barrymore had once tried to rape her.

In a wheezy, raspy voice intended to be Ethel's, the answer was, "Well, he didn't have to try very hard, did he, darling?"

We both cracked up at this, and I accidentally sprinkled some lavender powder on her cheekbone—which I decided to leave there where I felt it gave her a certain *je ne sais quoi*. She then swung into another of her favorites about a famous grand dame of the London stage who had fallen on hard times and was relegated to touring in rundown theatres in remote towns throughout England. Her lodging accommodations were equally decrepit, and in one of the shabby hotels where she was forced to stay, a wooden crucifix of Jesus hung on the wall of her room.

She looked at it and mused, "Oh, how I envy his comfortable cross."

This, she said, came from her old actress buddy, Estelle Winwood.

At this point I realized that I had put two false lashes on one of her eyelids, with one on the other.

Before I could do anything about it, she sat up to look in the mirror and I swished a brush with nothing on it across her eyelids and said, "Now close your eyes and let that dry."

She sat back to allow something to happen that wasn't even there while I deliberated how to pull off one of the doubled lashes without removing the other. With time slipping away and close to total exhaustion, I decided to leave it.

She always applied her own lipstick and I then corrected it. This time, with both of us out of our minds working on it, her lips were rapidly approaching her nostrils. It was uncomfortably becoming a déjà vu of the freaky make-up I had done on the woman at the Revlon Salon.

I complained that I wasn't too sure about this, but she said, "Don't worry, darling. My head'll be moving so fast they'll never even get a beam in on me."

After another drink, she paid no further attention to her make-up, and by then we were both too smacked out to even care. Quickly getting into our evening clothes, she, Jesse, and I went downstairs to the waiting limousine and before we knew it, we descended onto a red carpet in front of Sardi's with a crowd behind the ropes on both sides in a frenzy at seeing Tallulah going inside. As I had with Lucy, I got another taste of what it was like to be hounded by a mob. It was somewhat unnerving, and I sensed the strain of the upkeep on both these women.

Though the party was for the premiere of Patricia Neal's new film, Tallulah insisted that the Sardi cartoon portrait of her—which hung with the many others of the famous there—be placed to the left of the entrance where she could sit under it, forcing everyone who entered to first greet her. She reasoned that it was from her original creation of Regina Hubbard in *The Little Foxes* that Neal had followed and been successful, and she wanted recognition for that. No one was allowed to upstage Tallulah, but she had no compunctions about upstaging them.

Among the first guests to arrive were Otto Preminger and his wife, who were neighbors of mine with a townhouse a few doors down from me. When I worked at Fabergé, Preminger and I seemed to hit the sidewalk the same time each morning and ended up several times walking together to work, with him on his way to his office on Madison Avenue. It was an experience that was uncomfortable for both of us, which we endured until I, and perhaps he, too, arrived on the sidewalk at another hour to avoid a chance meeting. I'd put up with his crabbiness years before at the Cannes Film Festival when I was there doing drawings for the London *Sunday Times*, and I'd had my fill. Now, here I was again with—of all people—Tallulah Bankhead.

As he greeted her, he glanced at me and his expression read: "How the hell does he know her?"

I think I was a continuous enigma for this man. I seemed to pop up everywhere.

On one of our walks, I insisted that I send him a gift of Fabergé's new men's line. He protested he didn't want it, and I sent it anyhow. Years later, I wrote a screenplay with one of the minor characters inspired by my experience with Preminger. A friend sent it to him and told him the part was written for him.

"I don't do bit parts," was his rejection.

Had he known I had written it, his rejection might have been even stronger.

Sitting with Tallulah on the banquette by the entrance with Jesse on the other side, I noticed that the top lash of the double set of false lashes on her eyelid was creeping up and becoming unfastened.

Accustomed to this being my job, I thoughtlessly reached to push it back down when she stopped my hand and said, "No, no, darling. I'll do it."

Not wishing to make a public display of her make-up, she discreetly took out her compact mirror and adjusted it when we saw Shelley Winters approaching our table.

"Dear God," I prayed inside, "please don't let Tallulah tell anyone I did this make-up."

I had sobered up enough by now to see what I had done.

Tallulah had recently had an encounter with Winters at a Hubert Humphrey rally where Tallulah was seated and Winters wanted to get past her.

"Move it!" Winters had ordered.

"You move it, darling," Tallulah had responded stubbornly.

She distinctly disliked this woman.

"Oh, my God," Tallulah muttered, "here's that horrible woman again."

Before we knew it, Winters was standing over us observing Tallulah as if she were under a microscope. Then I heard Tallulah crumple my prayer and throw it in the toilet by announcing that I had done her make-up. Winters looked at me, looked at Tallulah, and nothing further was said. That was my answer to what I already knew.

Eli Wallach and Anne Jackson stopped by our table and, afterwards, Jesse went to the banquet table to get Tallulah a bit of food, which she barely touched. She didn't mingle with the crowd, but remained seated throughout the party. Patricia Neal never came over, asserting that this was her night and not Tallulah's.

I suspected that these outings were increasingly fatiguing for Tallulah. She appeared frail and not in good health. She would drink and then be disinterested in food. I advised Jesse that something should be done about Tallulah not eating, but he complained that there was nothing he could do. Tallulah was strong-willed and not one to be told what to do.

The party was still in full swing when we left, and the maneuver back across the red carpet to the limousine—with the rampaging crowd on either side of the ropes waiting for a glimpse of a star—was unnerving to Tallulah, as well as us.

With the help of the police, the crowd reluctantly parted when our limousine pulled away, but our windows were slammed with their fists, and the sides of the limousine were kicked. It wasn't an act of admiration, but, rather, hostility, perhaps from Tallulah not signing any autographs.

She was tired and weak, but the crowd cared nothing for that; they wanted their demands met. This was a new crowd for Tallulah, and it clearly frightened her, as it had Lucy. With a war raging and a president, his brother, and a civil rights leader murdered, this was an era of protest and rebellion, not at all the world these women had begun in.

Safely back at Tallulah's apartment where I returned to pick up my make-up case and the casual clothing I had removed, I sat with her in her darkened living room with only the hallway entrance light on. Jesse had gone to pick up some milk for their morning coffee with the limousine driver who would take me home.

We sat silently, relieved to be away from the madding crowd, each of us deep in our thoughts.

"Darling," she finally broke the silence, "I'm not going to live much longer."

I knew that she had been distraught about the recent killings of our country's leaders and the war and because it looked like Hubert Humphrey, the democratic candidate she supported for president against Richard Nixon, might not win the November election. Politics were bred in her, having come from an Alabama family with a long history of politicians and with her father being the speaker of the House of Representatives.

I also sensed the strain that these events, like the one that evening, were taking on her. She had said many times that she had done everything and met everyone, with most of them dead now anyhow. At 66, getting herself together to be Tallulah Bankhead once more was a burden. When one has that distinguished persona, they're expected to deliver it. For Tallulah, it was as much of a burden and a bore as it was for George Sanders, who committed suicide four years after she died.

"It's a bore," he said, and ended it.

I understood. I had seen how hard it was for her to endure an agonizing hour of make-up, with an hour or so of hair preparation before that, and I could imagine that it was a burden and a bore. Sometimes I felt the same having to do what I did, especially sitting next to one of my worst make-ups all night. I consoled myself with: "Well, you can't be perfect all the time," but I was a perfectionist, like Tallulah, and we couldn't just slough it off.

"Tallulah," I said, "it won't do you any good getting out of here. Jesse and I will just conjure you up in a séance every afternoon."

With the quick retort she was famous for, she said, "Just as long as you let me sleep till four o'clock, darling."

The following week, Jesse called to tell me that Tallulah had been taken to St. Luke's hospital suffering from flu that quickly turned to double pneumonia, complicated by emphysema from her heavy smoking. She had tried to cut down, even hiding her cigarettes, but she knew where to find them, and each effort had failed.

"Why didn't you make her eat?" I scolded Jesse. "She's been starving herself to death. I would have made her eat if I had to haul her to the hospital to do it."

"I couldn't," he protested. "She wouldn't listen to me."

He was right. No one could have saved her. Her prophecy came true. On December 12, 1968, Tallulah was dead. The official diagnosis was death from pneumonia, but my unofficial diagnosis was that she was fed up with all of it and the only way out was to just stop eating and wait.

On a cold, dismal December day, I watched from my window smoke curl from the chimneys of buildings across the street from my apartment and scatter in the wind before I attended a gathering in Tallulah's apartment for a kind of wake. Her burial would be in St. Paul's Church Cemetery in Chestertown, Maryland, where some of Maryland's distinguished politicians are also buried. Though her sister Eugenia chose the final resting place close to where she lived in Louisa Carpenter's guesthouse, I suspect that Tallulah herself had a hand in carefully selecting her preferred company, as she did in life.

At the gathering in Tallulah's apartment were Eugenia and her adopted son, Billy Bankhead, along with the usual assortment of Tallulah's gay male friends introduced to her by Jesse, as I was. Eugenia was already vying for my make-up services, which I would provide a couple of times as part of my mourning for the real thing.

Eugenia was no Tallulah. She was flighty, spoiled, and superficial, with little apparent depth and seven disastrous marriages to prove the point. She was currently involved with a handsome younger man who probably considered her a meal ticket, but, in truth, she had no resources and was mostly provided for by Tallulah or Carpenter, her du Pont–rich lesbian lover.

With her naturally flirtatious manner which, in her sixties, was wearing thin, Eugenia easily attracted men all over the world in exotic places like Tangiers and Morocco, and when she invariably got into money trouble, Tallulah or Carpenter would regularly bail her out. With Tallulah gone, she could now expect an inheritance—but perhaps not what she might have liked.

Recognizing Eugenia's tendency to extravagant spending, Tallulah shrewdly set up a trust that paid Eugenia $250 a month for life—not a lot for a woman who thrived on plusher times. She also received $5,000 outright, along with Tallulah's mink coat that she had always coveted, and was absolved of all her considerable debts to Tallulah.

Jesse, too, benefited by receiving $10,000 and her Baldwin grand piano, but it seemed likely he would need a new position with another "prominent" woman with room for a large piece of furniture.

Following family tradition, the bulk of Tallulah's estate went to family members, mainly Eugenia, with personal effects bequeathed to close friends like Estelle Winwood and Carpenter. There were those who complained they had been left out, but, for me, I had my memories and the letters she had written me, which would suffice a lifetime. I was honored just to have known her.

I reported to Mother that Tallulah had died. Unable to imagine that I could be friends with someone of Tallulah's stature—or perhaps threatened by the fact—Mother considered her merely one of my clients, not someone I could relate to human-to-human.

There was no way that I could convey the nature of my relationship with Tallulah that Mother would understand. How could I explain that I had been respected as a fellow artist and given unconditional love, something my family could never do for me?

Mother's scathing remark: "What do you know about make-up?" Tallulah never questioned my ability. Mother could never have understood what that had meant to me.

So, I tucked my loving memories inside to preserve them for a time when life might not be so good, to remind me that I once had a life that was.

6

An Affair in L.A.,
Make-Up Competition

In 1969, the Vietnam War had reached its highest peak of fighting. The toll of American war dead in April that year was 33,641, and rising. After three decades of fighting, the final cost of human life for all participants would be estimated at 1.75 million.

That summer in June, the police raided a gay bar in the Village, the Stonewall Inn, and gays and transvestites were hauled off to jail kicking and screaming. It was the beginning of the gay revolution. Gays, like blacks, were fed up with their mistreatment from police and others and were not going to take it anymore.

As a show of America's might, astronauts Neil Armstrong and Buzz Aldrin landed on the moon in July with "one giant step for mankind," and in August, rock and roll stars performed for four days in a 300,000-acre field in Bethel, New York, that became known as "Woodstock."

As Tallulah had feared, Hubert Humphrey lost the presidential election to Richard Nixon. In November, the largest antiwar protest of the Vietnam War descended on Washington, D.C., with 250,000 demonstrators, and in December, Nixon began America's withdrawal.

My fast crowd from Arthur led me to the Hamptons where we partied in the beach house of one of the member's parents, smoked a lot of grass, and consumed whatever stimulants were available. The occasion was to send off a younger member of the group who was being drafted into the army. Everyone had tried to talk him into heading to Canada, like many others, but his father had been an officer in the army, and he was doing this to honor him. He would be killed in Vietnam, and his parents would receive the customary government notification—a small compensation for the honor he had intended for them.

On the beach in West Hampton, I had met an attractive blonde woman, Valerie, several times married with two grown daughters and 12 years older than I was. It was apparent that Valerie had once been a looker but was now on the other side of it. We immediately became friends and began to run around together in New York.

Valerie's father had been quite rich and had left her a substantial trust fund, which gave her a monthly allowance that she always managed to overspend. It allowed her a luxurious lifestyle to travel widely and live in many parts of the world. Spain, in particular Barcelona, was her favorite, and conquistadores were her weakness.

She had a bull's head given her by one of her conquistador amantes that hung on the wall of her Spanish-decorated East Seventies apartment with a surrounding terrace overlooking the East River. Tattered and worn after years of traveling wherever she made her home, the poor thing's stuffings were coming out, but travel it continued to do, perhaps, like Valerie, in search of a lost love that always seemed to elude them. It was a fact—Valerie and her bull had seen better days.

Our favorite haunts in New York were Elaine's, a fashionable East Eighties bistro, and a rundown bar directly across the street from it that was then called Wilfred's.

Wilfred's was owned by a man named Wilfred and his wife, Lettie, whose idea of decorating their apartment was strewing tin cans over the floors. Whenever one was opened, it was tossed on the heap with the rest.

To save on electricity, the bar was purposely kept dark, using street lights to see, and usually had only one bottle of booze on the shelf. Customers were encouraged to have whatever the bottle contained, but if they insisted on something else, the bartender would run up the street, purchase it, and bring it back. Anything, no matter how bizarre, could be had at Wilfred's. With tin cans decorating one's floors, what could be bizarre?

A bartender there once asked Valerie if she knew where he could get a dildo.

She turned to me and asked, "Why would he think I knew where to get a dildo?"

The truth was that she looked like she knew where.

Unable to remain in business this way, Wilfred's changed hands and became Eric's. Murderers, thieves, drug pushers, addicts, drunks, pimps, prostitutes, even police, detectives, and celebrities frequented this bar. Patrons from the fashionable Elaine's across the street would dart across to slum for a bit before returning to their safer haven. Many times at late hours, Liza Minnelli stopped by to sing with the jazz band in the back room. Finally, the drug dealing at Eric's sent the owner, Eric, to jail, ending nearly a decade of decadence.

At the time, Elaine's was owned by Elaine Kaufman and Donald Ward, who had worked as waitress and waiter in a Village restaurant. From the time they started Elaine's restaurant, it immediately became a favorite hangout for personalities from the film, theatre, and literary worlds who came there nightly to gab, gossip, and dine. Elaine would eventually buy Donald out and purchase the building, further establishing Elaine's as one of the primary New York restaurants.

Donald held bacchanal parties at his apartment where drugs and liquor flowed freely until the wee hours of the morning. At one of them, a black man called Scooby-Doo, who was an habitué at the bars with the rest of us, began yelling that he was going to jump out of the kitchen window, convinced by the acid he had swallowed that he could fly.

A girl lighting her hash pipe nearby, and irritated with his constant yelling, challenged him with, "Go ahead, you asshole!" and he did.

The drugs were quickly flushed down the toilet before the police were called to find his shattered body in the courtyard below.

Donald later became a drunk and committed suicide, a sad ending to a life that had had every opportunity.

At Elaine's, people who worked in other restaurants and bars on the East Side would come to visit the staff that worked there. Valerie and I became friends with all of them, especially a group that worked in a popular East Seventies restaurant and bar called Surabaya, named for an Indonesian city and major naval base in Northeast Java.

Kurt Weil wrote a song called "Surabaya Johnny" for his 1977 musical *Happy End*—"sura" meaning hero, and "baya" meaning danger. Prophetically, it was the danger in this bar that would bring about a tragic ending for nearly everyone connected with it, including the owner, with diseases, suicides, addictions, and overdosing.

Valerie and I particularly became friends with a pretty, young blonde waitress there, Mary, and Billy, a handsome, tousled dark-haired bartender with a roving eye, who lived platonically together in an apartment above the restaurant. Valerie foolishly succumbed to Billy's charms and became his latest jilt, while Mary would become my official date for all important events.

After the restaurant closed in the evening, the "in" crowd, which now included Valerie and me, would hang around until dawn consuming the free booze, food, and drugs that were always plentiful. At daybreak, someone would phone Stereo Mike, who drove a limousine with the best stereo and the best cocaine, too. With Black Sabbath or Led Zeppelin blasting on Stereo Mike's stereo, and with whatever had been smoked, swallowed, or snorted, the crowd headed out to Ocean Beach, a community on Fire Island that was the preferred vacation spot for New York's grooviest restaurant help.

Billy the bartender once scaled a water tower there—about a half mile high—and refused to come down until someone threatened to trash his stash of dope, the culprit that had gotten him up there in the first place. That got him down fast. For him, a day without dope would be a day wasted.

Valerie frequently spoke of her older sister, Barbara, whom she insisted I should meet, with both of us being Geminis. One afternoon in Valerie's apartment, I met the notorious Barbara. Twice married with grown children like Valerie, and a small boy from a second marriage that was rapidly falling apart, Barbara lived in Glen Cove, New York, and also had a summer home in West Hampton.

In the Hamptons, where infidelity was as common as a game of tennis, Barbara had recently slipped getting out of a man's bed and sprained her ankle. With her gregarious personality, she was invited to all the fashionable Hampton parties, and because she had no intention of hobbling unattractively to such affairs, she persuaded a woman friend to dress as a nurse and push her to a party in a wheelchair. This kind of craziness was the last thing I needed, but searched for constantly.

Barbara and I quickly became an item, and the buzz of her Hampton crowd was that she was running around with a much younger, single man. Word got back to her husband, a self-made millionaire who had amassed his bucks in construction and was just looking for a corespondent to blame for his crumbling marriage. Barbara convinced him that I was merely her make-up artist, and gay too, which wasn't entirely true since I hadn't declared an end to my heterosexual philandering.

One weekend when I was a houseguest in their West Hampton home, I had had too much to drink, and her husband and a female houseguest caught me stark naked in their kitchen in the wee hours of the morning looking for something to eat. Barbara was in her room, so that let me off the hook that time. My real embarrassment came over breakfast the following morning where I confided to the female houseguest that I believed I had been naked in the kitchen the night before—too drunk to remember.

"I know," she replied. "I was there."

In Barbara's New York apartment, I had to flee to the closet when her husband unexpectedly arrived one morning for a visit. It became a game to see how much we could get away with, and I was always a step away from being named corespondent. When her divorce became final, her deception reaped her quite a substantial settlement.

But life with Barbara was far from easy or tranquil. She had a manipulative, possessive nature with a voracious sexual appetite, and her demands were frequent and unreasonable.

Valerie believed that Barbara was in love with me, which was certainly not the case for me, but it may have accounted for why she had pushed for a divorce so soon after our meeting. She thought we would marry. Had I even been inclined, her two failed marriages made that unthinkable. She had met her second husband while cheating on her first, as she had done with me—not what one might consider good marriage material.

That summer, Mary, my blonde waitress friend from Surabaya, was refinishing her apartment floors and lent me the sander to refinish mine. I stained them a dark brown and painted all the rooms of my mostly empty apartment a different color, adding, at the same time, a bit of furniture. My place was slowly becoming the home I had always wanted.

I painted my living room completely red, including the ceiling, which prompted Mother to ask, "Why did you paint this all red?"

"Because you wouldn't," I answered, which was the truth.

She would never have had the nerve. She never got that we were different and that I wasn't her.

In the late summer, Barbara rented a house in Malibu, California, and invited me out. I wanted to talk with Lucille Ball about my working with her, and I had also contacted the president of NBC in New York, Julian Goodman, the brother of a neighbor of ours in my hometown, to inquire about my doing make-up for one of their shows. In turn, he had contacted an NBC representative in Burbank, California, in case I wanted to relocate there.

I had also been talking with the Polly Bergen Company, an L.A.–based cosmetics company, about selling them false lashes that I had been cutting and Barbara had been peddling for me at the Georgette Klinger Salon. If I accepted Barbara's Malibu offer, I could kill all of these L.A. birds with one stone. I was aware that this could mean trouble, as my experience with her had been in the past, but I decided to chance it.

As it turned out, the trip was a disaster. When I arrived in Malibu, Barbara insisted that we wear eye masks over our eyes to make love in the morning, the time she preferred to do it. Since the basically one-large-room house she had rented had no blinds or curtains on its glass doors, which faced the ocean where the sun came up like a spotlight had been switched on, she was worried about being seen in that much light. I told her we'd look like Tonto and the Lone Ranger with those masks on and immediately nixed the idea of lovemaking in the morning, anyhow. Bad breath is not to be incorporated in lovemaking.

As her behavior had previously been when she couldn't have her way, she made all the arrangements I had set up difficult, if not impossible. I missed my appointment with the Polly Bergen Company when Barbara wouldn't allow me to use her car or drive me into L.A. The NBC representative I had an appointment with became interested in Barbara, which she encouraged hoping to make me jealous, and that messed that up. Lucy, too, was now disinterested, partly from my money demands and partly because she had made up with her old make-up artist.

In the end, the trip was an unpleasant experience, and when I returned to New York, I resolved to end my affair with Barbara and accept myself as a gay man once and for all. For that, the trip was a success.

The worst backlash from my being away from New York so long was that my make-up work had suffered. Also, there was a new make-up artist on the block: Way Bandy.

Way had previously been the make-up director for the Charles of the Ritz House of Beauty in the Ritz Tower on Park Avenue and was used to the antics of salon clientele. That was what had bothered me the most at the Georgette Klinger Salon, where the bratty, spoiled women with their constant demands had worn me down. With his easygoing, accepting manner, Way was far more suited to this than I was. Then, too, Way had always wanted to be a make-up artist. That thought had never crossed my mind until I needed a new line of work to support myself. If it hadn't been for need, I would never have ended up a make-up artist—hardly a good criterion for choosing one's life's work.

Like me, Way had first studied art and approached make-up, as I did, from an artistic standpoint. But his make-up designs were usually far more exaggerated than mine. I preferred to stick closer to realism, making women look as natural as possible, while Way liked more exaggeration and drama. Both approaches are equally needed in make-up, and each of us created both natural and dramatic make-ups in our careers, but our preferences made the difference in our styles. One thing we did share in common was clean, flawless make-ups that required little retouching and saved magazines, advertising agencies, and photographers that expense later.

For a time, there was only Way and me in the freelance make-up business, which was then in its infancy. This was before agents organized make-up artists, hairdressers, stylists, and photographers and clamped their control on the business. We were the first and strictly on our own. Our errors and triumphs, not only in business matters but also in make-up design, would be the road map that others would one day follow.

Way's entrance into the freelance make-up business wasn't that welcomed by my finances. His make-ups were now appearing in *Vogue* in Avedon and Penn photographs, as mine once had been, and advertising jobs would soon follow. It had been my choice from my insecurity to bow out of a lot of this, and Way was far more adept at dealing with the temperament of models, whom I found trying, to put it mildly. Still, I needed to support myself. I wasn't jealous of Way's success; in fact, I applauded him for his ease with handling the business. Artistically we were neck and neck, but I needed some of the business for myself.

At the time, an older ex-model-turned-agent, who had been representing a photographer that wasn't working out for her, was casting around for a new photographer and she consulted Zoli, owner of the Zoli Model Agency. He referred her to Francesco Scavullo, who was looking for an agent.

Scavullo had been an apprentice with renowned German photographer Horst, whose uniquely stylish photographs of the rich and famous appeared in *Vogue* for six decades. Scavullo's father had made his money selling brass kitchenware to restaurants, and the family was also reputed to have some interest in a restaurant in Central Park that later became Tavern on the Green. With his bucks, Scavullo's father purchased a carriage house in the East Sixties for his son to do his photography.

With only *Cosmopolitan* magazine covers and occasional jobs with other magazines, and having fallen out of grace with *Harper's Bazaar* magazine, one of his primary accounts, Scavullo desperately needed to get his career back on track, which the agent seemed to promise to do.

In the fashion world where news travels faster than the rise and fall of a hemline, Scavullo had acquired the reputation of being difficult and temperamental, which discouraged clients from working with him. Also, most of his photographs were old and showed make-ups and fashion that were dated. The agent spent weeks shuffling through masses of old photographs in his carriage house basement and eventually came up with an assortment where the fashion could pass as current, where hands, turned heads, and other obstructions hid the dated make-ups. From these she created a new portfolio.

Armed with this portfolio of old work that was now passing as new, the agent headed to Bloomingdale's department store, where she convinced the art director of Scavullo's talent and changed attitude. For her effort, she received a job order for several thousand dollars for black and white photographs for newspaper ads, more than Bloomingdale's had ever paid for such ads, and more money than Scavullo or she had seen in a long time.

With the Bloomingdale's ads, the agent then convinced Barney's department store that they, too, should have Scavullo doing their photography, and once again received more for that work than the client was used to paying. This clever girl could apparently talk her way into anything. She had passed Scavullo off as the new, happening thing, and it had paid off. He had a name already, and all it needed was redefining and a determined push, which she gave it.

By another stroke of luck, a new magazine was forming: *Pageant*, a small magazine that yearned to be big, with celebrity gossip and fashion news. Having heard that Scavullo might need the exposure and suspecting they could get him for an affordable price, they contacted his studio to inquire about his doing their cover color photographs. The agent seized the opportunity. With these color photographs she could then head to Clairol for a chunk of their advertising, and then on to *Vogue* with those photographs and the black and white ones from Bloomingdale's and Barney's. Her plan was working.

For *Pageant*'s covers, she suggested that they use top models who had gone or were going into the movies with the promise of an inside story about them. In this way the magazine could avoid the models' usual enormous rates because the magazine would be doing them a service. It paid off. Models like Cybill Shepherd, who would soon make her film debut in *The Last Picture Show*, Jennifer O'Neill, who would appear in *Summer of '42*, and Marisa Berenson, who would be in *Cabaret*, appeared on the covers, along with other Hollywood hopefuls, for far less than they would have ordinarily received. It even became prestigious to be on a *Pageant* cover. The magazine had a top photographer, top models, and now they needed top make-up.

Enter me.

My name had been around with *Vogue* and *Harper's Bazaar* for a while, and now there was Way, too. The agent contacted us and convinced us of the advantage of working with these top models and a top photographer, and everything else that was the top too, and we did it for no money. It was the exposure we got: Like everyone else, we were convinced that we couldn't turn it down. And so, my work began with Francesco Scavullo, and his work took off from there.

Through the agent's efforts, Francesco got two pages in *Vogue* for an upcoming issue, which began his work there, and from the *Vogue* photographs, *Bazaar* was lured back.

Unfortunately, Francesco's nerves took a spin from the sudden success and the pressure of it all and he was carted off to a hospital to recover from one of his several nervous breakdowns that popped up now and again in his career. When he came out, he headed to Fire Island for a vacation where he met and became infatuated with a young man: Sean Byrnes.

Convinced that Sean, who had had no experience, should take over as his agent and also oversee his studio, Francesco let the ex-model-turned-agent go, and Sean took up the job she had begun.

Things would continue this way for two and a half decades with many photographs in and on the covers of *Vogue*, *Bazaar*, *Cosmopolitan*, and other magazines throughout the world, but Francesco's advertising work would suffer from his temperament and Sean's, as they managed to alienate many of their advertising clients.

Francesco even went so far as to send photographs he had done for *Vogue* in a garbage can to art director Alexander Liberman to indicate his dislike of the layouts Liberman did with his work. It was his way of saying, "They're garbage," and it ended his work with *Vogue*.

Because of antics like this, he ended up working primarily with magazines—which he preferred anyhow because they gave him more control, but which paid nothing close to what advertising would have paid, which he envied in photographers like Avedon and Penn.

Like these men, he would produce several books, but only one was truly successful. His portraits would go for five-figure amounts, and as he became more and more comfortable with his celebrity, perhaps his greatest achievement would be his own self-promotion. With appearances on any TV show that wanted him and always up for a mention in a magazine or newspaper article, his reputation would eventually span the world.

But demons of his self-worth would plague him throughout his life, until his death in 2004, just before his 83rd birthday—reported in some publications as his 73rd birthday, a spin he himself concocted to disguise the truth.

A final note: the agent who had jump-started Francesco's career became disenchanted with the agent business after her episode with him, became a clerk in a small women's boutique, and disappeared into fashion industry oblivion like many others.

Scavullo was a good photographer in that his photographs were in focus, which, surprisingly, many photographers' were not. The work was clean in that the lighting was attractive and crisp and the background was uncomplicated and well lit. Everyone looked well under his lighting, which he perfected and carefully guarded.

The huge tub of lighting was usually placed on the left of the subject being photographed, unless they alerted him otherwise or he detected a facial need to adjust it. He had a good sense of the moment when to click the camera, and a good sense of fashion and how to present it to its advantage. His photography rejects were probably better than many photographers' best work.

However, he took few, if any, risks. Unlike Avedon, whose restless spirit was continually experimenting and would chance anything, or Penn, whose photography searched for the inner layer of the subject to locate the soul, Francesco exposed no more than the exterior and intended to penetrate no further. What you saw was all there was. It was usually a pretty face, dramatic make-up, or garment that attracted him, but the search ended there. To probe deeper might have brought out a deeper emotion that would require handling, and that wasn't Francesco. He presented little more than the surface of himself and may well not have known any more, afraid to probe further to find the demons that he feared the most lying beneath.

Avedon, on the other hand, intended to penetrate, locate whatever was there and even become combative over it, if necessary. Penn intended to penetrate, too, never content with merely the surface, but seeking the mystery of its creation. From this point of view, Francesco's photographs missed greatness, in my estimation. They were clean, pleasant, and good at what they did. It depends on what one is looking for and what one is willing to risk to get it. He found what worked and stuck with it throughout the two and a half decades that were his primary work.

Francesco wasn't the only photographer of pleasant photos; there were others, like Albert Watson and Neal Barr, though Barr's stylized work had more of an edge. Others were somewhat combative and edgy, like Hiro and James Moore. Others, like Bill King, had limited imagination and used tricks like having everyone jump in the air to give them something to do and make the garment move. King had everyone jumping, regardless what the subject was: fashion, politics, or show business. But Scavullo, Avedon, and Penn far outranked them all in the best of what they did.

(After doing the *Cosmopolitan* covers more than 30 years, Francesco would be booted off by Patrick Demarchelier, who produced work that had the combination of it all. With Demarchelier, for the first time, women would look warm, sexy, and real—rather than cold, exaggerated stereotypes of sexuality. But that would be decades later, in the mid 1990s.

Francesco and his new studio manager and companion, Sean, who now lived in the carriage house above the studio, had heard of my difficulty at Avedon's studio and knew I needed the work, as Francesco once had. They took advantage of this, playing Way Bandy against me and me against Way. Sean would show me Way's work and rave about it, making me work harder to keep up, as he did with Way. By this means, they kept us both on the skillet competing with one another, which pushed Francesco's work to the top.

The competition was less rigorous on Way, who eventually had more work than I did. I was booked several times a week with Francesco's studio, which kept other photographers from using me, and they had to go elsewhere for an artist. The control they exercised over me, which I allowed, would dictate my entire make-up career.

I was flattered that Francesco wanted me and endured this condition when, with a little effort when I had the chance, I could have gotten many photographers to use me, as well as magazines, too. It was laziness on my part. I felt that there should be agents, as actors have, to organize the artists' work life—which there would be some day—but I didn't want to do it. I wanted the time to do other things: like fool around.

Way was enterprising and ambitious. I was along for the ride until I could figure out how to have the life I wanted—whatever that was. It always seemed up ahead someplace. Mother had so confused me as to my identity that I really didn't know who I was or what I wanted. I assumed life would eventually lead me to it but, until then, I accepted that I would just have to wait.

People in the business would say I was good, and I thought it was clever to have a "so what?" attitude—especially when they said I was good. If they had said I was bad, that might have alarmed me. As it was, I enjoyed watching their faces when I threw it back at them. It was an attitude that was doomed to backfire.

One of my first jobs with Francesco was with Jaclyn Smith, before she was a "Charlie's Angel." It was on location and not in the studio. I asked to bring along Mary the waitress, and, with this being a minor shoot with a model who had done little work of importance, Francesco agreed. Mary got along better with Jaclyn than Francesco, who was always somewhat distant with his subjects, preferring the camera between them for protection.

Soon following this, there was a studio booking with Kris Kristofferson, who was there to shoot the cover of his newest album, *Easter Island*. Kris was quite jittery, and I did my best to calm him down. By this time, I was quite adept at being in a photography studio and not at all the frightened self I had displayed at Avedon's studio.

Because of Francesco's new-found success, *Vogue* was more willing to try him out on other things. A *Vogue* cover (March 1, 1974) was scheduled, and I was to do the make-up. This was a new chance to be a part of *Vogue* without the coattails of Avedon. I had bet a large portion of my career on Francesco—many times without pay—and it was paying off.

The model was Pola, a beautiful blonde girl with plump, pouty lips and sultry eyes. I had done Pola's make-up before for a *Cosmopolitan* cover, and because artists who had worked successfully with a model were often chosen again, I got the job.

Pola was a sweet girl—maybe

Kris was jumpy until he was in front of the camera (courtesy Francesco Scavullo Foundation and Sony Music Entertainment).

not bright, I felt, but lovely to look at. As I made her up in the most beautiful pastels to complement the soft pink sweater, peach chiffon scarf with lace trim, and coral and diamond pin and earrings that she'd wear on the cover—quite a contrast from the hard look I'd created on her for *Cosmo*—I identified with her story of losing a boyfriend she loved to another model. I, too, didn't feel I did so well in the love department, perhaps from my lack of security with my sexuality and Mother's continuing dominance in my life. I never felt sure of myself, and Pola seemed to be suffering with the same lack of self-esteem.

I sympathized with her, even felt a bit protective. After two shoots with her, I had grown quite fond of Pola—though I still had my convictions of her being on the dumb side. She seemed fragile and vulnerable, and my heart went out to her. And she was young: only 19.

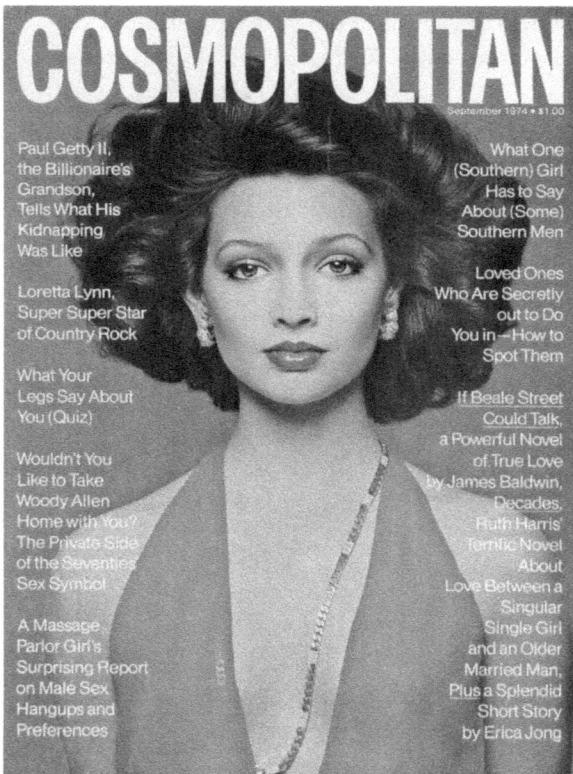

COSMOPOLITAN

September 1974 • $1.00

Paul Getty II, the Billionaire's Grandson, Tells What His Kidnapping Was Like

Loretta Lynn, Super Super Star of Country Rock

What Your Legs Say About You (Quiz)

Wouldn't You Like to Take Woody Allen Home with You? The Private Side of the Seventies' Sex Symbol

A Massage Parlor Girl's Surprising Report on Male Sex Hangups and Preferences

What One (Southern) Girl Has to Say About (Some) Southern Men

Loved Ones Who Are Secretly out to Do You in—How to Spot Them

If Beale Street Could Talk, a Powerful Novel of True Love by James Baldwin. Decades, Ruth Harris' Terrific Novel About Love Between a Singular Single Girl and an Older Married Man, Plus a Splendid Short Story by Erica Jong

Model Pola on the cover of *Cosmo* not long before her suicide (courtesy Francesco Scavullo Foundation and Hearst Communications).

Soon after the shoot, Pola committed suicide, and *Vogue* had the dilemma of bringing out a beautiful cover of a dead girl. I hoped they would do it as a kind of tribute to Pola and her only cover of *Vogue*. They finally did, reasoning that the public wouldn't know she was dead, and I was grateful because it would be my only cover of *Vogue*, too.

Polly Mellen worked on the Pola cover, and with the work I had done on that, I was requested for a reunion at Avedon's studio. I had my reservations. Life had become too short to suffer, and perhaps my apprehension followed me there.

As it turned out, I was right. Maybe I had a

chip on my shoulder from being bounced out, even at my own request, but a little gratuitous coaxing to stay might have relieved that. It would have been nice to think I was a little necessary. Clearly, that was not Avedon's style. He didn't need to coax; you coaxed him. Our parting had been mutually agreeable, and it should have remained that way. But here I was, back for more.

This time it was a newcomer from California, Rene Russo, who would one day be a major movie star. She had been accustomed to no more than a bit of lipgloss on her beautiful 19-year-old face while she frolicked about with the surfers on the California beaches. Avedon instructed me to shadow Rene's strong, square jawline to soften it for his camera—not the best approach with a young girl inexperienced in studio make-up and used to only lipgloss and a sea breeze to send her on her way.

To make matters worse, as I was beginning the make-up, she went to the phone for a call and returned in tears. Someone said it was her boyfriend, who announced an end to their relationship—a most inopportune time. I was left with a girl dissolved in tears explaining to Avedon that her condition was from her dislike of the make-up. Maybe so, but not the entire truth, and I had hardly begun. Would Leonardo da Vinci have allowed Mona Lisa to scream "foul" at this stage of his painting? Not that I was painting the Mona Lisa, but things change as we paint, and it is unfair to judge until the final results. And even then it's hard to tell until the hair and costume are in place, and certainly success should never be judged by the model—unless she has had an enormous amount of experience in the business. Certainly never a novice just starting out.

For the second time, the bounce came with Avedon stating as cordially as he could manage, "You!" (That was me.) "Get out of the studio."

That was the last of that treatment.

Gladly, I walked to the door—and with a spring in my step, I might add—relieved to be away from these egomaniacs.

Avedon attempted to soften the exit with, "Sorry."

I wasn't sorry. It was another example of photographers allowing a young, inexperienced girl to control things in order to get their photos. It was over for all of us together again, and the last time I had to hear Polly Mellen's inane utterance, "Divine," for everything. I returned to Scavullo's studio with a new resolve to accept my future with one of the best photographers in the business. After all, Avedon wasn't the end of the line but a new beginning elsewhere—and I embraced it fully.

(One final note: At a time when I was looking for an agent for my book, I contacted literary agent Peter Riva. The name struck a bell with me, and after hearing some of my Avedon war stories, he reported that his grand-mother had had trouble with the man. I inquired who his grandmother was and he revealed that she was Marlene Dietrich, as I had suspected, remem-bering that Dietrich's only daughter was actress Maria Riva and Peter was Dietrich's grandson. He elaborated that Dietrich had been photographed by Avedon and asked to see the photos and he refused, so they were never published. Dietrich's demands were no more controlling than Avedon's own controls through the Avedon Foundation that he set up for that very pur-pose, and it is gratifying to know that my problems with him were not uniquely mine. It goes to show that genius is not necessarily accompanied by a charitable heart.)

7

Katharine Hepburn, Helen Hayes, Joan Sutherland and Bette Davis

If I had done something that displeased Francesco, like a so-so make-up on a so-so face that hadn't inspired me, I'd be out of favor, until Way did something that displeased him; then I'd be back again. And so it went—on again, off again—throughout my career. So it wasn't unusual when I had a lull. It was disconcerting because I would be out of work, but something would always turn up to rescue me, like a booking with a magazine, another photographer, a TV commercial, or some source out of the blue.

When a friend and stage designer, Larry—whom I had met at the gay bar Harry's—called to tell me about a new musical, it was one of those rescues. The musical, *Coco*, was based on the life of Coco Chanel, the French couturier. Music by André Pervin, book and lyrics by Alan J. Lerner, choreographed by Michael Bennett and costumes by Cecil Beaton. The star was none other than the legendary Katharine Hepburn.

The trouble *Coco* was having, Larry said, was that the show's ingénue was supposed to come on stage directly from the country looking completely natural, and Chanel was supposed to make her up to become one of her top Parisian models. The ingénue needed a make-up that looked like she wasn't wearing any, and Hepburn would then add something on stage that would change her. The question was, what was that something? And how do you create a make-up that looks like it's not there? That's show business for you.

Like the make-up I had done on Lucille Ball for the *Ed Sullivan Show* where I had no experience, here I was again, at the top, doing something I had never done before. In fact, I don't know any artist who has ever created a make-up that looks like it isn't there. My risk-taking nature kicked in: I would attempt it.

I spent a couple of hours in the ingénue's dressing room carefully constructing a make-up that I hoped would project a pretty face without make-up. With the bright theatre lights that wash out everything, it is essential to have some make-up, and, in this case, it couldn't be too much or too little. Because of a lack of stage time, I determined that the make-up I would create should require no more of Hepburn than a brighter lipstick to effect a change. I had observed the stage lighting earlier, and I carefully calculated each step, but it was a tricky tightrope I was walking on.

When the make-up was complete, I went outside to the theatre's audience seats to observe the girl's entrance in the rehearsal they were having. In the audience, also observing the rehearsal, were Cecil Beaton and Alan J. Lerner, while Michael Bennett was on stage directing the cast, including Katharine Hepburn. Transfixed on Hepburn, I was caught off-guard when the girl suddenly appeared in a drab olive suit that could have been left over from the First World War.

A few seats behind me I heard Beaton complain, "She looks awful."

I had no experience in these matters, certainly none compared to Beaton, but I knew when I had been challenged, and I knew drab olive would make a rose look bad. The girl was supposed to be from the country, but she didn't have to look as though she had just trudged in from the trenches.

As if a jug of caffeine had surged through my veins, my head snapped around, and before I realized it, I addressed Beaton with, "Excuse me, Mr. Beaton, but I did the make-up."

Both he and Lerner riveted their attention in my direction. I had come on so strong that they were prepared to either greet me or dismiss me.

I continued, "The drab olive outfit she's wearing is draining her of all her color. If she were to have a navy blue outfit with a pink blouse, for instance, it would be more flattering to her face, and she would still look like she was from the country."

I quickly snapped my head forward before Beaton could call me an "impudent upstart" or something worse. Neither man said a word. There was no telling what carved and quartered plan they were already cooking up for my demise. I was concerned that it might reflect on Larry, too, but it was how I felt, and I had to say it to defend what I had done. At least, I deserved the chance to see if I was right.

Unlike Avedon's studio where I wasn't allowed to complete my work, these men graciously heard me, and the next day for rehearsal, when the girl walked on stage, she was wearing a navy blue suit with a pink blouse in the exact same make-up I had recreated.

"Well, that's more like it," I heard Lerner say.

I turned around, and both men were beaming. Alan gave me a thumbs-up, and Beaton smiled, but no more acknowledgment than that. I felt exonerated. These were great men, and they were gentlemen.

I think as artists, the greatest gift fellow artists can give one another is the respect and dignity of their art. I found a great deal of uncaring in the fashion world, which was why I gravitated to writers and people in the theatre where I did my best work and received the most recognition.

I had given Katharine Hepburn a pair of my hand-cut false lashes, which she never wore, preferring, instead, to go on stage with only a couple of black lines at the outer corners of her eyes, to give them depth and definition, and a slash of red lipstick across her lips. Her face was ruddy from her tennis and being outdoors in the sun, and she needed no extra face color. She was right, to reject the lashes. She looked glorious on stage and fully made up.

Even with Hepburn and the other greats connected with Coco, it lasted only around ten months. It really wasn't that good, with no memorable music like Lerner's other shows, and Hepburn couldn't sing, though she made up for it with her exuberance and personality.

Standing in the wings of the Mark Hellinger theatre observing her on stage my last night there, I thought, "This is one of the last of the great legendary actresses."

Besides Tallulah, I was fortunate to have been around some of the great legendary women. In the 70s, I made up Helen Hayes for a Blackglama mink ad, whose slogan was "What Becomes a Legend Most?" shot by photographer Bill King.

Throughout the make-up, Hayes sat wrapped in a mink coat the company gave all the legendary women who were shot for the Blackglama campaign at the time. When she got up, the coat trailed completely to the floor and engulfed her tiny body.

"Miss Hayes," I said, "that coat is too large for you."

"I know that," she snapped, "and I'm not taking it off until they give me another one."

She told me that she and her playwright husband, Charles MacArthur, were once weekend guests at a producer friend's house on Long Island. Tallulah and Robert Benchley, the well known '40s humorist and part of the Algonquin Round Table, also attended. That night when Hayes and MacArthur got into bed, they heard giggling, and when they snapped on the light, they discovered Tallulah and Benchley under their bed. The pair confessed they were there to find out "what an old lady and her husband do in bed."

Though only two years older than Tallulah, Hayes never looked young, even when she was. Totally guileless, she wasn't concerned if she was thought of as an "old lady." While other actresses of her generation sought glamour and fretted about their fading beauty, her ego remained intact, and she went on to become the greatest actress of them all, lasting into her nineties.

With Francesco for *Harper's Bazaar*, I was to have made up Bette Davis, but, suspecting he might not have a make-up artist to her liking, she hired one of her own and came to the studio already made up. Nevertheless, it gave me the chance to chat with another legend before the shoot began.

"My mother is a Damn Yankee, too," I said, knowing that with her residence in Connecticut she considered herself a Yankee.

"That's right," she returned in her feisty way. "That's exactly what they call us."

Then there was the shoot with Joan Sutherland for which I was late. I had to literally run to the studio to try to make it there in some reasonable time.

Entering the make-up room panting, I found Sutherland already positioned in the make-up chair.

"Miss Sutherland," I attempted an excuse, "you're the only woman I've ever run to meet."

"Of course," she said. "You were late."

Ouch! Legends also have sharp tongues.

Joan Sutherland's mouth sizzled as much as her golden voice (courtesy Francesco Scavullo Foundation, from *Scavullo on Beauty*, Random House, 1976).

Before large, expensive office and high-rise apartment buildings were constructed, Third Avenue consisted mostly of small shops,

neighborhood bars, and tenement houses, of which few still remain, and it was a fertile cruising ground for gays. Once there had been an elevated train, known as the Third Avenue El, running above Third Avenue from Chatham Square in the Chinatown area to 149th Street, but that was closed and demolished in the 1950s to make way for the more upscale neighborhood it would become.

On Third Avenue, one could meet the most interesting men in whatever variety one might want. And this was how I met Lee.

Handsome wouldn't even begin to describe Lee. Tall, blonde, part German and American Indian, with a natural physique that Adonis would envy, he was gorgeous by any standard. I fell in love at first sight. But Lee was too gorgeous to tie down. He was in his prime and making the most of it. Three lovers a day, he once told me, and so, as with his many conquests at the time, we became friends. There was no seeming permanence in the world then, nothing one could hold onto. With a quick shift in partners for both single heterosexuals and homosexuals, too, most preferred the party to coupling.

Bette Midler was singing at the Continental Baths at the Ansonia Hotel, with Barry Manilow as her pianist, and men, in between their sexual liaisons, stood around and watched wearing no more than small white towels. The Fillmore East, a downtown rock and roll arena for stars like Janice Joplin, Jim Morrison, and Jimi Hendrix, drew audiences from both the heterosexual and homosexual communities, and drugs were always a big part of both these places. Doubtless few, if any, attended these events sober.

Lee worked for a well-known interior decorator, Howard Rothberg, who had a townhouse in the East Seventies. When Howard was in Florida, where he also had a home, or was away on business, which he was frequently, Lee, Mary, her roommate, Billy the bartender, Valerie, and I regularly partied in his spectacular five-floor townhouse, which was a showcase for Howard's considerable talent.

Joan Crawford was a frequent guest there and had explained to some guests one evening—using a napkin to cover her face up to her eyes—how, in her then current movie *Straitjacket*, she had popped out from behind a partition and "fucked the audience" with her unexpected entrance.

Our favorite spot in the house was the "horse room" on the top floor, with bronze horse heads and horse figures everywhere, antique prints of horses hanging on the inlaid wooden walls, a leather bridle for a seat, red plaid couches and chairs, lamps with horse figure bases, and a huge red brick fireplace that accommodated a luxurious fire. It was the coziest place in the house to be, particularly on a cold winter night. I also brought my favorite model friends there—the ones who weren't so self-absorbed—and we all partied together until dawn.

Off from the "horse room" was an all-mirrored, marble bathroom with a sunken tub where, after an acid trip, or whatever we had sniffed, smoked, or swallowed, I found myself immersed in bubbles with whatever partner or partners had decided to join me.

On one occasion, Lee gave me a taste of a 200-year-old wine that he insisted we drink in Howard's expensive Baccharat crystal glasses. He said the wine cost a couple of thousand dollars a bottle—as well, the glasses may have too. It was like Tallulah's diamond bracelet: once you've had the best, you'll always know what that is.

The experience, which can't even be described as "taste," grew and grew inside my mouth, penetrated my nostrils, and expanded throughout my head. For every year the wine had been cradled and nurtured in its wooden vat, I experienced each of them in rapid-fire sensations that recalled the history of the time the wine had been in there. Even the green moss that surely grew on the vats in a moist forest, where I sensed it had been kept, became part of the experience. It was amazing and forever spoiled me for all the rest.

Howard had a Rolls Royce, circa the 1920s, that was a curiosity and an antique, complete with window shades that pulled down and a small wooden bar in the back. Lee would take Howard to the opening of a play, and with a few hours to kill before he had to pick him up when the play ended, he'd swing by and get me. We'd cruise to a gay bar where we'd bring drinks out to the car, not daring to park it, and the men would gather around to admire the car, while we admired the men and got a few phone numbers. Lee would then go back to Howard at the appropriate time, and he never knew what we'd been up to.

In this silver and maroon relic, we attracted so much attention that our date book was always filled. They thought we were rich, and we did nothing to discourage the illusion. Lee had an advantage over me, pretending the house was his too, as well as the car. However, I had a small claim: I was the passenger, so I pretended he was my chauffeur. He wasn't getting all the glory. With all the men this car attracted, it was time well spent.

When Mother came to New York for Thanksgiving—which she had decided she would do and then have Christmases with my sister—Lee and I prepared Thanksgiving dinner in Howard's house, complete with his finest china, glassware, and silver. After dinner, our friends stopped by, and Mother and a woman friend of hers enjoyed themselves along with us, even when marijuana was introduced. (Mother thereafter liked to say, "My son took me to a pot party.")

We loved Howard's house, even if he wasn't around long enough to enjoy it himself. The splendor and decadence it provided would not be easy to give up.

Lee had a friend, John Barrett, who had an antique shop on Third Avenue, a couple of blocks from my apartment. We began going to John's shop after-hours for red wine spritzers before continuing on at Lee's. It became our social thing and even included Barbara on occasions. This had become my crowd—Lee, John, Mary, Billy, Valerie, and Barbara—and replaced my old Arthur crowd, which had long since dispersed after Arthur closed.

John had been in the army, had no family, and was tall, good looking, and dark-haired. He was also a bit queeny, with a deranged mentality when he was drunk—which was frequently.

Mother couldn't stand John. She thought he was a fool, and he acted like one when he was drunk. I couldn't stand him then, either.

Hopped up on red wine spritzers and who knows what all, he said to Mother, "You know what I've learned, Kathryn?"

She didn't care what he'd learned and didn't want to hear it.

He continued anyhow, "I've learned to never shit in your pants."

Mother thought he was shitting in his pants already and couldn't wait to get away from him.

John got himself a boyfriend, a bartender in an Upper East Side gay bar, but I thought something was seriously wrong with the much younger man and told John this. He dismissed the idea and took him in as his roommate. He was totally taken with the man.

Not long after that, John showed me wounds on his stomach that he said were from the young man attacking him with a broken beer bottle. I begged him to get rid of the man, but he said the man was leaving soon to live with his sister and did nothing about it.

On a cold December day, around the same time Tallulah died, Lee called to tell me that the man had killed John. He said the police had contacted him from John's address book and they wanted Lee to come down to the morgue and identify the body. He asked me to come along.

I wasn't as close to John as Lee, but I wanted to support Lee, and so I went. At the morgue, Lee signed a bunch of papers, and then they said it was time to identify the body. Lee was intending to go downstairs with the police where bodies were kept in cold storage, and I told him that if he was going, then I wouldn't. I preferred not to have those memories. And so, Lee went down. When he returned, he was as white as a sheet. He said the man had stabbed John 120 times. His face, he said, was almost unrecognizable, with his eyes stabbed out, and the man had stuffed John's penis into his slit-open mouth.

The story was that the man and John had gone out one night and consumed two bottles of cognac. When they came home, an argument ensued—and John could be infuriating when he was drunk—and the man stabbed him, threw all the furniture out of the apartment window, and turned on the gas in an attempt to blow up the apartment and everything with it. The police arrived in time to prevent the explosion. I never knew what happened to the man, and I didn't care. I was glad that I hadn't witnessed the results in the morgue. It was bad enough to hear about it and have my imagination working on it.

I believe Lee was spooked the rest of his life about this, and periodically he would say, "John has been dead such and such years."

I had no idea how long it had been, but I believe Lee may have known even the days, and perhaps the hours too. I was thankful that I hadn't gone down those stairs with him.

In a veterans' cemetery somewhere outside New York, John was buried. Lee, Mary, and I, and a couple of women who identified themselves as John's friends, whom I didn't even know he had, were the only mourners. John had been raised by foster parents who were now dead, and no one from that family attended. There didn't seem to be anyone else. I didn't even know who had arranged the burial—perhaps one of those strangers I had never met.

Someone muttered a prayer, and one of the women quoted from the Bible, and as I stood on that lonely, windy hilltop with the others, surrounded by acres dotted with hundreds of white crosses marking the graves of those who had served their country, I knew I would never be back. I was sure many others, like John, would soon arrive in this desolate place. It was sad to leave someone so unattended, but I couldn't have found my way back if I had to. I didn't even know where I was. And I was sure Lee would never be back, either. Like the others, I was here to bury someone I had known. It was brief, but I had known him, and this was his ending and his final tribute.

Somewhere in a cemetery close to New York is someone with only a name, like many there, perhaps, whom no one knows, in a grave that no one will ever visit again—lost soldiers, fallen one way or the other, with no place to go but there.

8

Bette Midler and
No, No, Nanette

In May 1970, students protesting the Vietnam War sparked a riot at Kent State University in Kent, Ohio, and the Ohio National Guard opened fire, killing four students and wounding 11 others. The photograph of an agonized girl kneeling over the body of a fallen friend etched itself into the American fiber, as had police dogs attacking blacks in Birmingham, Alabama, in the '60s and Governor George Wallace standing in a doorway at the University of Alabama to prevent blacks from attending there. These, and photographs of the dead and dying in Vietnam, were becoming our legacy, a war that our obsession with Communism had driven us into, of which we now wanted out. Nixon was trying to wind it down, but the American war dead that year would reach 4,204.

These were dangerous times, as further exemplified by Martha Mitchell, Senator John Mitchell's boozy, loudmouth wife, who beat the Washington scandal drums about Nixon's wrongdoings and landed on the November cover of *Time* magazine in a glamorous shot by Francesco, with a startling makeover by Way that helped promote his name faster than I could write mine.

My day would come several years later when the Republicans, still miffed over the Watergate fiasco and Nixon's resignation, found a Democratic scandal in Elizabeth Ray, the alleged mistress of Democratic Ohio Representative Wayne Hays, and blew it all out of proportion. (Who didn't believe that every one of them had a mistress?) I did a make-up on Ray for the cover of *The Washingtonian* magazine that made her look as virginal and innocent as freshly fallen snow. I could play dirty politics, too.

In 1971, Diana Vreeland was replaced at *Vogue* by Grace Mirabella,

Sonny and Cher brought their pop and kitsch to TV, and I did Cybill Shepherd's make-up for *Harper's Bazaar* magazine at Bill King's studio where, thankfully, he didn't have her jumping up and down.

While I was making her up, Shepherd gobbled down a plate of food that would challenge a field hand's appetite and threw the empty plastic container into a trash receptacle with such force that the sound resounded throughout the studio. I mused to myself that either she would be as big as a house someday or the angriest woman alive. Later that year, she would create a sensation in her first movie *The Last Picture Show*.

It always amazed me how many models, with all their advantages, could still be unhappy. However, having things doesn't necessarily bring happiness, and gratitude doesn't necessarily accompany youth.

News of Nixon's involvement with the Watergate break-in the following year flooded the country with a new scare. Now we would have to get rid of him and end the war, simultaneously, with as little egg on our faces as we could manage. The only good news that year was that with a truce called, only four Americans lost their lives.

For Francesco, I did make-up on several popular female singers for album covers and magazine editorials: a bubbly and upbeat Linda Ronstadt for *Rolling Stone* magazine, a somewhat brooding Carly Simon for *People* magazine, a funny and entertaining Shirley Bassey for the cover

With a face as innocent and pure as this, who would believe that Elizabeth Ray had ever been otherwise (courtesy Francesco Scavullo Foundation and Garrett Graff, editor, The *Washingtonian*)?

of her album, *The Magic Is You*, a soul-satisfying Roberta Flack for an article in *Harper's Bazaar*, and for a bit of funk, Chaka Khan, also for *Harper's Bazaar*.

At seven in the morning, I did a complete body make-up on a model from head to toe for a bath oil commercial—a most bizarre procedure in that I made up her face first, got acquainted, and then directed: "Okay. Drop your jeans." (Thank God we got acquainted first.) When the commercial was aired on TV, the camera panned up her nude body from her toes up to her head and she had a line that read: "Happy Birthday, skin," at which point she blew out a series of candles that appeared to extend down her entire body.

An upbeat and fun Linda Ronstadt (photograph by Francesco Scavullo from *Rolling Stone* issue dated October 19, 1978 © Rolling Stone LLC 1978 all rights reserved. Reprinted by permission).

For drama, I made up a dreary and down Faye Dunaway, who seemed to take herself much too seriously, before her successful 1974 film *Chinatown*, directed by Roman Polanski and also starring Jack Nicholson.

For photographer Bill King, I made up Bette Midler for *Rolling Stone* magazine. Andy Warhol also attended the shoot. He obsessively photographed my make-up case that, by now, had grown to astronomical proportions with every make-up in the world in there for whites, blacks, young and old, and body make-up, too. The case weighed a ton, and I lugged it like a small cosmetics store, prepared for everything—which I was now getting.

Bette had been a smash at the Continental Baths during her two-year tenure there, and would receive a Tony award in '73 for her concert at the Palace Theatre—quite a jump forward. Already she seemed to have her eye on Hollywood, a dream that wouldn't materialize until '79 with her first film, *The Rose*. She was concerned about the proportions of her nose and may have been considering how it would photograph on screen.

I felt that her nose gave her face character and discouraged her from making changes by suggesting that a nose change might affect her voice, a theory totally unfounded that I invented to sidetrack her. She considered it, but character didn't seem to be what she was looking for—beauty, perhaps, but not character. She may have also feared that she'd end up in only funny roles—which she basically did. Those were her best roles, but she may have preferred to be taken more seriously.

She had consulted several plastic surgeons but had made no decisions, and when I said I had a friend who was a plastic surgeon, she immediately wanted to meet him and add him to her investigative list. I was to set up the appointment and go with her.

To prevent her from being overcharged because of her star status, I suggested that she use a fictitious name. It was my paranoia from not wanting to be accused of leading her down an expensive garden path if that's how it turned out, but it seemed to lock into her paranoia, too.

Having no fictitious name yet prepared when the nurse in my friend's office called to ask me my client's name, I sputtered, "Bette ... I mean Bet—sy ... uh, Brown."

When Bette asked what name I had used and I told her "Betsy Brown," there was a pronounced silence on the other end of the phone that I took as "Too stunned to speak."

"Well, it's better than Betty Boop," I defended it.

"Well, barely," she said.

To add to our clandestine intrigue, Bette arrived at my apartment incognito with no make-up, her then distinct curly red hair totally hidden under a big black fur hat and a bolero-style, faux leopard fur jacket. She looked like a strange, mad Russian from a Tolstoy novel.

On our way to my friend's office, unfamiliar with her work, I asked about her act.

"Well," she said, "it's me and three trashy girls. But I'm not as trashy as they are."

I asked what drove her to become what she was.

"Hate!" she answered.

Okay.

We arrived at my friend's office, with me now looking as strange as she because I was about to lie to everyone. I didn't think my phony name idea was such a good one anymore, with Bette done up like she was on a spy mission for the KGB.

A nurse gave her forms to fill out, and when the nurse left, Bette needed to be reminded what inane name I'd given this bunch for her.

"Betsy Brown," I said quietly.

"What?" she asked, loud enough to be heard by the nurse, who had resumed her spot behind a glass partition.

"Betsy Brown," I repeated, trying to be discreet, but I was sure the nurse had heard me and was wondering why this woman couldn't remember her own name.

When the nurse returned for the filled-out forms, she looked at Bette suspiciously and said, "Don't I know you?"

Good God. All that fur cover-up for nothing.

"No, no," Bette said, hiding her face in the forms. "You don't know me."

The nurse took the forms and reluctantly left the room, still checking Bette out like she was in a police line-up. We were both acting so oddly that I'm sure the nurse thought that at any moment we could grab the doctor's scalpel and attack.

"The doctor will see you now," another nurse entered to announce, obviously sent in by the first one to validate her suspicion. We got up, and she, too, checked Bette out, which was beginning to rattle both of us.

Her expression read, "Whoever this chick is, she looks dangerous, and the doctor better watch it."

I introduced Bette to my doctor friend, and she immediately wanted to see every boob, face, and nose that he had ever done. He rang for his nurse to bring in his file, and when she did, it was the first nurse who had first checked Bette out, which she did again. When she left, she left the door partially open, and Bette got up, stomped to the door, slammed it, and returned to her seat. The nurse re-entered with more photographs, and again she left the door partially open.

It occurred to me that she might be doing this on purpose to eavesdrop. Or maybe it was in case the doctor yelled for help. Whatever it was, something must have occurred to Bette, too, because she again got up, stomped to the door, and slammed it. This girl was clearly getting on her nerves.

Thumbing through the photographs, Bette mumbled, "She looked better before. She looked better before."

There wasn't anyone who didn't look better before. Convinced that she was on the right track already with her old nose, she got up, thanked my doctor friend, and that was the end of her nose job.

At an earlier meeting, Bette had asked me for improvement advice. With nothing better to offer, I suggested that I had heard that June Allyson had to learn to smile for the movies without crinkling up her eyes, as Bette was prone to do. Watching Bette trying to smile without crinkling up her eyes was like Muhammad Ali trying to fight with his hands tied behind his back. It was an organic part of her, and that's what made the divine Miss M. divine. Like Tallulah, she was a unique commodity, and needed to remain untouched.

No, No, Nanette had been a hit on Broadway for several months when I received a call from Cyma Rubin, the show's producer, whom I had been referred to by *Vogue*. She was looking for a fashion make-up artist, as opposed to a union one, to spruce up the show's make-up. She complained that the boys all looked like girls in their present make-up, and that the girls didn't look sparkling enough.

The show was directed by Burt Shevelove, with musical director Buster Davis, and choreography by Donald Saddler. It starred the legendary Ruby Keeler, then in her 60s, who tap danced with a long line of chorus boys and girls and thrilled audiences, as she had in her '30s film *42nd Street*. The show would start a trend of other revivals in the future and movie stars appearing on Broadway.

A book by Don Dunn, *The Making of* No, No, Nanette, came out shortly after the show opened and chronicled Rubin's dealings with the original co-producer, Harry Rigby, from whom she managed to take over the show. The book painted Rubin as not that ethical, a fact that would not stand her in good grace with the Broadway community. My personal experience was that she had a keen sense of quality and style, but an aversion to paying for it.

All of this was unknown to me when I trundled over to her Chinese-red office, where I sat across a black lacquered desk observing the dark-haired, attractive producer with a distinct profile flip through my portfolio, as I had on many of these kinds of interviews. With plenty of work at the moment, I didn't care if she liked the book or not. It displayed make-up for camera and had nothing to do with stage, and though I had a sixth sense about projecting make-up for different mediums, nothing in the book could actually verify that. I considered this merely a courtesy call in response to her call, as well as an acknowledgment to *Vogue* for having recommended me.

I had enjoyed my time with *Coco*, but doing make-up for Broadway entailed climbing a lot of stairs backstage in search of particular dressing rooms, and I wasn't eager to repeat that. Studio work was far easier and less physically demanding.

Cyma slammed the portfolio shut, sat back in her chair, narrowed her eyes to size me up, and brusquely delivered, "How much do you want?"

It was the cat and the canary, and I was about to be swallowed up. She was far more adept in these matters than I was.

Since I had only my hourly rate for camera work to draw from, which I felt would be too much, I finally agreed on a flat fee for the job. I figured that it would take me a day to spruce up the New York troupe, which mainly consisted of the chorus girls and boys. I'd do each group separately, and then swing into the two principals she was concerned about, Helen Gallagher and Bobby Van. Not anticipating the complicated schedules of all these performers, I would discover that a day to do all that would be impossible.

Then she wanted me to design the make-up for the entire cast of one of *Nanette's* national touring companies, which was presently in rehearsal in New York and would open in Dallas, Texas, in a month. My job would be to design the make-up in New York and fly to Dallas to oversee it.

Somehow, I had agreed to a flat fee for each of these troupes, and for one of them I'd have to go to Dallas. What was I thinking? Cyma was getting the biggest bang for her bucks, and I clearly needed training in negotiating. Better yet, I needed an agent, but they weren't around yet. Even when they were, they were a bigger pain in the butt than my negotiating.

My biggest job in the Dallas troupe was the lead, Evelyn Keyes, a movie star in films like *The Seven Year Itch* and one of Scarlett O'Hara's sisters in *Gone with the Wind*. She used this for the title of her 1977 book, *Scarlett O'Hara's Younger Sister: My Lively Life in and Out of Hollywood*—cleverly using lower case for the "in" to emphasize the "Out."

From years of neglect and disinterest, Evelyn's copious beauty had been dormant. My job was to resurrect it and bring it out. Her mousy brown hair had to be transformed for the audience to recognize her as the redhead she had been in movies.

I began by taking Evelyn to Suga, the famous hair stylist for fashion magazines who had a salon at Bergdorf Goodman's. There she got the most flattering cut and the right hair color that was the first step in restoring her glamour. Cyma insisted that glamour was the primary ingredient the show should have. I basically agreed with Cyma on everything; she was a great show person with impeccable taste. It was her tactics that I, and others, disagreed with.

Then I had the challenge of transforming both the New York and Dallas troupes of chorus girls and boys. With all the girls gathered in one large room at the rehearsal studio rented for the show, I began by using one of the girls as my model for my demonstration.

As I was about to start, one of the girls asked, "What do you do when you're not doing this?"—perhaps suspecting that I did other make-ups besides theatre.

"Oh, a little of this...," I replied, and did a bump to the left, "...and a lot of that," and did a vigorous grind and another bump to the right.

The humor entertained them and immediately won their confidence.

I had studied Jules Fisher's lighting of the show and observed that it had a kind of white-blue tint that gave the show a sparkle. I knew that I wanted the make-up to complement that and the costume colors, which I intended to incorporate into the make-up.

With no more than that to go on, I concocted a make-up on the spot that would be repeated in many shows on Broadway for years to come. I began with an ivory foundation base and powdered it with baby powder to give the skin a fragile, porcelain quality. A lavender eye shadow went on either side of the eyelids with yellow in the middle of the lid to create a shimmer. I lined the eyes with a navy blue eyeliner to give them definition without the heaviness that a black liner would have created. I used black mascara with black false lashes, an apricot color on the cheeks, and a cherry-red lipstick.

All of the colors combined to give the Technicolor look of the movies, which seemed appropriate for *Nanette*, a movie kind of a show that was pure "old Hollywood."

Next came the boys. I determined that the reason they were appearing too effeminate in their make-up was that they were being too precise and perfect with it. Girls' make-up can be perfect, but men have to approach their faces with a rugged intention, as opposed to perfection. It's all about our intention.

They were using a water-based, pancake foundation all over their faces that completely covered their own natural skin as well as their beards, an important part of masculinity. Their faces were looking too perfect, which is fine for women but not for men.

I researched water-based foundations in theatrical make-up stores and found a color that was a tawny rust. Used with water as it was intended, it would have made the face too red, but used dry on a sponge, it was a perfect color for men's stage make-up.

The technique I came up with was to dig up a bit of the hard pancake foundation with a knife or other sharp object to create a kind of powder, rake the dry sponge, or a sponge with a drop or two of moisturizer on it, over the dug-up foundation to transfer it to the sponge; and stroke it lightly over the forehead, cheeks, chin, and nose. The trick was to use the foundation like a blush, a transparency, as opposed to an opaque mask as they had been doing, and let their own natural skin show through. They had been covering up too much.

It worked. They were a handsome group of men on stage.

With the chorus girls and boys completed, I gave Helen Gallagher some make-up tips and even cut Bobby Van's hair, an art I had taught myself. My cuts didn't always turn out so great but, thankfully, this one did. My work over with the New York troupe in I don't know how many days, I flew to Dallas to oversee the make-up for that troupe.

I had not yet done Evelyn Keyes' make-up because I needed the stage, the lights, and all the rest to direct me. I liked Evelyn. She was a witty, feminine, intelligent woman with a gentle soul. Not to imply that she was a lightweight; she exuded strength, too. She'd need that with Mike Todd being her lover, before Elizabeth Taylor snatched him up. Three of her four husbands were directors Charles Vidor and John Huston, and the popular '40s bandleader and clarinettist Artie Shaw—certainly no lightweights either. Shaw, himself, was married eight times, and his wives included Lana Turner (seven months) and Ava Gardner (a year). The whole group might be what one would call "heavy."

Evelyn and Artie's marriage lasted well over 20 years, far longer than any of their others, so there must have been something there. She told me that they had once taken acid to see what all the hoopla was about and that during their experience on it, she could see right through Artie.

I thought to myself, "I think I could see through Artie Shaw and I wouldn't even need acid to do it."

I only knew that he was a man about Hollywood, with Cary Grant good looks, who had dated or married nearly every available woman there. It would seem that those ladies needed to wake up. Perhaps, in Evelyn, he had met his match. She was a Scorpio, and although she denied that I'd learn much about Scorpio women from her, from what I knew, I thought she was a perfect Scorpio example. She was intelligent, charming, dynamic, and sexually charged, which, I believed, was what corralled men to her like bees to honey. Evelyn had what it took.

Completing Evelyn's make-up my first day at the Dallas auditorium where *Nanette* was playing, I went outside to the audience seats to observe what I had done in the rehearsal that was in progress.

When Evelyn came on stage, as if prompted by Cecil Beaton at the *Coco* rehearsal, Cyma echoed, "I don't like the way she looks."

Neither did I. Either the lighting or the make-up was creating unflattering shadows under Evelyn's eyes, and I couldn't discern which it was. It would certainly be easier and less expensive to adjust the make-up, and that's what I was expected to do.

Backstage I examined Evelyn's face and didn't see any shadows. It looked perfect to me. But unquestionably there had been shadows under her eyes. I concluded that the black false lashes I had applied must be too long, too dark and overpowering for her small, fragile face, and they were casting shadows under her eyes. I pulled them off and replaced them with shorter brown ones. When she returned to the stage, everyone breathed a sigh of relief. She looked great. In make-up, the subtlest thing can make a difference. The eyes, eyebrows, cheeks, and lips form a unit that creates a balance, and if one of them is off—too dark, too hard, or not enough—the whole thing can look off. Anyone involved in make-up must be alert to catch what that is.

Evelyn's leading man in the Dallas troupe was the great Don Ameche. I remembered Ameche from his two film roles as Alexander Graham Bell, and I was impressed that I was going to be involved with the make-up for the inventor of the telephone.

As I approached Ameche's dressing room, I heard him inside tuning up his voice.

I knocked on the door and waited to hear him say, "Come in."

I opened the door and was surprised to find Alexander Graham Bell standing there in nothing but a jockstrap.

Embarrassed, I ducked my head and muttered, "Sorry, Mr. Ameche. I'll come back," and turned to leave.

"No, no, no," he said. "That's all right," and went for a robe. "I wear this so I'll look neat on stage in my suits. Don't want things hanging down."

That was certainly more information than I had solicited. I explained that I was doing the show's make-up and offered my help if he needed it. He didn't, but there was one thing he did want from me.

"Make sure all the ladies' lips are powdered so their lipstick doesn't transfer onto my tux," he said. "In films, their damn lipstick was always getting on my clothes and I hated it."

That was it, and he went back to tuning up his voice.

Nanette thrilled audiences in Dallas, as it had in New York. On my way to catch a plane back, I left Evelyn jogging on the road outside the auditorium—which I understand she did well into her eighties before she passed away in 2008 at 91, preceded by Artie in 2004 at 94. It might be presumed from these two that the hotties live the longest.

With the success of my make-up for *Nanette*, Cyma wanted me to tutor the chorus girls and boys in the Chicago troupe, whose leading lady was Virginia Mayo, and then fly on to San Francisco for June Allyson's troupe. My negotiation skills hadn't improved because I was still accepting far less than I would have made had I remained in New York—but I was having the time of my life. I was more hooked on theatre and films than ever and vowed to do something there myself some day.

The Chicago troupe was easy. Virginia Mayo's make-up was perfect as it was and needed nothing from me. The old troupers, like her and Ameche, with all their training, knew more about make-up than I ever would.

As I was leaving my hotel my last evening there, I saw Virginia and her husband, the actor Michael O'Shea, having dinner in the dining room, and she motioned for me to come in, which I did. She introduced me to O'Shea, and I didn't think he looked well. He died shortly after that. Paraphrasing the title of her 1946 film about soldiers after the war, *The Best Years of Our Lives*, she would write her autobiography, *The Best Years of My Life*. Her 26 years with O'Shea, her only husband, which by Hollywood standards is exceptional, were doubtlessly what made them the best.

The San Francisco troupe was a noisy bunch. Exhausted from my trip out, and from lugging my heavy make-up case up and down steep backstage stairs in search of dressing rooms in New York, Dallas, Chicago, and now here, I was in no mood to put up with the noise in the room when I began my make-up lecture with the chorus girls. I scanned the room and located the main noise source. It was Cyma, the director, and a group around her all chattering away on what I considered my time.

Unable and unwilling to shout above the din, I stopped everything and said firmly, but politely, "No one in this room should be talking now but me."

That shut 'em up. The point was that if the make-up turned out badly,

I would get the blame. I was merely guarding my territory, which would save me grief later. I learned not to be afraid to speak up when it involved my job.

My reason for leaving my hotel that last evening in Chicago was to search for a gay bar, which I found right around the corner from my hotel. I had a sixth sense about these things. I could track a gay bar like a beagle tracks a rabbit. It was something about the exterior of the place; it always seemed dark and moody and promised more than a drink. For my effort, it had produced a one-night stand. When I arrived back in New York, I discovered that it had also produced the "clap"—gonorrhea, for those who don't know.

I went to a Fifth Avenue doctor known to mainly treat gay men for sexually transmitted diseases, "Doctor Crotch," as Lee called him. In his office were photographs of his male clientele, mostly models, either nude or scantily clad. No doubt, they had all been there for the same reason I was: Doctor Crotch's miracle crotch treatment.

This was my second time there that year, and as he was giving me a penicillin shot, he said, "What are you doing, loaning that thing out?"

Actually, I was. AIDS had not yet made its appearance, and at this time, everyone thought all we had to do was get a penicillin shot and in three days, we'd be back in action. We would discover that there are penalties for the mistreatment of our bodies. AIDS may have already been around, and many of us were just lucky; that's the only explanation as to why we survived. We were all playing Russian roulette, and the loaded gun would surely fire someday.

I had asked Mother to join me in my suite of rooms in Chicago. It seemed a shame to let all that space go to waste with only me in it. She declined, saying that Chicago wasn't where she wanted to be in the winter. Instead, she met me back in New York, and one evening we went to *Nanette*. After the performance, Cyma suggested that I take Mother backstage to get a look at show business behind the scenes. I wanted to check out Bobby Van's hair, so I took Mother along.

I left her on the stage outside Van's dressing room while I went in. Coming out, I could see from the wings her small figure standing in the middle of the huge stage with only the stage light providing light, while she gazed out into the now empty theatre. It was a scene eerily like Mama Rose in *Gypsy*. Like Mama Rose, she had been with me throughout it all, pleading with me to be a success as if it were the only sedative for all her painful years with my father's drinking. I wondered if she had had dreams of acting (like me), or of being something other than a homemaker and mother, which, when she was young, few women were allowed to do. Was this her real desperation—some dream she'd had at some faraway time that she had passed on to me? Is that why she had begged me to do this for her—to fulfill an unrequited dream whose distant murmur was so faint that she could barely remember where it came from anymore? But it still gnawed at her, and the only relief was through me.

As I approached her, she said, "Just think ... only minutes ago there was color and life here, and now there's just this bare stage."

It was like a child's lament. The fantasy was over, the clowns had gone home, and this was the true reality: it had all been make-believe. In some way, it was a sad comment on our life together. We were the fantasy. I had wanted a friend, but she refused to give up the mother role. Without that, who would she be?

I was slipping away. She had wanted my success, but now it threatened her. She couldn't admit that her performance as Mother was over, that my continuing to play the son who needed a mother had passed. She wanted to hold onto the illusion.

I felt guilty that I could no longer provide this and was torn between her needs and mine. We had our usual arguments from her continually trying to control my life, and I would explode. My sister had long ago laid down the rules, and I needed to do this, but I didn't have the strength. And so, I exploded—an ineffectual way of dealing with it.

Maybe the truth was that I was afraid if I took a stand, she might take me up on it and I wouldn't be able to go it alone. I wanted Mother in my life, but not how she was accustomed to being. She couldn't be the friend I needed; she could only be "Mother." And that, to her, was telling me how to do my life.

When she left, we both knew we were at an end. She would have one more visit to New York to see me before we finally called it quits.

Once she said, "When I'm dead, I'll still be looking down on you from a cloud."

"Oh, Mother," I said, "please don't."

I meant it. I wanted this pain over—whatever it took.

9

Michael: The Young Man
Who Would Change
My Life Forever

With the country's violent climate, further evidenced by the war's disregard for human life, a kind of lawlessness was creeping over the land. Old laws regarding family, church, and sex were being challenged and alternatives sought. Wife swapping, Indian gurus, and same-sex partners were being explored. Pop idols like Mick Jagger and David Bowie flirted with ambiguity and hinted at bisexuality. Having same-sex partners was in vogue.

The new freedom and empowerment that gays felt after the Stonewall Inn riot encouraged the opening of more gay bars, baths, and after-hours places. Gays were becoming a political force to be reckoned with, and everyone wanted to appear broad-minded. It wasn't politically correct to challenge them. It was their drumbeat leading the party, and no one wanted to be left behind.

The greatest malady the country had was the fear of being out of date and over the hill. Everyone wanted to appear young and "with it." Women, way past their prime, piled on their little-girl make-up, enhanced their hair with exaggerated hair falls, and hiked their hemlines to the limit to appear young and still desirable. Straggly, grey-haired, balding men let what hair they had grow long, wrapped it around their heads, and squeezed their protruding bellies into tight, provocative bell-bottom pants and fantasized that they were back in their youth.

Everyone wanted to be sexually desirable, and in the clubs, enhanced by drugs and the disco beat, they believed for that moment that they were. The war had created a desperation in people to live as much as they could before they were dead. In a land where leaders could cheat and lie, where others were assassinated, and where police were called "pigs," nothing that had existed before seemed relevant anymore. It was every person for himself—like a shootout in the Old West.

Lee was still reeling from John's tragic ending, and to avoid his feelings, he went on a sexual rampage with his three partners a day. I was alarmed that I was being left behind, and I tried to up my activity to compete. Without the accoutrements of a fabulous townhouse, a cool Rolls Royce, and Lee's great looks, I could barely keep up with even one of these. We prowled the usual gay bars and after-hours places in search of prey, and our score was about equal, but it was becoming more of a full-time job than my make-up work.

Often Valerie and Mary would accompany us. We'd begin in some above-the-ground place like Elaine's or Eric's. After a few drinks, puffs, or whatever, we'd move our party to an after-hours joint where, after compromising ourselves just short of free sex on the sidewalk outside to get in, we'd enter and crawl out—with or without a "catch"—sometime in the early morning.

Once Mary and I had been up all night drinking, and all the rest, in one of those sleazy joints when someone told us of a local TV show that was interviewing couples the following morning about the current dating situation in New York. Though we were certainly no example of that, after a few more drinks to while away the hours before we were supposed to be there at 9:00 AM, we staggered over to the studio to fill out the forms to be on the show. The "suits" in that studio couldn't have been more surprised seeing us roll in there. They gave us the forms, anyhow—probably afraid we'd start a riot—and that was the end of it. The condition of our clothing alone would have eliminated anyone. We were too stoned to know any better.

On another occasion, I was asked by an editor at *Town and Country* magazine to participate in a national cosmetic event that was being held at a midtown West Side hotel ballroom, where I was supposed to create on stage on my model's face the new fall look—whatever that may have been.

With our usual debauchery, Mary and I stayed up all night preparing for it. In my stupor, I plucked out nearly all of her eyebrows and did such a bizarre make-up that she resembled one of the "Children of the Damned." Then she got into a medieval-looking, brown velvet gown she'd borrowed from a friend with a slit up to the crotch that constantly flapped open, exposing her panties underneath. She then completely wrapped her head in a black satin scarf and pinned what looked like a feather duster in the front. From her neck up, she looked like a flapper who might be a maid. From her neck down, she looked like Attila the Hun who might be a stripper.

Spending so much time on our preparation, we arrived at the event too late for the part for which we were scheduled. Besides that, they hadn't told me we were to have shared the stage with several other artists. That really ticked me off. And what would Mary now do, done up in the middle of the day, looking like a medieval stripper who cleaned houses?

They thought the error was theirs—even our lateness—and to compensate they offered us a solo spot after lunch, and even offered lunch, too.

Now they were talking.

After a sumptuous meal that included wine right to dessert and coffee, we hit the stage and gave them a show they'd never forget.

With Mary sitting paralyzed like a zombie on a high stool, I expounded on the colors I'd created, having no idea what I was talking about. A man in the audience questioned the face I'd created, which, by now, with Mary sitting like rigor-mortis had set in, must have looked like an Egyptian death mask.

"What you see is what you get," I answered him curtly, no doubt slurring my words.

Mary even answered a couple of questions, but her speech by now sounded like sputtering through crackers. The audience quickly caught on that we were stoned out of our minds—as were many in the audience after lunch—and they kept it up. A woman who appeared to have some official position with the event came out frequently from the wings trying to get us off the stage, but we were having too much fun. If she'd had a hook, she'd surely have dragged us off.

Afterwards, several photographers besieged us to photograph us, and, as it turned out, we ended up representing the entire event in the industry magazine articles that followed.

That's what they got for expecting me to share the stage with other artists.

My increased marijuana intake enhanced my grandiose conviction that I was a star. Though I was considered one of the best make-up artists in the business by now, that didn't give me the right to behave as arrogantly as I did at times. I was on top of something at last, and I wanted everyone to know it for all the times I had been put down. I didn't consider that what goes up will assuredly come down.

I wanted Mother particularly to acknowledge my new position, but she granted me no recognition. To concede it would be admitting that I was standing on my own and didn't need her anymore. Her fear of being left alone made that totally unthinkable. No, I must continue to believe that without her I would be nothing.

Of course, I didn't believe that; but then, I did believe it. It had been so ingrained in me that it was impossible to rid myself of that idea. In some sick way, it was comforting to know I wasn't doing it alone. But there was an imprisonment and emptiness I felt—like everything was constantly being taken away from me. The only thing I owned was the marijuana, booze, and sex. Those were mine, and I coveted them.

I was always conscientious to make sure that I was well rested for the amount of work I was now getting, but on my days off I was burning my candle at both ends. Everyone around me was doing the same, so I had nothing to compare how it was affecting me.

I would hear: "Oh, cocaine isn't addictive," and though I didn't do much of that because of the cost, I believed it because I wanted to. I heard: "Marijuana isn't as bad for you as cigarettes," and since I was trying to give those up, I used marijuana instead. Unable to tolerate hangovers from booze, I let pot become my thing. I didn't realize how it muddled my brain and made my behavior erratic and out of order.

At an advertising shoot for Revlon, I, the four models, and even the photographer were so stoned on marijuana (which one of the girls had brought with her) that the shoot turned into a disaster. The girls, some of the top models in the business, laughed so uncontrollably and constantly that it became annoying. When the art director repeatedly tried to explain how she wanted me to apply the facemask that was the product being advertised, I became so frustrated that I angrily threw the tube of it on the floor. The photographer stomped off the set and had to be cajoled to return. Undoubtedly, Revlon had to re-shoot it. But we were all making so much money and had so many bookings, we didn't even care. There was always the next job. It was a kind of merry-go-round that never stopped spinning.

Perhaps my bad behavior on the Revlon shoot was due to an incident beforehand. I had designed a series of eye shadow colors for a company called Andrea that manufactured false lashes. I went to their lab in New Jersey (the same lab used by Elizabeth Arden) and sat there all day diligently working with the chemists mixing original colors like eggplant, rust brown, midnight blue, emerald green, and the like—all standard today but quite unique then. Andrea first brought out the colors in a set of three: light, medium, and dark, and then all together on one board and they were very successful.

Soon after they came out, I stopped by Revlon to consult with them about the shoot I was about to do for them. I was speaking with their products designer when she pulled from her drawer the series of colors I had designed for Andrea that she was copying for Revlon.

"How do you like these?" she asked.

"I like them a lot," I said. "I designed them."

She immediately shoved them back into her drawer and nothing further was said.

Tell me those companies don't copy.

As for Andrea, I mixed my colors like a painter and therefore created original colors. That episode with Revlon convinced me once and for all that unscrupulous product designers regularly snatched their ideas from whatever source they could and then claimed they had originated it. The reason the Revlon products designer was copying the colors I had designed for Andrea was that they were new and too tempting to pass up. The make-up artists who originated the idea got nothing—little pay, if anything, and certainly no acknowledgment—but the products designers, I'm sure, had no compunction about receiving whatever they could from their snitch. Maybe Revlon deserved having their facemask product thrown on the floor. Who knows where and from whom the idea originated?

In 1973, Nixon's tapes connecting him to the Watergate break-in would force him out of American politics for good. He managed, however, to get a cease-fire in Vietnam, where Johnson had failed, which, thankfully, spared the loss of human life that year.

Everyone's favorite New York mayor—tall, elegant, handsome John Lindsay—was out of office after eight glamorous years, replaced by short, fat, squat, unattractive Abraham Beame—quite a come-down. Not only was the country looking unattractive, but New York wasn't looking so good either.

The hippie musical *Hair* had closed the year before, signaling changes brewing. Now, *No, No, Nanette*, a throwback to a simpler time, closed too—perhaps signaling further changes. Hippies and naiveté were out of fashion. The country was moving on—but to where?

Valerie and her crumbling, decrepit bull's head made yet another pilgrimage, this time to Santa Monica, California, where she took up temporary

residency in a big white rented house with a swimming pool in the back surrounded by Grecian statues of naked men. Doubtless, her landlord was a
gay man. She asked me to come out, but hanging out with a rich woman
with money to burn would get me nowhere. I had to work. Her restless spirit
would soon drive her back across country—south on this junket—to Miami
Beach, Florida, making her sojourn in California a short one.

Lee's decorator boss, Howard, was selling his East Side townhouse and
permanently moving his business to his other home in Coconut Grove,
Florida. This meant that Lee would soon be leaving, too. Like a migration
of birds, my friends were en route and leaving me behind.

Cleaning out Howard's basement in preparation for their move, Lee
offered me the choice of anything down there that struck my fancy. Everything was to be sold indiscriminately as a lot at auction, and it seemed
humane that some things should be given a home with me. There were wonderful objects on table after table that Howard, with excellent taste, had collected over the years from his worldly travels. I discreetly chose only the
things I liked, and Howard even threw in a large white rug that had been
in his townhouse dining room that nearly covered my entire living room
floor.

Lee was also salvaging some things for himself and wanted me to store
them: paintings, glassware, engravings, and a large mirrored disco ball that
had once hung in a 1920s ballroom and belonged to John Barrett. When
he was murdered, Lee was storing it for him at Howard's, and now I had it.
At first, I was slightly creeped out, but when Lee hung it in my all-red living
room and placed on a table the light that reflected the mirrored prisms, I
loved watching the dancing lights reflected on my walls and ceiling like tiny
planets roaming the universe.

Using his decorating skills, Lee also hung other things and placed
objects I had collected in a way that I probably wouldn't have thought of.
My apartment had become a home, a refuge for me, and Howard's hand-
me-downs would now assist me in my pick-ups as the townhouse had assisted
Lee. I would miss him and Valerie, but the world was moving on, and so
were our lives.

Superheroes had always fascinated the public in comic books—who
didn't remember Superman and Flash Gordon on TV? Although *Star Wars*
wouldn't be in movies until 1977, its predecessor on Broadway was *Warp*. A
science fiction fantasy set on some planet in a faraway galaxy, it had a Flash

Gordon leading man, a damsel in distress to rescue, ray guns and other special effects, and a villain that would make Darth Vader seem as docile as the family pet.

With my previous Broadway experience, I was asked to design the makeup. One by one, the cast came to my apartment for me to design their makeup in my living room. I had the leading man's brown hair changed to Flash Gordon's yellow blonde, painted the leading lady's lips bubble gum pink like in the comic books, and made the villain look more treacherous than Ming the Merciless. A crowd of druggy potheads from Eric's bar showed up opening night and applauded Mary and me as we walked down the aisle like celebrities. But alas, no make-up, not even the second coming of Ming the Merciless, could have saved that awful show. It closed in four days.

By this time, I had worked with several minor rock and roll artists—too minor to recall their names—and with Edgar Winters, brother of Johnny Winters, two better-known rockers whose stars were fading fast. One evening, while I was working with Edgar on an album cover, Mary and I went out with him and his girlfriend to have dinner at Elaine's. Mary worked there, but she had this night off. Sipping Dom Pérignon in the back of a stretch limousine, we pulled up in front of the restaurant where, inside, everyone was immediately aware of our arrival. As we walked through the door, the help and clientele who knew Mary greeted her like she was a celebrity. There was no recognition of Edgar, even though, being an albino with snow-white hair, no eyebrows, and pinkish eyes, he was quite distinguishable.

"Who is this Mary?" he inquired, impressed with Mary's status in this restaurant where he got nothing.

I shrugged and never told him she was part of the help.

I had also worked with other minor celebrities, like transvestite Candy Darling, predecessor to Lypsinka, with whom I would work in the future, and Viva, one of Andy Warhol's underground stars—so my repertoire included both offbeat and mainstream people. Not that Art Garfunkel wasn't mainstream, but he sure was offbeat.

He and his partner, Paul Simon, had split in '68, and Art had done a couple of films: *Catch 22* and *Carnal Knowledge*. He had a new album coming out and some photographer from California was shooting the cover. I was recommended to make up Art, and, as an added bonus, they wanted me to cut Art's hair. I had cut Bobby Van's hair and some minor rock and roll guys' hair, so I was quite capable of cutting Art's hair—if he had let me.

Before I began, his publicist took me aside and said, "Art loves those two puffs of hair on either side of his head, so don't cut them."

I had already eyeballed in on those two frizzy puffs of hair that looked like fuzz horns on either side of his receding hairline and instantly hated them. I knew I could cut his hair in a way that would make him look less bald without those hideous horns, and I set about to do it, ignoring the warning. It was that risk-taking thing again, which sometimes got me into trouble.

As I was cutting his hair in the garden outside the apartment where the photographer intended to shoot, I said to Art, "This is a 'cut-see-kill' haircut."

"What's a 'cut-see-kill' haircut?" he asked.

"I cut it, you see it, and then you kill me."

He chuckled, but when he considered it, he jumped up and ran for a mirror. I had cut off those beloved puffs—and worse, I was bragging about it. That was it; I was dismissed.

Well, I had been kicked out of better places, to echo Lucy's line to Tallulah in their TV show together. I had, actually—Avedon, for instance. To say nothing of Club 21, when my brother-in-law and I went in there drunk once—but that's another story we're not getting into here.

When the album came out, there was Art on the cover in the haircut I had given him, and he never looked better. And he looked less bald, too, as I had planned. I doubt he would have given me credit, but I'm taking it now.

One of my art instructors at Pratt, describing how I attacked a drawing, said, "Richardson goes in where angels fear to tread." The actual phrase is: "Fools rush in where angels fear to tread," which may be a more appropriate way to describe how I waded in where a more cautious person might pause to consider.

The experience with Garfunkel was like my lightening of Lauren Hutton's eyebrows that sent her off her rocker. On the other hand, Avedon wanted me to do something about Anjelica Huston's then thick eyebrows that were too dark and heavy. I created a graceful, thinner brow line that Huston still uses to this day. That happened because of trust. Without trust, it's impossible to create. Those who had trust got results.

Donald Saddler, the choreographer for *Nanette* and one of Broadway's finest, suggested me for the make-up for Harry Rigby's new show, *Good News*. It was previewing in Boston and he intended to bring it to Broadway.

Following in the same mode that he and Cyma had started with *Nanette*—that he lost to her, which only made him more determined—Rigby had hired another legendary screen star, Alice Faye, as his leading lady. John Payne, the wooden actor in such film classics as *Miracle on 34th Street*, was her leading man, as in several of her films.

Primarily a '30s and early '40s film star, Faye had not been in films since her last appearance in the Rodgers and Hammerstein 1962 film musical *State Fair*, so it seemed an appropriate time to trot her out for one last look. At 58 now—after several face lifts and boozing with her husband, Phil Harris—all traces of baby fat that had once characterized her face had long since disappeared. What was left was an Alice Faye who was still recognizable in person, but somewhat scrambled across the footlights of a stage. With very little good bone structure to begin with, and needing the baby fat to resemble her original self, Faye simply didn't know how to make herself up for the stage. Her features had always been rounded: eyes, cheeks, nose, and lips, but now on stage they seemed to melt into a blob.

In that medium, the lights and the rest of the stage atmosphere make projecting oneself a bit tricky. Even in the best conditions, it's not easy. With no professional guidance telling actors how they look at a distance throughout the theatre, it is impossible for them to know how to make themselves up to their best advantage. It would be like trying to give a performance without a director. Yet, invariably, when a show is being put together, make-up is the last thing thought of—if it is thought of at all. For examples of how hard it is, we need only to reflect on Evelyn Keyes in *Nanette* and the ingénue in *Coco*. Even I had to hop to get those right. Still, directors and producers continually rely on actors to know this art.

In Rigby's case, he was wise enough to see that his leading lady needed help, and with Donald there, they solicited that help from me.

I took one look at Alice's face and could see that it was stretched like a balloon across what bone structure she had. Unless the make-up was carefully planned, I sensed that she might not project as herself across the footlights. I was also told that her eyes were appearing squinty and small on stage, but they weren't in person. She must have been doing a lot of things wrong, limiting the possibilities she had.

My job was to map out the right make-up and train the show's make-up artist to recreate it on Alice every night (no one was trusting her to do it). They also wanted me to buy the make-up, which I had always balked at with everyone. Since they didn't seem to trust either the make-up artist or

Alice to do this, and since she was my favorite childhood movie star—whom I had adored in movies like *Hello, Frisco, Hello* and *Alexander's Ragtime Band*— for her, I'd do anything.

Estée Lauder had just come out with a new line of eyeliner pencils with a dark color on one end and a light, pearlized version on the other. I bought a whole slew of these, along with the lightest color of Revlon's cream foundation and their colored moisturizer that I had used on Tallulah and Lucy.

As I had done with them, I began with the colored moisturizer to give Alice's face a youthful glow, and followed that with the light color foundation, which I powdered with baby powder, as I had with the *Nanette* chorus girls. The light color foundation with the baby powder over it lightened all of Alice's features, and now I was able to select the features I wanted to bring forward.

Again, as I had done with the chorus girls, I lined Alice's eyes with a navy blue eyeliner, sensing that a black liner might have been too overpowering; penciled a light, pearlized blue inside her lower lids to open up her eyes; and added a lot of light blue eye shadow all around them. I followed that with a deeper blue in the creases of her eyelids to give her eyes depth, and then mascaraed her lashes with a deep blue mascara. On top of them, I placed black false lashes, which I had cut and feathered so they wouldn't be too long and cast shadows, as they had with Evelyn Keyes in *Nanette*. I kept her eyebrows light and away from her eyes so that nothing pushed down on them to close them.

A brown shadow went under her cheekbones to bring out her bone structure, with more brown under her chin and all around her jaw line to define it and bring her face forward. A light blush of peach went on her cheeks—too much color would have flattened them out—and her lips were lined and filled in with a bright red lip color that complemented all of her costumes.

Everything on her face was open, light, and airy. Heavy make-up, as Lucy was also doing, was why these women were looking older and why Alice's eyes were closing up on stage.

When I finished, I went outside to view the work in the theatre and joined Rigby, Donald, and several others gathered in the back waiting for Alice's entrance. When she came on stage and faced the audience, her full, round blue eyes shone to the very back of the theatre. The entire group gathered there gasped in unison at the clarity and projection. Even I was startled. Gone were the squinty, small, non-projecting eyes, replaced by

Alice's big, round blue ones. Her skin looked soft and contoured, and her lips were plump and juicy. The Alice Faye we had all known and loved in films was back in town. Hello, Frisco, hello!

Third Avenue was still cooking with the endless parade of gay men who strolled there, but the hunt was somewhat dimmed without the competition of Lee to fuel it. Before he left for Florida, he had introduced me to comedienne Totie Fields at a party after a show she had given. She was a friend of Howard's and lived in my neighborhood.

One evening on Third Avenue, I was talking to a young man I had just met whom I was considering taking home with me, when Totie stepped out of a cab and, taking me aside, said, "What are you doing talking to him? Go on home."

She then went inside her apartment building, and I thought to myself, "She's got a nerve telling me to go home. What business is this of hers?"

Taking no heed of her attempt to warn me, and perhaps as a kind of spite, I took the man home.

In the middle of some preliminary stuff between us, the man suddenly jumped up and said, "Give me all your money!"

I was startled and realized, too late, what Totie had been trying to tell me. I later learned that she had seen the man cruising Third Avenue before and had heard he was a hustler and some other scary things about him that I was now going to experience firsthand.

I had little money on me, having spent most of it earlier buying mescaline, which I had taken with Mary and Billy the bartender. Coming down from it now, I found this man threatening me in my living room even more frightening.

"I don't have any money," I answered him truthfully.

"You have money," he said. "It's the weekend. You have money."

Well, I did have $1.70, which I gave him.

Snatching it up, he shouted, "You have more!"

That did it. No one was shouting at me in my own space. Something inside me snapped, and I grabbed him by the neck of his shirt and ripped off his pants pocket, where he had just put my $1.70, spilling the contents over the floor.

I dragged him to the door, slapped him across the face, and yelled, "There's no God in you!"—wherever that came from.

I opened the door and threw him out, slamming the door behind him. The man could have had a knife or a gun. What was I thinking?

Now he was timidly knocking on my door.

"Please," he pleaded outside, "the keys to my apartment fell out of my pocket. I need my keys."

Continuing my reckless behavior, I threw open the door, dragged him back inside, slapped him again across his face, and this time yelled, "What would your mother think?"

What would my mother think, for that matter?

I opened the door again, threw him and his keys out behind him, and slammed the door.

"I'll kill you if I ever see you again!" he screamed, kicking the door. "I'll kill you!"

He did see me again, but he came nowhere near me. He probably thought I was crazier than he was.

As if that wasn't enough, on Third Avenue again, soon after that incident, I ran into a Vietnam veteran I had been introduced to by Lee. I liked this young man when I first met him and sensed that he felt the same way about me. Certain this time that it was okay, I asked him back to my apartment.

When the subject of bed came around, he unscrewed his legs, tossed them in the corner of the room, and said, "Carry me there."

I was speechless. As much as I wanted to support our boys in the armed forces, I was not prepared for this. If this was a test, he had handled it badly. Perhaps he was angry, which was understandable, and wanted to be treated like everyone else, but I had feelings too. Unfortunately, there was no way, and it was an unpleasant experience for both of us.

All of these mishaps aside, with the activity on Third Avenue it was no wonder that my life would eventually careen in the unlikely direction of Donnie. Dark hair, medium height, and vaguely attractive, he'd eyed me on a Third Avenue bus coming home one evening and after a one-nighter that I fully intended to leave at that, we became what might best be described as ... friendly.

Unquestionably, Donnie was gay; in fact, he may have invented it. But this didn't deter him from becoming involved with a much older, rich woman, Nora, who owned a large duplex penthouse with a wrap-around terrace on the Upper East Side. Money, obviously, took precedence over Donnie's gayness.

Nora had been a mother to two grown daughters and wife to her now deceased husband, and had inherited a fortune from her wealthy family whose familiar name had been on American household products for generations. As far as Nora was concerned, if this gay young man wanted to service her ... why not?

Donnie would insist, as if trying to convince himself, "But I love Nora. I really do."

He also loved the expensive Italian suits, Cartier watches and gold jewelry, trips to exotic places, and lavish dinners out that always included his hang-around pals—and when it came time to pay, guess who picked up the tab? Nora would learn there was a price to pay for Donnie's attention.

Riddled with personal insecurities and jealousies, they competed to extremes with one another. Both Nora and Donnie fancied themselves singers, and Nora rented performance spaces and threw extravagant parties in her penthouse for the sole purpose of performing, regaling her captive audience of friends and acquaintances with the most atrocious cat screechings. Annoyed at being relegated to part of Nora's audience, Donnie would invariably butt in with what he had to offer vocally, which, after excessive booze and cigarettes, sounded like gravel grinding over sandpaper. Each talked incessantly throughout the other's "performance," and between the screeching, grinding, and chattering, the place became a bedlam.

Obsessed with Donnie's continuous infidelities, Nora had extensive plastic surgery: arms, legs, butt, a tummy tuck. She even had silicone pumped into the tops of her hands to make them look less old and veiny, but, instead, the procedure made them resemble small boxing gloves. Having nearly died on the operating table from the butcher-surgeon who would do that much work on someone at once, she now presumed she looked as young as Donnie—who, with all of his debauchery, didn't look that young himself.

Fretting with his own bag of insecurities, increased by his rapid hair loss, he'd had a hair extension woven into what was left of his own hair and became paranoid that it could be detected. With his constant combing and fiddling with his extension, desperately trying to make it look natural, and with Nora adjusting and readjusting her make-up and wigs, these two were a very nervous pair—and made everyone nervous around them.

A friend of Donnie's, Sandy Wilson, the creator of the musical *The Boy Friend* (which was turned into a 1971 movie starring Twiggy and Tommy Tune), came to Nora's penthouse for a drink one evening. Down the spiral stairs floated Nora in a gauzy caftan, wearing an enormous pair of sunglasses that covered most of her face, and a long red fright wig that kept tipping to the side—more so as she drank. After an hour or so of primping in front of the bathroom mirror, Donnie also appeared in sunglasses, with his hair extension fluffed to absurdity. Wilson, too, made his appearance in sunglasses. I was the only one fool enough to appear as myself.

Sipping drinks on opposite couches by the fireplace with this bunch of spooks trying to hide their age and flaws behind sunglasses, I felt like I was with the cast from *The Munsters*.

Donnie had all of his jewelry and a watch that Nora had given him stolen from his apartment, as well as his car. Nora chalked it up to "one of those New York things," but I suspected he'd been picking up hustlers and they had ripped him off. When he showed up at my apartment one evening with a handsome young man that he passed off as a friend, my suspicions were confirmed.

When Donnie disappeared into the bathroom to re-fluff his extension, the man pulled out a gun and said, "I don't want you to think I'd use this on you"—thank you very much. He continued, "I'm looking for a guy who owes me 30,000 bucks, so put it away until I leave." It would seem he had the misconception this was to be an extended visit.

Recovering from my shock, I accepted the gun and when Donnie emerged from the bathroom with his wig sufficiently teased, I ordered him and the man out of my apartment. Holding onto the gun until they were both completely out, I tossed the man his gun, and quickly closed and locked the door behind them. Whatever they were up to was their business; mine was staying alive.

I'd had it. I wouldn't have been with this ridiculous bunch if Lee, and now Valerie, hadn't moved to Florida. And Mary now had a boyfriend who was taking up all of her time. I yearned for companionship that was real and fulfilling—and that's when destiny stepped in.

Donnie would be allotted one last go-around. On a particularly warm day in early spring that conjured up thoughts of summer, he called to ask if I wanted to drive with him and a visiting friend from California to the beach in Jacob Riis Park in Brooklyn. After some grilling to make sure this "friend" wasn't a repeat of my previous experience with him, I agreed.

Since the beach he was going to was en route from photographer Bill King's studio where I was working that morning, when I finished making up a fat man to look like Santa Claus, I packed up my make-up case and waited downstairs in front of the building for him. He arrived in a tan convertible, a replacement for his stolen car, with the visiting friend already in the back seat. I climbed into the front seat with my make-up case, and we whizzed off. Typically, it turned out that the visitor from California wasn't an acquaintance at all, but a friend of a friend who needed a place to stay until he got his own apartment. His name was Michael.

With Donnie sitting between Michael and me and chattering endlessly, we perched on the nearly empty beach at Riis Park, notoriously known for being gay, and watched a foolish young man running by the water in front of us waving yards of pink chiffon over his head like a banner. Our laughter filled the warm spring air and mixed with the sound of gulls and the ocean as a prelude of the summer to be. Little did I know that this man from California sitting on the other side of Donnie was the destiny that would change my life forever.

10

David Bowie
and Gloria Vanderbilt

At the top of the stairs leading into his plane, Richard Nixon waved goodbye to his presidency in August of '74 and was whisked out of Washington. Thankful to be rid of Watergate, the country embraced Gerald Ford to complete Nixon's term, but not enough to grant him one of his own. Mayor Abe Beame wrestled with New York's economic woes while Patty Hearst brazenly brandished a machine gun for her Symbionese Liberation Army captors, and with American ground forces pulled out of Vietnam, the North and South Vietnamese were left to their own carnage. When the whole fracas was over in '75, after three decades of fighting and 1.75 million dead, the gains would be no more than when it all started.

For the men who had fought the war, there was no homecoming celebration or tribute. The party that had started at the beginning of the decade to drown out the gunfire going on in some foreign place was in full swing, and no one wanted to be reminded of anything depressing. We had become addicted to fun, wild times and we wanted more.

For their new liberation, the gays were awarded more baths and downtown bars and dance clubs in seedier sections of town, like the Lower West Side waterfront in the meat packing district, where the cobblestone streets at night were dark and dangerous. To heighten the danger, sex and drugs regularly took place in the backs of large parked produce trucks in lots there and in vacant rotting waterfront warehouses. Danger and lawlessness had been taking over New York City, whose economic difficulties meant less police, and this fed into a kind of sexual thrill for gays that naughty behavior might be punished by violence. Downtown leather bars played into this fantasy, and everyone wanted to appear more menacing than the other guy.

Aware that Donnie had gone out of town and suspecting that Michael might feel disoriented in New York by himself, I called him a couple of days after our meeting on the beach. He said that he was moving from Donnie's as soon as he could find himself an apartment. I sensed that he was concerned about Donnie's possible advances. Being 23 with a fine physique, quite handsome, with soft puppy dog amber eyes, dark hair, and a moustache, Michael would surely have been on Donnie's hit list. Donnie was not one to leave many stones unturned or at least trifled with. Michael was having none of it.

I met him that afternoon after my call, and we took mescaline and walked around the city observing things inside shop windows and commenting on them. He told me that he was originally from Brooklyn. His father, an accountant, had accepted a job with Bill Cosby in L.A., and Michael, his two brothers, and his parents had moved there when he was a child into a big house with a swimming pool. Their apartment in Brooklyn had been small, and the big house in L.A. was an amazing luxury for all of them.

Unfortunately, Cosby's company didn't pan out as planned, and Michael's father was out of a job. By then, he had made contacts in L.A. and continued on, keeping the house and the lifestyle. However, the lifestyle had played havoc with his marriage, and Michael's parents divorced. His father had since become part owner of one of L.A.'s trendiest restaurants, "Ma Maison," and he had moved with his new wife to Encino, California, to raise avocados and other produce for his restaurant. Michael's mother had moved to a house in Palm Springs, complete with a swimming pool and an outdoor Jacuzzi.

In some ways, the move to L.A. had paid off handsomely, but in other ways, it had destroyed the lives of Michael and his younger brother. They were the youngest and the most hurt by their parents' divorce. His older brother was now a model in L.A. and had been on his own for several years. He was the least affected.

Competing with his older brother, Michael had come to New York to try his luck at modeling. With years of my own modeling experience and working with photographers, I knew exactly what steps to take. Michael and I bonded immediately, with him offering friendship and me offering my expertise, but it soon blossomed into a friendship that made us inseparable.

He found an apartment a few blocks from me, which was no accident. I was delighted to have him as a neighbor I could reach at any moment. We had dinners together, went to movies, the theatre, rock concerts, and all kinds of social events. All of my friends loved him. Without realizing it, we were forming a partnership.

We went back to the beach at Jacob Riis Park, where I took photographs of him sitting on the sand with the ocean behind him. I styled him with a jean jacket of mine and even cut his hair. The look was handsome and strong, just what we wanted for the model agencies. He began modeling, but the work was sparse and he needed more to make his mark in New York, the reason he had come here. I recognized it as the goal of a younger me, and I gladly extended my help.

After graduating from UCLA, he had been doing macramé on a beach in California while he formed his New York plan. This gave him the idea to create macramé plant hangers and sell them to New York florists. He began small, creating the plant hangers in his new apartment, but soon the orders poured in and he outgrew the space. He moved into a business loft in the West Thirties off Fifth Avenue, illegally living in the back of the large space. There he set up shop, training handicapped workers to do the macramé, and it quickly became a lucrative business.

When the florists became saturated with plant hangers, he turned the business into macramé belts, selling the belts to New York department stores and other stores around the country. The problem was that the workers he trained to do the macramé constantly left, forcing him to train others, and that became a burden for him. To deal with this, he got rid of the macramé and turned his business into belts he designed and jobbed out to small manufacturers to make for him. His earnings the first year were several hundred thousand dollars. He was on his way.

I admired Michael. He had a knack for making money, and I was impressed. I struggled with my work, making good money to support a nice lifestyle, but nothing like his. There was something else that I also felt, something more than just close friendship, nothing sexual, though we tried that and decided to be friends. It was a connection I had felt that afternoon on the beach when we first met, like a spiritual thing neither of us understood.

Some clairvoyant astrologer told us that we were soul mates, which she said meant that we were from the same source and had known each other in other lifetimes. It was all so mystical and sounded romantic, and that became our problem: were we friends or something more? If it wasn't sexual, then what were we? We would try to find out.

Michael had come from a dysfunctional family like my own, and maybe that was what I first related to about him. He said his mother prepared dinner for the family by opening cans. As a child, he snuck candy for his dinner, which substituted for love. My mother was an excellent cook (though instead of doing the cooking herself, she trained our maid to cook like her). So this wasn't my problem. But Michael's father, being a workaholic, was emotionally and physically missing in the family, and this I related to.

He told me that when he was a child he would wait by the elevator in their building in Brooklyn for his father to come home, and when he did, he would walk out of the elevator, pat Michael on the head, and go inside their apartment, never realizing how glad his son was to see him.

When his father suggested divorce to his mother, she said, "I can't talk about that right now. I'll be late for my tennis lesson."

Apparently, L.A. had gotten to her. Was it any wonder that Michael would substitute candy for the love and compassion missing in his parents? He would substitute a lot more than that in the future.

In the late summer, I flew out to L.A. for *Mademoiselle* magazine to do the make-up on Valerie Harper, whose TV series, *Rhoda*, was beginning that fall. Not being an avid TV viewer, I had never heard of Rhoda or Valerie Harper, and I had never even watched the *Mary Tyler Moore Show* where the character, Rhoda, originated. But I was glad to be going back to Hollywood, my childhood dream.

Before I left, *Mademoiselle* called to ask me to bring some clothes for Valerie who, they said, was no longer the size of the clothes they had already sent. I had enough of my own stuff to carry with my heavy bag and an even heavier make-up case, so I requested that they send a limousine if they wanted me to carry Valerie's stuff too, which they did.

The magazine editor, the photographer, David McCabe, the hair stylist, and I stayed at the Beverly Hills Hotel. My room faced a wall with no view, but since we would only be there a couple of days, I made the best of it. I had lunch in the Polo Lounge and lay around the pool playing movie star, a pleasant fantasy that no one believed but helped pass the time. Our first night there we dined at Le Bistro, enjoying their first-rate food and excellent service. I could have gotten used to that life, but there was work to be done.

Early the next morning, I faced Valerie. They had sent a bus for us because the shoot was to be outside at various locations around L.A. This meant that I had to do Valerie's make-up on the bus, not where I did my best work, but I managed and the make-up came out fine. She was a down-to-earth person, real and warm, with a ready, accommodating smile and disposition that made it easy to like her and easy to do her make-up. I was sure her show would be a success, and it was.

The last shot was late that afternoon, and the sun, which McCabe needed for his outdoor shooting, was sinking fast. I had to repair Valerie's make-up that our lunch had smeared a bit, and I was hearing a demanding "Hurry up!" from McCabe. It was the end of a grueling day with a lot of shots and make-up on a bus that bounced every time anyone entered or left. Fatigue was rapidly setting in, and I was fading like the sun, unable to go at a faster pace.

"Hurry up!" I heard McCabe demand again.

Valerie and I rushed from the bus and over to a fountain, where she sat and McCabe clicked just as the light from the sun faded from view. When the photograph came out in the magazine, Valerie looked beautiful, calm, and serene, with the late afternoon sunlight bathing her in a rich golden glow. It was the most beautiful of all the photographs McCabe took that day and certainly belied the tension going on around us. Valerie was a trouper and deserved all of her success.

Soon after I arrived back in New York, I got a call from Cyma Rubin, the producer of *No, No, Nanette*. Coming from the success of that, she was planning a new show called *Dr. Jazz*, starring Bobby Van from *Nanette*, and she wanted me to do the make-up. It was a big and costly show with lots of set changes and glamorous costumes like *Nanette*, and it was being presented at one of New York's largest theatres, the Winter Garden. The book and lyrics were written by Buster Davis, who was also the show's musical director, as he had been with *Nanette*.

One afternoon later I stopped by the Winter Garden theatre for a rehearsal where I viewed the most convoluted, mishmash presentation I had ever seen. It appeared to take place in the 1920s, like *Nanette*, but the period seemed ambiguous and unable to make up its mind whether it was then or now. Then there was Bobby Van still doing his cutesy *Nanette* schtick, which worked for the syrupy *Nanette*, but had nothing to do with this show which was darker and edgier. It was obvious that the show was in trouble.

The problem was that the people involved were still doing *Nanette*, and this show needed an entirely new concept to pull it off. Buster Davis was simply wrong as the writer, and so they brought in others. That didn't work. Then they had the idea to bring in Lola Falana, the Josephine Baker–like Las Vegas dancer and headliner, which required new sets and costumes and pushed the costs sky high. Falana was supposedly Bobby Van's love interest, with not a drop of chemistry or believability between them, but it was all a bit vague. Their racial difference, too, was never dealt with, which, in the '20s, would surely have been an issue.

They seemed to want to keep the show light like *Nanette*, which it wasn't. It ended up that Van did his *Nanette* thing while Falana did her Las Vegas act. Nothing came together. The complexity of the relationship of the two main characters would certainly have made an edgier show, perhaps a better one, and might even have broken new musical theatre ground in the '70s.

While the show was in the middle of its total of 42 preview performances, Cyma and I were talking on the phone one day when I revealed that I was on my way to an apartment on top of the Plaza Hotel that belonged to a Victor Posner. When she heard the name, she immediately insisted on meeting him.

"You know Victor Posner?" was her reaction.

"No," I said, "I know his daughter, Gail. She's a client. I'm going there to cut her boyfriend's hair."

Some time before, Gail had contacted me from a credit of mine in a magazine, and I had been doing some make-up on her. To me, she was a spoiled, rather attractive rich girl who craved her father's affection but never got it because he was involved in his business deals and with his girlfriend.

The name was all it took for Cyma; she was practically on her way there. It turned out that Posner was a Miami real estate tycoon who was considered a piranha of hostile corporate takeovers that raked in extravagant executive salaries for him while risking his workers' pension funds. This was the reason for Cyma's sudden interest. Simply put: the guy was loaded.

Not one to pass up any opportunity, Cyma intended to convince Posner to invest in her rapidly deteriorating show, a far-fetched idea since he hadn't gotten where he was by bad investments and was probably the shrewdest man she would ever meet—no match for even Cyma.

Going up in a small elevator that Gail had to instruct me to find, I landed on the top floor of the Plaza, walked down several corridors and buzzed through several doors and offices until I arrived at a suite in the back where Gail met me at the door. Inside was a long hallway that funneled into a maze of rooms, with an enormous living room and a poolroom with a pool table and bar. Each room contained more than 50 phones on the tables, couches, and floor, with many of the phones constantly ringing and no one to answer them. Who was calling on all those phones was anyone's guess—

perhaps some disgruntled real estate person or current hostile takeover victim intent on telling Posner off, but he was nowhere around, and doubtlessly wouldn't have cared or wouldn't have answered, anyhow.

Gail, her boyfriend, and I began a small dinner that she'd had sent up from the Plaza kitchen when there was a knock at the front door down the long hallway. I had told Gail about Cyma, who I wasn't completely certain would show up. I was equally uncertain that she could get past all the doors and offices that she'd have to navigate through to get to the apartment. Gail had made it clear that she didn't want her there, and she certainly hadn't rung her in, but when I heard the screaming outside the door, I knew that Cyma had somehow managed to get past all the barricades. She was a determined woman, anyhow, and when she was intent on money, nothing was stopping her.

I tried to fight off Gail, who was pulling on me as I went down the hall to open the door. We stood at the locked door arguing about my opening it, while Cyma, hearing a fracas going on behind the door, continued banging.

"I know you're in there," she yelled, hearing our argument on the other side. "Open up!"

Finally, I managed to get away from Gail and unlocked the door. Cyma bolted through with her handsome young lawyer boyfriend behind her.

"What the hell's going on?" she demanded.

"We weren't sure it was you," was my lame, if not unbelievable, excuse (how could we have mistaken her with all the yelling?), and we went down the hallway into the living room with the ringing phones and Gail's boyfriend (who was also her lawyer) calmly finishing his dinner unperturbed.

Gail informed Cyma that her father wasn't there. She would wait, was her response, and I concluded that it would be all night if it took that. *Dr. Jazz* was in bad shape, and she had already spent well over a million dollars keeping it going. She wasn't losing that money if she had to camp out on a couch at the Plaza.

Gail went back to her dinner and didn't even offer her guests a drink. As far as she was concerned, Cyma was where she didn't want her to be, and there would be no hospitality from her. This was a girl who had told off several Hollywood movie moguls, and she was unimpressed with this big-time Broadway producer sitting in her father's living room.

Like an apparition, Posner suddenly materialized in the doorway with his girlfriend, a young woman a third of his age, in a red silk harem-girl outfit with balloon pants, a midriff top, and her belly button showing. Cyma immediately shot up, scarcely allowing time for introductions. Bored with business, the girlfriend retreated to their bedroom down the hall while Posner graciously remained to allow this unexpected guest to rant about her show.

With all of us sitting like a pow-wow in a circle of chairs around Posner, with Cyma directly across from him ploughing through her figures, the late afternoon sunlight shone through the window and hit Posner's snow-white hair. With his healthy-looking Miami-tanned face and glowing white hair, he looked like God next to me in a wingback chair.

Occasionally, he would glance at me as if wondering, "Who the hell is he and what does he want?"

I was just trying to figure out how one becomes God.

It was a good question, though, considering I had come here to do a simple haircut and Cyma's desperation had consumed us all.

At the end of her spiel, or at least all that Posner was enduring, he got up and said, "Send the information to my lawyers. I'll have them look it over," and he faded out as he had faded in: without fanfare. After all, God doesn't need trumpets—that's for mortals.

Unfulfilled, Cyma slumped out, and I did my haircut in Posner's gymnasium-sized kitchen, which I doubted was ever used. Afterwards, on my way out, I passed his bedroom where, sitting in their king-sized bed, his girlfriend watched TV and he flipped through the newspaper, perhaps scouting for future investments with Cyma assuredly not one of them.

"Good night," I said, though I doubted he yet knew who I was or why I was there. I thought I heard something audible from inside, and I left.

Cyma's show went down the tubes, and I had to fight, with my lawyer's help, for the money owed me. After over a year of monthly installments, it was finally all paid up. I was told by Cyma's stage manager that if I went the legal route, I would never work with her again. She had made some enemies on Broadway, and *Dr. Jazz* would be the last show she produced there. It was an example of biting off more than she could chew. Broadway is too expensive to be cocky.

Harry Rigby, Cyma's beginning co-producer with *No, No, Nanette*, from whom she wangled the show away, went on to produce many shows after *Good News*, with Alice Faye, failed to make it to Broadway. One of his best-remembered shows, which ran from 1979 to 1982, was *Sugar Babies* with Mickey Rooney and Ann Miller.

Apparently, the trick with unethical behavior is not to get caught doing it. Posner, too, would learn his lesson when, toward the end of his long life, he would be caught at tax evasion and do community service by feeding the homeless.

How hard the high and mighty fall when they dare to play God.

I was beginning to write. Sensing that I would one day have my fill of make-up, I had consulted an astrologer and a clairvoyant. Both told me that I should write, though I had no idea what to write. I had always been fascinated with films, so I began writing plots and dialogue that I would one day turn into full screenplays.

The clairvoyant also told me that I should write music, and having sung in church and everywhere when I was growing up, I began to write songs. I consulted with Michael about all this, and he was as fascinated as I was. He began studying music, which he had also done when he was young. We were becoming partners in that we planned to work on music and lyrics together. I would write the story and dialogue, and, with his ability to attract money, he would produce the show. It was crude at first, but we intended to hone in on it until we had projects to peddle. This gave us a goal and something to strive for besides our everyday existence. Our partnership would eventually go far deeper than we ever imagined.

I had mentioned some ideas to Cyma and had even been working on a plot line for *Dr. Jazz*, but to her, and everyone but Michael, I was a make-up artist and that was the extent they were willing to see me. Michael believed in me, far more than they did, and certainly far more than Mother ever had. I loved him for that belief. It made me feel that I could do it. I was sure that with Michael I could do anything, and he felt the same way about me. Supporting each other was the foundation of our friendship, which was budding faster than a rose.

Michael's apartment, in the same loft space where he also had his belt business, was becoming too confining and intruding on his personal life. He located an apartment quite similar to mine in an East Thirties brownstone, and his first gift to himself was a beautiful white baby grand piano. It was quite elegant and dressed up the place considerably. He began studying music seriously and writing songs, as I was. We were certain that if we pooled our resources, we could write a hit musical—deluded by our youth and inexperience that this would be easy. His belt business had taken off with more orders than he could barely handle, and my make-up career was in high gear.

We had every intention of going to the top and doing it together. We didn't see that the increasing spin of our lives was beginning to spin out of control.

Michael found a lover for a while, and when I visited them at Michael's new apartment, they were sitting in bed snorting coke. I wasn't concerned. Everyone I knew snorted coke, and I even had a line myself. I rarely used it, so it was a kind of treat for me.

Mary, on the other hand, used it regularly, as did most of our friends. It was considered a luxury, even a status symbol, and not habit forming—a falsehood we now understand. Michael had worked hard for what he had, with his belts regularly credited to him in fashion magazines and articles written about him, a situation that I, too, was enjoying. If a little coke helped him get through his busy day, what of it?

The problem was that his business was growing almost faster than he could keep up with it. Besides overseeing a staff of people that now worked for him at his loft, he dealt with the manufacturers that made his belts, chose the material for each belt, and also designed them. He was also his own salesman, contacting department stores and speciality shops all across the country and attending trade shows in Dallas, San Francisco, Atlanta, and Chicago. Coke was becoming the necessary steam to get all of this done. But it was a far greater habit than I ever imagined.

As my work was escalating, so was the rest of my life. Though I didn't use coke to get things done, I did use marijuana, which made my behavior erratic at times. I was also picking up several men a week for sex and that was becoming more of a focus than my make-up work. Lee had taught me well. I missed him and Valerie, and even visited them from time to time in Florida, but I no longer needed them, or Mary, to make the rounds of the city's hot spots. I knew them all and had no problem going there alone.

Many times Michael would accompany me or I would run into him in some bar, usually on the downtown West Side waterfront where gay bars lined the streets.

S & M bars were prevalent here, and baths were opening everywhere. The abandoned ramshackle warehouses that extended out into the Lower West Side Hudson River and the parked produce trucks had become the favorite haunts of gays who met to have sex after the bars closed.

Michael and I never went there because of the danger; we would either leave from a bar with someone or hook up together later for coffee somewhere. He had long since given up his lover, which I knew he would and was glad because it gave us more time to be together. Mary, too, had given up her last squeeze and was now into another one. As for me, I was getting plenty of sex, so it didn't matter. Since the war and during it, nothing was permanent, anyhow.

As a friend used to say, "Get a fresh one."

Or, as another one said, "Had 'em, hate 'em."

It was a quick turnover and on to the next. Everyone was having too much fun to pause for long. Life was going fast.

When I made up David Bowie at Scavullo's studio for some shots for *Rolling Stone* magazine, I had no idea who he was. Later, when his publicity people called me to make him up for some publicity shots and for the Grammy Awards being held at the Uris Theater in the West Fifties—later renamed the Gershwin Theatre—I had more knowledge of his considerable talent.

David was a charming man, undeniably handsome, with eyes that were a different color—quite unusual, like Edgar Winters' distinguished albino-pink eyes and white hair and skin. I pondered whether all rock stars had unusual characteristics and concluded, that in some ways, they all did.

While I was making up David at the Uris Theater, white powder kept appearing on his nose. I couldn't figure out whether it was from my powder sponge or from David. Since I wasn't using white powder, it had to be from David.

In the middle of the makeup, for no reason other than idle conversation, I casually asked, "Do you have a mother, David?"

Unless she was dead, I figured everyone's mother, like

Preparing David Bowie to go on camera (courtesy David Bowie).

my own, was around someplace. I was vaguely curious if she had been in any way instrumental or involved in his career, as mine was.

Without a word, he got up and disappeared into the bathroom until minutes before he was to go on stage. Either I had unwittingly hit a sensitive nerve or it was time for him to spend time—a lot of time—in a bathroom.

Later, while I was standing in the wings watching Moms Mabley, the octogenarian black comedian, performing on stage, I saw David darting about backstage like a caged bird trying to find a way out.

"Over there, David." I pointed to a doorway clearly marked "Exit."

As if the birdcage door had suddenly sprung open, he flew outside and disappeared into the night.

When I arrived home where Michael had been watching the program on my TV, he said that David appeared on stage stiff as a corpse, done up in a wide-brimmed black fedora and black suit, looking like Lurch, the zombie-like butler on the popular '60s TV show The Addams Family. That clinched it. The white powder was definitely from David.

I also did his make-up for his "Young Americans" tour, where he stepped onto the stage from a large, unfolding hand. When he was preparing to do his first film, The Man Who Fell to Earth, his publicity people again called me. At first, I agreed to a price, but after considering the early morning calls required for film and being in the desert several months where it was to be shot, I called them back and asked for a much higher fee, to which I knew they wouldn't agree.

They didn't, and, instead, that summer I did the make-up for a small independent film that was being shot on Long Island, Through the Looking Glass, a naughty adult version of Lewis Carroll's Alice in Wonderland. However, fearing the film might not sell in its more conservative form, the producer would have footage edited into the film that turned it into a porn film. Those of us who worked on the film, including the female lead, knew none of this when we signed our contracts. Soon her image and all of our names would be on the large screen connected with a porn film.

When they yelled for make-up on the set, it was to wipe an orgasm off a female actor's face. I refused, as did others for various other reasons, and our non-compliance nearly shut down the production. Our contracts forced us to finish the film, but stricter guidelines of what we would and would not do were hastily initiated.

When the film premiered, not realizing the extent or extreme nature of the added footage, the female lead invited some of her family to attend.

After the showing when the lights came on, not a smile was left on any of their faces. In the film, the chauffeur was screwing the maid, young Alice's father took his daughter to bed, the Mad Hatter was sticking a carrot up an Alice double's ass at the tea party, the Queen of Hearts was blowing the rabbit, and Tweedledee was buggering Tweedledum. They even had a camera travel anatomically through a woman's vagina—whatever was sexy about that. Europe would embrace the film as some art piece, but, thankfully, America barely got a glimpse of it. Some of us even considered having our names removed from the credits, but quickly the film passed into obscurity and let us off the hook.

I had one last run-in with the porn industry at another time when I was low on cash and needed money. A young straight man I knew, who was aware of my previous porn experience, called about a film he was working on for which the producers needed a make-up artist. When I arrived at an upscale Upper East Side apartment where they were shooting, I was ushered into one of the bedrooms where cameras were set up, as they were in all the bedrooms there, filming separate films.

In the bedroom, the director was instructing a man and a woman in a bed where to put this or stick that so the camera could get a better view of the activity. With so many instructions, the couple was getting confused and couldn't get on with what they were doing there.

In exasperation he finally yelled, "Don't you know the camera from your ass?"

"Yeah, I know it," the woman yelled back, "but ya got too many goddam things goin' on here at once."

It was so sterile I couldn't believe anyone would be interested. I was told that my job would be to make the girls look different for each film with wigs and make-up so they could be used over and over without having to get new girls for each film. They said that men get tired of the same old girl.

I went into the living room where three women were passing the time filing their nails and applying layers of make-up. One of them was standing by a window observing the street below.

"They better hurry and get me over with," she said. "My husband's gonna be here at six and he'll be mad as hell if I'm still up here working."

Her husband? And where were the children? This was too tawdry for me, and I told my friend to forget it. I'd already had one round with a bunch like this, and I didn't need money that bad.

Martha Mitchell, Senator John Mitchell's wife who blew the whistle on Nixon's Watergate shenanigans, died in 1975, as did Charles Revson, head of Revlon; and that year, I did the most complicated make-up I had ever done, for the cover of *Esquire* magazine, with photographer-art director Onofrio Paccione.

One side of a model's face I painted young and the other side I painted old, while holding my hand in front of one eye to cover the side I wasn't painting so it wouldn't interfere with the side I was painting. It was the most confusing make-up of my career, and the most challenging. By now I had a bit of a name in the industry and people assumed if you were a make-up artist you could do anything. I was untrained in the art of make-up, and certainly couldn't do the miraculous things they could do in Hollywood, but my risk-taking nature was always willing to pitch in and try. This time I lucked out.

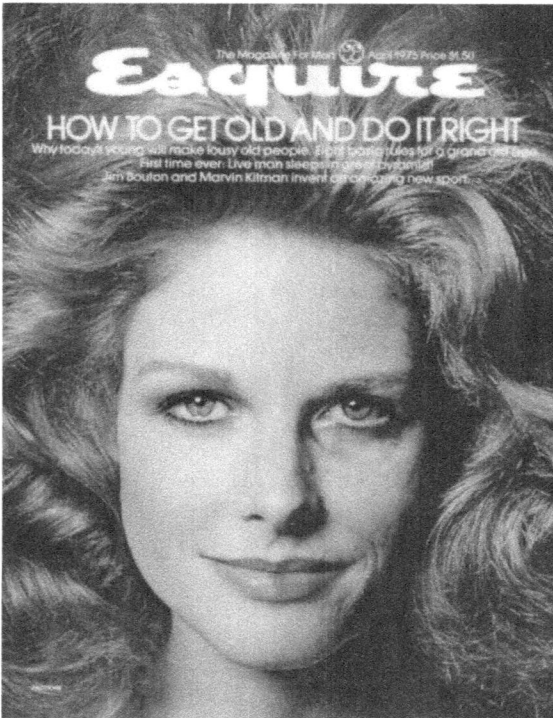

Painting one side of the model's face young and the other side old was a daunting task (courtesy photographer Onofrio Paccione and *Esquire*).

When the cover came out, one side of the girl's face looked as though it was in advanced deterioration while the other side remained youthful and intact. Perhaps it prophesied the deterioration in the make-up industry where privately-owned, "family" companies like Revlon, Elizabeth Arden and Helena Rubinstein would be gobbled up by corporate take-overs after their founders died, leaving Estée Lauder—led by the Lauder family—one of the only big "family-owned" companies remaining.

So it was that year that I began a professional relationship with Gloria Vanderbilt. The following year she would begin her fortunate climb to the top with blue jeans, assisted by an Indian corporation, Marjani, which licensed the use of her name. With Gloria as their spokesperson and a well-made product that flattered a woman's figure, the company reaped millions in sales from '76 to '85, when she bailed out and retrieved her name for (she told me) a million dollars, only to have lawyers fleece her out of most of it.

I began working with Gloria at Francesco Scavullo's studio. It was for a photograph of her for the cover of her new book, Woman to Woman. (Later, disappointed in the photographs Scavullo took, she would have the whole thing re-shot by another photographer.) She was charming enough in a studied way but not that warm—in fact, somewhat distant.

I knew nothing of Gloria other than there was some business about her when she was a little girl. I later found out that it involved her aunt, Gertrude Vanderbilt Whitney, founder of the Whitney Art Museum, suing for Gloria's custody from her mother, Big Gloria. Whitney insisted, as did Gloria's grandmother—and even inferred by Gloria herself in her own testimony—that Big Gloria was unfit as a mother because she was a fly-by-night party girl who had dalliances with both men and women—the stereotype of a reckless, carefree 1920s flapper.

When her aunt was awarded custody, she dismissed Gloria's beloved nanny, her one true confidante and ally who had been with her from the beginning of her life, leaving the little girl alone and lonely. This experience was etched into Gloria's persona and gave her the fierce drive she needed for her jeans venture.

Her first marriage in 1941 at 17 was to handsome Hollywood-playboy-turned-actors' agent Pat De Cicco, whom she had met at a party. They divorced in '44. The following year at 21, she married conductor Leopold Stokowski, who was then 65, and their union lasted 10 years, producing two sons, Stan and Chris.

When I asked her what her family thought about her marrying at 17, she said, "I don't think they much cared," revealing the lost, lonely child she had been.

From her beginnings, she seemed to enjoy living on the edge and was a self-declared risk-taker, somewhat like myself. I made her up for the opening of a clothing line she tried to start, which wasn't that successful. Two weeks before the opening, she had her eyes surgically altered and the bruises were still evident around them and hard to conceal.

"Why did you do this so close to your opening?" I asked her.

"I like to live dangerously," was her answer.

As she said, so she did. With the Vanderbilt name behind her and a natural artistic flare, she tried to market personal items, textiles, greeting cards through Hallmark, and a perfume, "Glorious," with her signature emblem, a swan. She took this from Hungarian playwright Ferenc Molnár's play *The Swan*, in which she appeared as an aspiring young actress at the Pocono Playhouse. (It was later made into a film in 1956 with Grace Kelly.) However, none of Gloria's ventures were as successful as her jeans.

Perhaps she saw herself as the swan—a beautiful fairytale princess hopelessly caught in her principality. Grace Kelly played it so well in real life, and Gloria might have, too, if she'd had the chance.

In '56, she married fiery film director Sidney Lumet as further proof of living on the edge, but that dissolved in divorce seven years later.

When I met her, she was married to Wyatt Cooper, a quiet, likable Southerner whom she had been with since her divorce from Lumet. He was a decent writer with a bit of substance, but not that successful. With Gloria's family resources drying up, she needed Marjani and the bucks they would provide, so she signed over her name and went to work.

Marjani had considered other name celebrities like Charlotte Ford, but their offer included appearing in TV ads. Perhaps preferring not to have the spotlight or the work, Ford turned it down. On the other hand, Gloria was used to the spotlight; in fact, she craved it after her dramatic childhood. Having entered and left many courtrooms with camera flashbulbs popping off all around her, she still entered a room as if expecting the same treatment. It had been a less exciting life without it, and with Marjani behind her, she could now expect to renew her fame, as well as her fortune. She immediately snapped up Marjani's offer that Ford had turned down.

After my first make-up on Gloria at Scavullo's studio, we were scheduled for more shots at her apartment overlooking the East River in the Fifties. To go there, Francesco asked that I not wear jeans, my preferred working outfit in case I got make-up on myself. To make his point, he even sprayed his studio with cologne when I walked in to infer that my jeans stank, which, of course, they didn't, but that was Francesco's own bit of drama. This pretension later amused both Gloria and me, considering that she became the jean queen of the decade and half of the next, and only showed more of Francesco's insecurity.

After the make-up at her riverside apartment, she immediately called me and said, "I just want to tell you that your make-up was the best ever."

She then went on to ask how much I charged for a party or whatever. After we became more comfortable with one another, with many more make-ups other than those for Marjani, she would pour me coffee from a silver coffee service when I arrived in the mornings and graciously ask, "Cream? How many sugars?" until she knew exactly without asking.

I could tell that she was happy with Cooper and their two boys, Carter and Anderson, who is now an anchor with CNN. She had once said that all she wanted to do was marry and have lots of children and make them happy, unlike her unhappy childhood. With her two sons with Stokowski and the two with Cooper, these were all the reasons for her happiness.

The riverside apartment was sunny and large, but not overly large, with perhaps three bedrooms, simple and modest looking, with unassuming, airy furniture and space around things. There was nothing pretentious about it or cluttered, unlike the place she lived following Cooper's death in 1978 when, as a newly single woman with her new fame, she moved to the same East Fifties apartment building where I used to go for Tallulah and brought in a lot of her family's furniture and treasures and grandiose, oversized family portraits that turned the place into a virtual Vanderbilt museum.

For 15 years, her life with Cooper and their two sons had been quaint and even simple, but now the drama returned with the heaviness of drapery and pretentious period furniture that made the rooms appear darker and overloaded and seemed to reflect the torment and confusion she must have felt inside. She had had the family life she had always craved, but now it was gone. Sure, she now had the money she and Cooper had wanted, but that was to have been for the two of them together. Now it seemed the money was all she had left.

In her dining room, where we went to do the make-up because of the good light, the massive family portraits hanging on the walls dwarfed the room. The one of her mother became our reference point.

"Make my skin white and porcelain like my mother's," she would say. "And make my eyes nice and slanty," referring to her frequently surgically altered eyes that were now permanently on a slant. As if there was another choice.

This was the mother she had scorned in court, rehearsed in what to say by her aunt and grandmother. Now, in a kind of apology, her mother's portrait hung, in reverence, in a prominent place in her home: where she ate.

She threw herself into the Marjani work, feverishly working to the point of exhaustion and enduring ridicule from comedians like Johnny Carson, who showed his TV audience a photo that appeared in *People* magazine of Gloria sitting amidst a large group of women bent over with their butts sticking up displaying her name on their jeans. Gloria sat facing the camera with her characteristic ear-to-ear smile that showed all of her teeth, seemingly oblivious to the absurd circumstances surrounding her.

In the first TV commercials, a spokeswoman would do the commentary while Gloria was seated in the background at a drawing table, supposedly sketching some new jeans. In reality, Gloria had nothing to do with their design and, at most, gave only a gratuitous nod of approval to Marjani regarding their appearance. Later, she was brought forward and participated more.

In one of the ads, an elegant Park Avenue apartment building substituted as Gloria's address before she moved to Tallulah's old building in the East Fifties. A grand limousine—rented for the day—pulled up in front of the building, and she got out and strolled into the lobby, allowing Marjani to preserve the rich Vanderbilt myth they hoped would rub off on their jeans. It worked: everyone wanted to live in rich Vanderbilt style, with Gloria's personal emblem, a swan, on their behinds.

Her jeans became status symbols and the discos rocked with them, as did the TV ads. Female models zoomed around on roller skates, with Gloria in their midst wearing her own jeans and looking as hip as any of them. Her life was on a roll, and she dared not stop to look back or it might vanish, as things had in the past. She would have seven more years of this after Cooper's death until she—and perhaps her family, too—couldn't take anymore.

After doing a make-up on her, I was waiting in the library of her East Fifties apartment to escort her to Marjani's when she went to get dressed and left a video on for me of our latest jean commercial.

In it, Gloria said, "Regardez le derrière," and then whipped herself around and displayed the most splendid backside—for a woman her age, or even for anyone.

I was amazed, and when she returned I commented on her splendid physique. She smiled and walked out of the room wearing her signature jeans, showing a backside that in no way resembled the one on the video. I couldn't figure out how she had done this.

At the studio where we were filming that day, a girl was sitting there knitting while she waited for her part of the filming.

"What do you do?" I inquired.

"I'm Gloria's ass."

"I beg your pardon?"

"You know that part when she says, 'Regardez le derrière,' and whips her butt around? Well, that's my butt."

Gloria didn't exactly lie to me, but she certainly left me with a false impression. It was my stupidity not to presume a body double. I just thought she was doing her own work.

In her book *Woman to Woman*, published in 1979, for which I did the make-up for her cover photo (working with another photographer after she rejected Scavullo's photos), Gloria wrote: "For special occasions, such as a photography sitting for a magazine, I always try to book the great make-up artist John Richardson [the name to which *Vogue* credited my work], who is so much in demand that he has to be booked far in advance. John is extraordinarily sensitive to not only the outer personality of his subject, but also to the inner beauty of the person. He never swamps a woman with a too-stylized make-up unless, of course, she asks for one. Instead, he will make you look your best self—accentuating rather than submerging the real you."

Gloria perfectly described what I always tried to accomplish with my make-up, with one exception: I would never have swamped a woman with a too-stylized make-up, whether she asked for it or not. To make one look their best was always my goal. It was against my nature to camouflage anyone. If they were wearing my make-up, they were looking like themselves in it.

The cover of the book demonstrated my philosophy perfectly. On it, Gloria looked soft, penetrable, womanly, and motherly, as I saw her then—not at all the exaggerated, hard-edged, perhaps even unpleasant woman she later displayed in her TV ads when I no longer worked with her. Maybe the times called for that exaggeration and hardness, but I feel that it separated her from the very public she wanted to reach. None of the vulnerability and femininity that had first attracted me to her was displayed. Perhaps it protected her at a time when she needed it, but I think it hastened the ending of her professional life with Marjani.

On one of my last TV shoots with her, the Long Island estate of one of the founders of Merrill Lynch was substituted as Gloria's estate. In the commercial's background, while a commentary was going on, her sons, Carter and Anderson, frolicked across the grounds with their dog—or, rather, a dog hired for the day.

A mix-up occurred about my ride out there, and Gloria's limousine was radioed to come by my apartment to pick me up. During our trip, Carter kept up a steady stream of political conversation, in which he had a great interest, but his youthful exuberance was, in truth, exhausting. I could see that it distracted Gloria, who had a job ahead—and an all-day one at that—to say nothing of an hour or more of make-up beforehand. She needed some down time to prepare for it, but wasn't getting any. I, too, wanted the same, but Carter was relentless with his chattiness, and my answering him didn't help matters, either. Anderson was young and bored and said little, unlike his TV persona today.

When we arrived, we were all frazzled out. There was no place with proper light to do make-up, so the electricians set up lights for us in the living room in front of couches on which women from the advertising agency promptly stationed themselves to get a good view of what I was going to do to Gloria. Steely she sat, poised on a high stool in front of them, as if giving a performance.

Her attitude was, "If you want to look, look. I'm getting paid a lot for this, and you're not."

When I was through, considering what I had started with, with Gloria worn out from the ride and from her life and then being gaped at for an hour by a bunch of nosey women, they almost applauded.

One wag even came over to me and callously crowed, "Poor thing. I felt sorry for her. She looked so old. And what you did with her."

I reminded her that she hadn't worked as hard as Gloria after her husband's death, so she had better be glad she didn't look as tired as Gloria. The woman sheepishly walked away.

When the day was over, the crew was loading up the trucks with their equipment. It would take a couple of hours before they were ready to depart, and the hairdresser and I were supposed to go back with them. I had been working as hard as Gloria and the boys, who were now in their limousine waiting to pull out. I went over to the car window where Gloria was in the back seat next to the boys with her feet propped up in the jump seat and asked if I could ride back with them.

"You'll have to sit in the jump seat," she responded. And then added: "But no talking."

Who wanted to talk? I was so exhausted I was afraid I'd go to sleep and fall out of the jump seat. The hairdresser saw me get inside, and he, too, not wishing to wait around for the trucks, came over to the car and asked if he could ride with us.

"We're filled up," Gloria growled, keeping her feet firmly on the jump seat, and motioned for the driver to pull out.

I felt sorry for the hairdresser and a little ashamed that I hadn't ridden back with everyone else. I was sitting here, and the hairdresser, who had worked as hard as the rest of us, was stuck back there. Gloria didn't seem to register anything. We had helped her look her best all day, and she couldn't even let the hairdresser ride in the front seat with the driver.

She and I were eventually at odds about many things. Getting up at five in the morning to be at her house by seven in order for her to get somewhere by nine, and then not being paid was one of them. My agency tried repeatedly to collect on unpaid bills until I told them to stop trying. Many times in my career, rich women—and especially those who were famous— simply didn't pay some of their bills. They thought they were doing you a favor by your being able to claim them as one of your clients.

That didn't cut any ice with me. I felt that everyone was equal and treated everyone with that respect in mind. I expected the same returned to me. Marjani's bills were paid, of course, but they went to the company. Personal bills for parties and appearances, for no apparent reason, were ignored—about three thousand dollars' worth. It was an eccentricity that many of the famous thrived on and a luxury that I was expected to offer, but it grated on me. I was just supposed to accept this.

She recommended me for a make-up job to a famous skin care woman, someone like Georgette Klinger, but she didn't consult me beforehand. Doing make-up on Gloria was one thing, but on someone I didn't know and to whom I hadn't given my consent was an entirely different matter. It hadn't occurred to her that I should be consulted before she offered my services—I was just supposed to do it. I didn't like anyone selling me without my having a say in it.

When the woman contacted me, I quoted her a hefty fee, but after considering that I had wanted to join friends in the country that weekend, I called her back and doubled it to make it worth my while to stay in town. She refused, which was what I had wanted in order to be with my friends, but Gloria was furious. She felt that it reflected on her, but then she wasn't doing the job and she hadn't wanted to go to the country. Things might have turned out differently had she consulted me.

My experience with many rich women was that they tended to believe the world revolved around them because they could pay for it. I was sick of this treatment. With marijuana making my behavior erratic, anyhow, and disturbed about her unpaid bills, we parted company. In fact, I courted it. I didn't want to work with someone who would treat artists, or anyone, like they were hired help who didn't matter, as she had the hairdresser when she refused him a ride back in her limousine. If there's no respect for others, there's no joy in the work.

In many ways, Gloria was like another businesswoman years later, Martha Stewart, who reached the top and reportedly treated many badly who helped her along the way. In Truman Capote's unfinished novel, *Answered Prayers*, there are passages about Gloria that are less than flattering. She told me that Wyatt had seen Capote on the street drunk, disheveled, pilled out, and babbling incoherently. He was a sore subject around that house and slandering him was a pleasure.

In 1988, Gloria's son Carter jumped from her 14th-floor East Eighties apartment terrace, while she pleaded with him not to. I went to the Frank E. Campbell Funeral Chapel on Madison Avenue to pay my respects. It was the same chapel where, in the late '60s, Judy Garland's funeral had caused such a crunch of onlookers. Inside, Gloria was standing at the head of a long receiving line greeting those who had come. This was what she was trained to do, and she did it well, but the pain and the sedation it took to do it were obvious.

"It's John, Gloria," I said to the faraway face that gazed at me with seemingly no recognition.

"John," she repeated, as though remembering or trying to put it into focus, but she appeared uncertain.

As a reflex—and from the pain I was feeling in my own life at the time— I reached out to give her a hug, and she quickly backed away, barely able to stand up much less withstand a hug without collapsing. I realized my error as she quickly resumed her frozen smile for the others in line behind me, while any memory she might have had of me faded from her mind like running paint.

I doubt that she has thought of me in these many years since, but I've often thought of her, especially after she lost what she had gained from all her work to unscrupulous lawyers. Wyatt Cooper's death had been a serious blow to all of them, and perhaps most to Carter, who idolized his father and showed so much promise with his political tirade in the limousine. Perhaps the giddy years of jeans and Marjani took their toll on everyone.

Gloria did what she had to do to provide and survive at a time when it was the hardest—right after her husband's death. For that, she deserves a great deal of credit. But I've often wondered, in hindsight, if it was worth it.

I must acknowledge Gloria's kindnesses, as well. When she had her first clothing show, she put my chosen name, Evan, on my seat, becoming the first to honor it. When Cooper's book, *Families*, came out in 1975, she gave me a copy, which she inscribed to me with both Carter and Anderson signing it. In it, Cooper speaks to Carter about life and death, growing old, and growing old with his sons. It was a sad fact that he would never do this, nor would Carter. When Gloria's book *Woman to Woman* came out, she made sure that I got an inscribed copy of that, too. These are the endearing, thoughtful things that will endure far past the rest.

But with Gloria being a Pisces—one fish swimming upstream and another swimming downstream at the same time, and me being a Gemini, twins, there were too many people in a room at the same time, all of us wanting our own way. The peaceful quiet of no more obligations finally brought blessed relief.

11

Barbara Walters, Supermodels, the Bee Gees and Studio 54

In 1976, Jimmy Carter became President, bringing with him Walter Mondale as his Vice President; David Bowie's people contacted me about *The Man Who Fell to Earth*, which I wangled out of; I traveled around Manhattan with dynamic Bella Abzug doing her make-up for her Senatorial race, which she lost; and I did Barbara Walters' make-up for Scavullo's book, *Scavullo on Beauty*, which should've been titled: *Beauty Artists on Beauty*, since I and the other beauty artists created the beauty that the book was about—and we did it all for free. If we hadn't we wouldn't have worked with Francesco again. With this kind of blackmail, the photographers got rich while the artists struggled.

I couldn't begin to calculate how many free make-ups I did in my career. With magazines paying so little, our only hope of survival was advertising jobs that were always promised if we did a freebee, but they were few and far between. The perks for our effort, however, were hanging with celebrities, the socially elite, and receiving inscribed books and thank you notes that didn't pay the rent.

Soon after Walters' make-up at Scavullo's studio, someone from her staff called me about doing her make-up for TV. I didn't want to be stuck with any one client any more than I had wanted this arrangement with Lucille Ball years before, so I discouraged it, and they went elsewhere. Many celebrities that I made up tried to engage me exclusively, which I'm sure they did with other make-up artists, but I felt this would limit my growth as an artist and in meeting others. They, of course, would say that I could do other things when I wasn't needed by them, but my experience was that their demands were constant and all consuming. Besides, no one was so interesting that I should limit myself that way.

Margaux Hemingway, one of the great supermodels created by *Vogue* (and one of Ernest Hemingway's granddaughters, which didn't hurt), made a film that year titled *Lipstick*. Scavullo and Way Bandy flew out to Hollywood to appear in the movie as shadows darting about Margaux, who was cast as a famous model pursued by an enamoured psychotic fan. The film was not well received and did little for Margaux in films, but it started her sister, Mariel, whom Margaux had suggested for the part of her character's sister in the film, on quite a substantial career.

I was doing Margaux's make-up for Fabergé ads, for which she was paid a cool million, when she returned from a private showing of the film.

She floated into the dressing room where I was waiting to apply

Though I was asked, I wasn't up for doing Barbara Walters' make-up full-time (courtesy Francesco Scavullo Foundation, from *Scavullo on Beauty*, Random House, 1976).

her make-up, sat down, and said, "I couldn't believe it. I was wonderful. I was really great," as if the strong assessment would make it so.

I knew nothing of the film, but it seemed prudent for an actress, and an untrained and inexperienced one at that, to wait until someone in the know appraised her work before making such a strong assessment. Most actresses I knew didn't even want to see themselves on screen, much less appraise their work so highly. It felt amateurish to me. My suspicions were confirmed when I saw the film. Borrowing what Dorothy Parker had once said about Katharine Hepburn—that the gamut of her emotions in a play she was in had gone from A to B—Margaux didn't even get the A part right.

I was again booked with her for more Fabergé perfume ads, for which the entire crew had to spend a weekend at a Long Island motel. Outdoor shots were to be taken at different locales, with Margaux in an inner tube

on a river—for which I had to wade out to do make-up retouches—and with her leading a donkey down the beach.

Margaux—whose name was derived from a brand of champagne, a shaky beginning at best—was difficult. She had overpowering, heavy dark eyebrows that I had to pluck nearly out of her head to make room for the make-up around her eyes, and she couldn't sit for the long periods of time that were necessary for the make-up to be applied with accuracy. She kept jumping up and roaming about, jabbering all the time, which broke all of our concentration.

She had married an heir to a hamburger chain, and when the crew on the Long Island shoot broke for lunch, she and her new husband spent their time in the motel screwing off the make-up that I had applied that morning. This required that I reapply it after lunch, for which I got hell because the outdoor light that the photographer needed for his work was fading, and we were still inside the trailer reapplying Margaux's make-up. It became a dreadful experience for all of us.

Even Scavullo said, "They're going to have trouble with her," and he was right.

She and her husband eventually went to Europe, where they lived quite comfortably on the generosity of friends. They finally divorced, and she returned to New York and tried to rekindle her modeling career, but drink, dissipation, and unprofessional behavior had done her in, and it would never happen. In July of '96, after many tries at getting off the hooch, she, like her famous grandfather, ended her life in suicide. It brought to mind that fame, and some fortune, do not necessarily solve our problems, nor do they bring us happiness. That's an inside job, and many of us can't survive our demons.

When I made her up at the Scavullo studio for her hopeful return to modeling, which I did free, she said, "I love alcohol," and therein lay her problems.

I had never heard anyone say they loved anything like that, but when I considered it, most of my friends, including myself in some cases, felt passionately about destructive things. We were all zooming down a very destructive road of which we were hardly aware.

To accomplish the heavy schedule that his belts now demanded, which took him around the country several times a year, Michael had been depending more and more on cocaine. He told me of a clothing convention in Dallas where everyone, like himself, was using coke to get things done. The problem was that he refused to delegate any of the designing or manufacturing of his belts to anyone but himself. I suspected that coke wasn't a good thing to regularly depend on, but the accepted theory was that it wasn't bad for you or habit-forming—a theory intended to justify doing it—so I paid little attention.

I, like many others, thought of coke as just a step up the drug ladder from marijuana, of which I certainly did enough. But coke, besides being expensive, made me jittery, so I rarely did it. Everyone I knew who was on it, including Michael, became Chatty Kathy. They never shut up, and I hated being around it.

One Christmas, concerned that Michael had been losing a lot of weight, I stayed in town to be with him instead of going home to Mother. When we met for dinner, he talked incessantly about his belt business, the new belts he was designing for the coming season, and a party he'd just come from where, I was sure, he and everyone there had been snorting coke.

Finally, after enduring his rapid-firing motor mouth for nearly an hour, I stopped him with, "Michael, I'm here! It's Christmas. I stayed here for you. I have a present for you."

Then, and only then, did reality return, and we began to relate and exchange like the friends we were.

At an all-night gathering with mostly black jazz musicians and the wife of one with whom I was an old friend, I had gone beforehand with Michael to his pusher on the Upper West Side to get some coke that he now wanted to share.

As the musicians began to jam, he pulled out a small vial of coke and asked a girl next to me if she, and the others sitting around our table, wanted some.

"You call that coke, honey?" she responded, and pulled out a bag as big as two fists. "This is coke."

When the session broke up at nine the next morning, long after my friend and her husband had departed, what was left of that big bag of coke was now about the size of a quarter. Everyone there had gone down on it until that was all that was left. I went home and didn't sleep well for three nights. After that, I rarely touched it, and if I did, it was no more than one toot and that was it. It was too nerve-wracking for me. But Michael continued.

Mary's new boyfriend was an alcoholic, and she was rapidly becoming one herself. Valerie had taken up with another alcoholic in Florida, a young man in his early twenties and nearly 40 years younger than she was. He rarely reported home for the dinners she cooked for them, and she usually ate alone. Lee went nightly to the gay bars in Coconut Grove, Florida, and sometimes missed his work with his decorator boss, Howard—sometimes not showing up for days while he crashed from whatever he had consumed. This prompted Howard to call me from Florida and ask where Lee was. I didn't know where Lee was all the way up in New York; I scarcely knew where I was.

The town of New York, too, was rapidly getting out of hand. Mayor Beame had never been able to manage the budget, and a lot of necessary things that a town needs, like cops and law and order, were missing from the mix. New York had become a dangerous place, and everyone was celebrating a kind of Sodom and Gomorrah it produced. In Central Park, drugs of any sort were easily available just by asking nearly anyone there. Whisper the name of anything you wanted, and in minutes you were surrounded by sellers.

One evening, I went with a straight male friend to a girl's apartment in the East Village where we all took mescaline, ran a tub of water in her bathtub, climbed naked into it, and sat there for hours rolling endless joints and talking. When we ran out of grass in the early morning, I climbed out of the tub, got dressed, and went downstairs where, across the street from the girl's apartment, I saw a black man standing in front of a closed shop. I went over and asked him if he had grass; he handed me a gin bottle he'd been swigging from, and while I took a few swigs from his bottle, he disappeared for a few minutes and returned with the grass. I gave him the five bucks he'd asked for the grass, returned his bottle after exchanging a couple more swigs, and returned back upstairs where I rejoined my comrades still in the tub, rolled a joint from the new grass, and kept on talking until we nearly shrivelled up like prunes.

That's how easy things were to obtain. And there was no one, like cops, to bother us.

Years before when Barbara and I were in L.A., we stopped in Beverly Hills to ask directions of another car, and immediately, out of nowhere, we were surrounded by cops. That's how strict things were out there. A friend told me he was walking barefoot through Beverly Hills and got thrown in jail.

Things of this nature didn't happen in New York, where the cops had joined the party. After the Stonewall bar riot, gays were no longer harassed by cops in gay bars. It simply wasn't politically correct.

As the world let its guard down, in April of '77 the greatest Sodom and Gomorrah of them all, Studio 54, opened in New York catering to every taste, mood, and indiscretion one could think of. The disco had once been a CBS TV studio and still retained audience seats in the back where drugs were consumed nightly by the truckload and carnal activity was conducted throughout any evening unencumbered. With Ian Schrager and Steve Rubell as co-owners (and who knows what underworld ties the place might have had), it became the most successful and world-renowned disco ever. But the real truth of its success might lie in the unique party mixing concocted by Rubell.

A small dark-haired man with big round eyes like a pug dog, Rubell kept a close rein over his domain like the pug watchdog that he was. With the help of big muscular bouncers out front, he knew whom to let in and whom to keep out to cook the joint to boiling and beyond. It was a kind of prestigious thing to be chosen, like the old Arthur disco, but this was far more select than that ever was. However, depending on which night you attended, and Rubell's mood, almost anyone with enough tenacity and time to wait could eventually be allowed in.

A long lobby—left over from the studio theatre it was—prevailed the inside the entrance, where, at the end, doors opened into a darkened atmosphere of small circular bars attended by handsome, bare-chested male bartenders surrounded by ear-piercing music. On the dance floor, bathed in blinding, flickering lights that confused one's vision, writhing bodies pulsated to the insidious, throbbing base rhythm.

Welcome to Sodom and Gomorrah. Don't look back or you'll turn to a pillar of salt—or, in this case, a mound of cocaine. It was rampant there. Stars could be seen going downstairs to the VIP lounge, where all manner of drugs were readily made available. Only the elite, the truly important ones, were allowed there, however—meaning those who contributed to the success of the disco by their presence, or who had the most parties there and spent the most money.

Scavullo had parties there when his books came out, and all of us who worked for him attended them. Others that I was associated with also had parties there that I attended. My face was known around there, and though I don't believe I was ever personally responsible for getting in (I credit the crowd of rascals I traveled with), I never had any trouble gaining admission. A big muscular bouncer out front would point, with occasional help from Rubell himself, and in you'd scoot leaving the mob at the entrance, as at

Arthur, whining outside. People who looked like they were from Kansas were let in, men in business suits were allowed in, obvious prostitutes went in, secretaries, blue-collar workers, cute boys—plenty of cute boys—the socially elite, the rich, the famous, the nobodies, all formed the unique mix that made Rubell's parties a sensation. The man knew how to throw 'em and throw 'em big!

Inside, people in costumes would be dancing next to the "suits," secretaries danced with the druggies, someone dressed as a nun would be paired with the devil, small people, extraordinarily tall people, fat, thin, every creed and color, from the lowest of society to the highest, all were at the party having a ball. At any given moment, the lights would flash and balloons would pour from the ceiling, or snow or confetti, or a bunch of lights would descend. One never knew what would descend or suddenly appear. Liza Minnelli might sing a song, or some other celebrity would make an appearance in the DJ's booth. The young, the old, the well-heeled, and the pauper all danced to the same incessant, compelling beat. It was a mad, mad, mad, mad night at "54."

Once I saw a young woman on the dance floor with an enormous plume, like a giant peacock feather, extending out of her costume, which was open in the back exposing a bare butt. The giant feather, which trailed way up in the air, was anchored by some attachment around her waist and made her butt virtually wag. When I traced its origin, it went right up her ass. What that must have felt like stuck up her ass and wagging high in the air is anyone's guess, but it didn't seem to bother her and may have even improved her dancing.

From the same party that evening, I took home a young man in a sultan costume: turban, balloon pants, bare midriff top, and sandals in the middle of winter. He left my apartment at nine the next morning dressed the same way. What did my neighbors think? Oh, well—just another scandal to add to the ones I was already creating.

Soon after Studio 54's opening, Scavullo had a party there to celebrate his first book, *Scavullo on Beauty* and I took Michael. Many of the people in the book were there, including Way Bandy who, like me, had done many of the make-ups. That evening, while Michael sat next to me on a banquette, a handsome man on the other side tried to pick me up, but he was so forceful and forward that I was turned off. It turned out to be Way Bandy. Though we were quite acquainted with each other's work, we had never met. The following day I knew he was booked at Scavullo's Studio and I called him to say how much I had enjoyed meeting him, a gross exaggeration because I could barely hide the discomfort I had felt. We had a laugh, but I believe we were both relieved that we hadn't consummated his attention.

Schrager and Rubell were convicted of tax evasion and sentenced to jail for three and a half years in 1980, only to get out in 13 months to reopen 54 the following year. Either they had a little help from friends or everyone wanted to return to the party. 54 permanently closed its disco doors in 1980, and Rubell would die of AIDS a year later, ending nearly a decade of the most sensational parties New York had ever seen.

In 1977 all the lights in town blew out again for the second time since the great Northeastern blackout in '65. During the first blackout, the city behaved responsibly, but the blackout of '77 brought widespread looting and arson, particularly in poorer sections of town that could ill afford the damage. Lack of adequate police protection prompted storeowners to stand in front of their stores with baseball bats to protect them. When all of the mayhem was over, the estimated damage was a billion dollars.

To add to the hardship, the city was already suffering from lack of services, with industries moving south to more affordable and safer areas. When Ed Koch took over the mayor's office from Abe Beame the following year, he inherited not only the city's financial problems, but the danger as well.

Bars, baths, after-hours places, and clubs capitalized on the excitement the danger produced. It was cool to be risky and slum in some sloppy, decadent place where you had no idea where you were. It was even cooler to be fucked there.

Everyone was looking for a hard cock to either match the one they had, use it, or just observe it. It was chic to be bisexual. Rock stars like David Bowie and Mick Jagger hinted at ambiguity. A heterosexual male friend of mine—intending to broaden himself—would meet with me, get terribly wasted, ask to see it, put it in his mouth, and squeal like a stuck pig because what he was doing blew his mind. It was only mildly amusing to me, if not boring, because this was how I did things. For him, it was a mind-altering experience.

More and more places were opening that catered to sex, drugs, and taking risks. Plato's Retreat, a heterosexual version of what was going on in homosexual places, was a sexual paradise for wife swapping—sometimes screwing on the tables or banquets in full view of everyone. For the more discreet, orgy rooms were provided where partners could romp en masse in a free-for-all sexual scramble.

Besides the familiar Continental Baths where Bette Midler began her career, other bathhouses had opened. One of the more infamous ones was the St. Mark's Baths on St. Mark's Place on the Lower East Side, sometimes referred to as the Ever-hard Baths. Inside was the usual male sexual frenzy going on in rumpus rooms and jacuzzis where, with the aid of poppers and every drug imaginable, things were continually hard and inhibitions were checked at the door.

Saturday Night Fever was a big movie in 1977, and for the cover of *Rolling Stone* magazine, I did make-up on the Bee Gees—who created the music for the film—and found each of them quite different from the other two. *Star Wars* was another blockbuster film that year, and I made up Carrie Fisher, who played Princess Leia Organa in the film. Fisher was most intelligent and hilarious, joking that Princess Leia's scant costume was kiddie-porn.

Cheryl Ladd replaced Farrah Fawcett in the successful TV series *Charlie's Angels*, and I made up the uncertain Cheryl, in a difficult situation replacing the beautiful Farrah. Her fears would vanish when the public readily accepted her as one of the motley three.

Also that year, Way Bandy came out with his make-up book, *Designing Your Face*, and it was clear he was outdistancing me in the make-up racket. Everyone wanted Way's book— not that it explained how to do your face with complicated formulas only he understood— but it was large, it had beautiful photos inside that were a joy to look at, it had stars, and it fit perfectly on a coffee table. Women were buying it. His name had become synonymous

Each of The Bee Gees was quite different (photograph by Francesco Scavullo from *Rolling Stone* issue dated July 4, 1977 © Rolling Stone LLC 1977 all rights reserved. Reprinted by permission).

with make-up, while mine was merely known in the industry. It even became prestigious to have Way's book.

Soon Scavullo would have a *Vogue* contract, and for the covers he would use only Way. My skirmishes with Avedon and *Vogue* had left a bad taste in everyone's mouth, and they were now reluctant to use me. Times Books would offer me a make-up book two years later, but I didn't know that then. All I knew was that Way was outdistancing me, and it was uncomfortable. He deserved the recognition because he was an exceptionally gifted artist, but I had been there long before Way, and now I was taking second place.

Carrie Fisher called her scant Princess Leia costume "kiddie-porn" (courtesy Francesco Scavullo Foundation, as seen in U.S. *Harper's Bazaar*).

Disenchanted, it was at this point that I consulted the clairvoyant who told me I should be write. I thought that I could hardly write my name much less anything else, but when I considered that I had always wanted to work in films, I began my first screenplay and found that I could do it. Having written a cameo part in the screenplay for Otto Preminger—permanently etched in my mind from our many encounters and particularly our morning walks together years before—Michael contacted him about the script. Regardless that he rejected it on the grounds it was a minor part, he did like the script, which was encouraging.

Then music began coming to me for a musical I would write that Michael helped me financially to record with an excellent musician. The problem was that he and the musician got so wasted on the coke they both consumed (I couldn't have had any even if I had wanted to because I had to sing) that it took hours to record one song and was an exhausting experience.

With Michael's own music studies, we also began to seriously consider collaborating on a musical together. All of this gave me hope and made me realize that I had never really cared about make-up anyhow. I intended to drop it some day—so why not mentally do it now? Let Way have his book that he wanted and deserved. With work and persistence, I could eventually have far more of what I had always wanted. This was the beginning of a move away from make-up that would revitalize my life.

12

Gilda Radner, Muhammad Ali and Washington, D.C.

In 1978, for a *Cue* magazine cover, I did make-up on Jill Clayburgh, who would marry playwright David Rabe and who appeared that year in the critically acclaimed film *An Unmarried Woman*. I marveled at Clayburgh's sensational body with the tightest, flattest stomach I had ever seen. It rivaled a trampoline. I also did make-up on a troupe of dancers in a Broadway musical called *Dancin'* that would have a respectable seven-year run, and a couple of make-ups on Gilda Radner, the brilliant Saturday Night Live comedienne.

On the second Gilda shoot, for which I literally covered her from head to toe with make-up, she asked for a bottle of vodka that she had stashed in the photographer's refrigerator. The hairdresser, an insensitive, arrogant twit if there ever was one, said that he did not "fetch" anything for anyone. I got Gilda her vodka. He reminded me that this was why I would never be as famous as Way Bandy. I decided if it took that attitude, I was glad. Way would never have behaved that ridiculously anyhow. He was a far bigger person than that.

I began going to Florida with a Canadian film company to shoot Avon TV commercials, which lasted several days and required the crew to be holed up in the Coconut Grove Hotel. Around the hotel's pool, the phones rang constantly for the pushers lounging there sipping their Mai-Tais. After the shoot, I would head to Lee's apartment in Coconut Grove to spend a few days dancing at all of his gay haunts. Then I'd swing over to Valerie's apartment on Miami Beach, where we'd terrorize all of her heterosexual haunts on the beach. It was a relief for her from her drunken, younger lover, who was never there when I was, which was fine by me. He preferred to board for that time with a buddy and return when I left to continue his irresponsible behavior. From my experience with drunks, I was sure this would not end well for Valerie.

It began with a boob job that she, 40 years older than he, got in her mind that she needed to keep him and entice him. I doubted that in his booze-induced state he would even register it or care—he was always too stoned to sexually perform anyhow.

In the mid '80s, Valerie would call me from Boston to report that she had just been diagnosed with lung cancer—she was a heavy smoker—and nothing could be done because her boob job would have to be removed first, and that would spread the cancer throughout her body. She would retire to Martha's Vineyard, where her two daughters lived, to starve herself to death—no second opinion or anything. Her failed relationship with the young man had left her emotionally scarred, and her age had convinced her that she had no more to live for—a vain notion from a life lived strictly for herself. Sadly, her two daughters might have benefited from her putting up a fight about her situation, instead of yielding. It might have given them time to come to terms with their life with her and her five husbands that they had had to endure. True to fashion, selfishly she left them with more emotional baggage to contend with.

In '79, for Scavullo I did the make-up on beautiful blonde model Patti Hansen, future wife of Rolling Stones guitarist Keith Richards, for one of my favorite *Cosmopolitan* magazine covers. I also flew to Washington, D.C., with society columnist Aileen Mehle, who then wrote her breezy, gabby "Suzy Knickerbocker" column for the *New York Post*. The reason for the trip was to do her make-up for a TV interview with the great Muhammad Ali (she had previously completed an interview with Frank Sinatra).

An agency that was now handling me had booked a British hairdresser, Allen Purver, whom I had first worked with in the early '70s for *Harper's Bazaar*. He was down on his luck but still a decent hairdresser. I had suggested him to my agency, and they accepted him. Assuming the introduction meant that we worked well together, they began booking us this way.

In truth, Allen had the best grass in town and lived close to me, where I could avail myself of it occasionally. For that only, we became friends. Riding on my coattails, he was now getting a lot of work, but I wanted to shake him loose. I had discovered too late that he was also a serious coke freak. Not wanting to cause him financial hardship, I had not yet said anything, but as the situation worsened, it was beginning to be at my expense.

My agency, of course, knew nothing of any of this and continued booking us together. I still considered Allen a good hairdresser, but he was stoned all the time—like many artists I worked with then—and this caused his work to be erratic.

One well-known hairdresser was so stoned on a shoot with model Christie Brinkley for *People* magazine that he kept spitting on her hair to control it. She endured it because either she didn't realize the extent of it, or she was afraid to rattle him. Now here I was again with Allen Purver stoned out of his gourd with Aileen Mehle, and it would be a bumpy ride for all of us.

To start it off, Allen had given me a puff before he and

Beautiful Patti Hansen was one of the most amiable models of them all (courtesy Francesco Scavullo Foundation and Hearst magazines).

I and Aileen had gotten into the limo that was to take us to the airport.

Sitting in the back with Aileen—a game girl, and beautiful too, with plenty of pizazz of her own—I got so wrapped up talking about the benefit of some exercises I was doing that I spouted out, "If I wasn't sitting in this limo, I'd take off my clothes and show you."

She laughed, but I wouldn't have put it past me at that point.

We stayed in a hotel in Georgetown, and the following morning—the day of the Ali interview—when Allen and I went to Aileen's room to do our work, he and she got into such a skirmish over her hair that I had to separate them.

"Now you be quiet," I said to Aileen, "and you do your thing," I said to Allen. "And when he's finished, we'll see what we've got and take it from there."

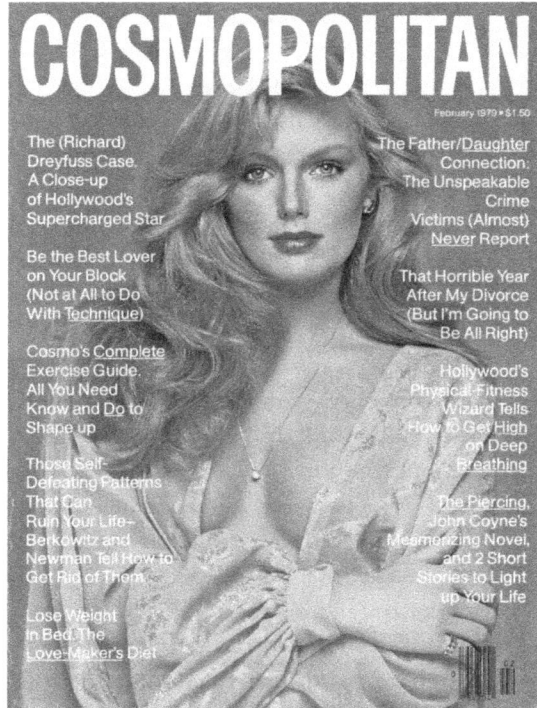

They agreed and then got right back into it. He simply wasn't doing what she wanted, and I knew she knew her own hair and was right, but he was unable to get it. Before we realized it, the producer of the show was in the room telling us we had to come downstairs immediately to do the interview in the ballroom where Ali was sparring with his partner or Ali would be gone.

In the elevator, with Allen trying to repair Aileen's messy hair and me doing final touch-ups on her make-up, we arrived in the ballroom downstairs where the champ was punching out his sparring partner. He came over to the ropes, where his trainer raked his hands down both of Ali's magnificent arms. What looked like a gallon of water rushed off them into a bucket as Aileen grabbed a microphone and began her interview. Whatever she looked like, straggly hair and all, it was too late to do anything about it now. She was on prime time.

I was booked again with Aileen to complete the taping, but this time Allen wasn't included, and Aileen wasn't as docile as she had been in Washington. She intended to get what she wanted this time from both me and the personal hairdresser she had booked. When the work was completed, she looked beautiful and far better than she had in Washington, but we had had plenty of time and better insight into what we wanted. I always found that when things were rushed, they never turned out right.

Michael had contacted some shops and department stores in the Miami, Florida area about his belts and intended to fly down there to show them personally. I thought that maybe we could go together and make a vacation of it, staying with either Valerie or Lee. Since I had bookings to attend to first and Michael had to get down and back because of his other obligations, he went without me.

I was irritated, but I understood. Perhaps I was more disappointed. His business always took priority over everything, and though I understood it, it always seemed to come between us and the things we could do together.

He called me from Florida, and he was with Lee. I had given him Lee's phone number, as well as Valerie's, but he chose to call Lee, and now he was with him. I knew why. He had never met Lee, but I had told him how handsome Lee was, and that's why he was there.

I knew I was acting like a jealous shrew. Why shouldn't he be with Lee? I liked him, too. Maybe it was because I wasn't there with them—or did I feel he had left without me so he could do this very thing?

When they called, they were too merry for me to be comfortable. I was certain that they would go to bed together—but why did I care about that, too? I had been to bed with Lee, and he was great, but I didn't want Michael to do it. For Lee it would only be another notch on his bedpost, but maybe it was also the same for Michael. At any rate, I was pissed. It seemed somehow indecent for my friends to be going to bed together. It was like ... incest—at least that's what I told myself.

When Michael returned, I confronted him with it and he confessed that he had gone to bed with Lee, but he said that had not been his plan when he left without me. He needed to get down and back, and that's what he did. But did he have to take a little nibble of Lee along the way?

I was still furious and stopped speaking to him for a time. When my work was completed, I took myself to Florida and stayed at Valerie's, ignoring Lee. I didn't know exactly what was wrong with me, but I was miffed and intended to stay that way. Michael called, which I was glad he did, and after a few soothing words about how sorry he was to have offended me, he asked if he could join Valerie and me and make things right.

Valerie thought I was acting like a woman scorned in a love affair, which I pooh-poohed. With her approval, I allowed Michael to join us. Soon after he arrived, I became deathly ill from something—probably my craziness brought it on—and Michael lay with me on Valerie's couch all day comforting me. It felt good having him there, but Valerie took no comfort in it. She couldn't clean her house with us lying around all day, but I was glad he was there.

The East was having a serious snowstorm, and we were grateful to be in Florida. Then my agency interrupted with a call to ask—no, demand—that I return to do a make-up in Washington, D.C., again, this time on Walter Mondale and his wife, Joan, for *People* magazine. I dragged myself from the couch, and Michael and I flew back to New York where I picked up my make-up case and headed to Washington with, of all people, Allen Purver.

We checked into a hotel in Washington where the next day we were to go to the Vice President's house to make up Mondale and his wife. It seemed likely that he might have his eye on the White House, particularly with Carter's poor rating in the polls sinking even further with his handling of the Iran hostage crisis. Mondale would get his chance in '84, but lose it to Reagan.

When I arrived in my hotel room, I called Michael. As usual, he was as glad to hear from me as I was to hear him. When I hung up, I knew why I had been so furious about him and Lee: I was falling in love with Michael.

Early the next morning the limousine was waiting in front of our hotel to take the photographer, his crew, Allen, and me to the Vice President's house. When we pulled up in the driveway, several police dogs were let loose, sniffing, over our luggage and equipment. I assumed they were sniffing for drugs. I was certain they'd find all sorts of stuff in Allen's bags and we'd all be hauled off to jail.

I could see the headlines: "Photographer for *People* magazine and crew caught with a stash of dope in front of the Vice President's house just in time before they turned the U.S. government into a den of iniquity."

Instead, they were sniffing for firearms—probably the only thing Allen wasn't carrying, with his stash in his pockets, anyhow—and we were allowed inside the house where we were ushered into a kind of sunroom in the back of the house. There we were supposed to transform Mondale's wife, Joan, into a more attractive woman. And transform her we did.

Each time Allen went to the bathroom—and he went there frequently—he left me the joints he was smoking there, hidden under a roll of toilet paper. Between the two of us, we nearly blew the poor woman's hair right off her head. When Allen pulled back her hair—which she usually discreetly wore over her high forehead to hide her receding hairline—we thought we saw something marvellous and convinced her that she should wear it back for the photo.

In truth, it was the highest forehead I'd ever seen and should have remained camouflaged with hair. With the hair pulled back, she looked as though she could be playing Queen Elizabeth I. All she needed was a ruffled collar and a white flour mixture plastered over her face. Thankfully, that was the only thing I didn't do. But we did expose that high, high-h-h forehead. In the heat of such things, and with two overbearing artists stoned out of their minds hammering at her, it was hard for the poor woman to stick to her convictions and know the truth anymore.

Then we got hold of the Vice President who came in exhausted, overworked, and pale as a ghost. I decided to make him look like he'd been on a skiing trip: tanned, rested, and looking great—which he didn't. To achieve this, I applied so much make-up that he came out looking like the politician-father in *La Cage aux Folles* when they made him up as a drag queen. When I was through with him, all Mondale needed was a wig and high heels to be convincing.

Into the large rotunda room at the entrance of the house we all went, with Mrs. Mondale's hair frightfully resembling Elsa Lanchester's in the

1935 horror classic film *Bride of Frankenstein*. As for Mr. Mondale, he could now pass for Dr. Frank-n-furter, the transvestite in the rock cult classic *The Rocky Horror Show*. The photographer was all set up—in fact, he had been set up for hours—waiting for Allen and me to complete our creations, which could now easily haunt a house.

As if I hadn't already applied enough make-up on Mondale, I proceeded to add more while everyone—secretaries, Secret Service, the photographer, and his assistants, all exasperated by now—stood about watching.

"That's enough," I heard Mondale's secretary order.

Arrogantly, I turned and said, "Not until I'm finished."

Oh, God. What was I thinking? The grass had muddled my brain.

"That's the way to tell her," Mondale kindly, but foolishly, backed me up.

So I applied more on both of them.

I worked once again with that photographer for *People*, and he said, "Don't put as much make-up on the model as you did on Mondale."

He had a point. When the issue came out, I'm sure they were the most made up pair ever to appear on a cover of *People*. I've always felt a little guilty that that cover may have contributed to Mondale's losing his bid for the presidency.

(I had intended to display the *People* cover of Mondale and his wife in this book, but when *People* read the text that was to accompany the Mondale cover, all negotiations for permission to use the cover in my book ceased immediately. Was it men wearing make-up on their covers, pot smoked at the Capital—as if it had never been done before—or my telling Mondale's secretary to f— off? They never said. Mondale's secretary was right: I should have stopped before that last powder puff.)

Without a doubt, I was getting more and more out of hand and didn't even know it. We all were.

Allen would drown in a friend's pool in Florida in the '90s, probably too stoned to save himself, after a failed marriage to a beautiful, blonde Swedish model we had both worked with for *Family Circle* magazine. It was a tragic ending to a talented man caught up in drugs in an era when they were an acceptable, social thing to do.

Mother and I had not been that close these past years. We spoke on the phone, but seeing each other was another matter. I could no longer contend with her meddling in my life. On her last visit to my apartment, I had come in at 4:00 AM, and, seeing me coming in at that time of the morning, she raised her head from the pillow where she slept in my living room and said, "What is it with you—booze, women, or pot?"

"All three," I exaggerated, "and some you haven't even thought of."

We had one last argument before she left, but it was the last I was going to tolerate. The unpleasantness had gotten to her too. She decided to spend more time at my sister's in Lexington, Kentucky, and I turned my attention to Michael. We needed this switch in our emotions to save ourselves. Together, it was too intense and damaging for both of us.

She didn't like my emotions being switched away from her, though her switch was fine by me. It was only a matter of time before her old jealousies of everyone I was with would surface. I wanted to bring Michael home for Christmas, but she balked at it.

"Very well," I said. "Then I won't come."

She paused and then said, "I'll have to think about that."

She realized she couldn't have it both ways and that she was going to lose. She quickly relinquished and allowed Michael to come with me. Actually, she thoroughly enjoyed him.

"Is he a Jew?" she finally asked.

"Yes," I said, ready to challenge her if need be.

Nothing further was said, and if it mattered to her, she never revealed it.

She was brought up in a very strict Pennsylvania family in a small town, moved to another small town in the South when she married, and had not been exposed to many people unlike herself throughout her life. She traveled extensively throughout the world later in her life, and perhaps this was her way of broadening herself and her understanding of the people in the world. She didn't mingle with the cultures she visited, preferring to gaze from a tour bus window at the activity outside, but she saw it, and perhaps that changed her perspective on life and about others. Whatever she understood, she kept it to herself in her own private world.

What I understood about her was only what I understood about myself. I loved her and, in spite of everything, was still dazzled by her, but who she was remained an enigma to me throughout my life.

I kept my feelings about Michael to myself and certainly never revealed anything to him. I wasn't even sure of them myself. I thought it was completely ridiculous that after all this time being friends he would be any more than that to me. I wasn't even that attracted to him. He was handsome— I'd always thought that—but I wasn't attracted to him.

I did love him, however, but I was having plenty of sex and saw no reason to suddenly cut that off and have an affair with Michael. It even sounded somewhat incestuous. We were like brothers. But if you love someone, isn't the next step sex? That was never what our relationship was about. And besides, how did he feel, anyhow?

It would be revealed.

I had gotten a contract from Times Books to write a make-up book. An agent had called Scavullo's studio to ask who, besides Way Bandy, was the hot make-up artist, and they told him about me. He called, and before I knew it, I was sitting in the Russian Tea Room on West 57th Street signing a contract.

I had also just finished my first screenplay, and to celebrate all of this, I went to Michael's for one of his scrumptious spaghetti dinners. In a long, white flannel sleeping shirt, while he was stirring a pot in his kitchen, I suddenly saw how domestic he was and what a partner he would make. At that instant, I totally lost it and began to cry.

What was happening to me and why it was happening I had no idea, but he saw the state I was in and came over to me. I got up and went into another part of his apartment where, in a darkened room by a window overlooking the city, I was trying to compose myself. I was uncertain how to handle these emotions. Homosexuals have no previous training about dating, emotions, love, any of it. We don't go to a prom with the one we'd like to go with; we don't hold hands with someone throughout our growing up; we're just supposed to somehow come out and know how to do these things. Heterosexuals have been doing these things all their lives. So I felt awkward about my feelings, and especially with a friend—awkward to say the least.

"What's wrong?" Michael asked, coming over to me.

I didn't answer him. How could I say, "I think I'm falling in love with you?" How crazy.

And so I said, "I think I'm falling in love with you."

There, I said it. I looked like a fool, I felt like a fool, and I said it.

"I am too," he said. "What should we do?"

God, where do we go from here? Have sex? This was crazy.

Before I got another thought out, he kissed me, and I knew my world had changed. Whatever it was going to be, it would never be the same. This was to be a celebration party, and I guessed in a way it was, but why was I feeling so sad? Wasn't love, or whatever was happening, supposed to be happy?

There was something wrong, but I couldn't figure it out. Like Scarlett O'Hara, I'd figure it out tomorrow. Tonight we'd celebrate with spaghetti and wine—no sex, just spaghetti and wine. Sex was saved for other people—we didn't want to ruin this special thing we had with that. And so it began, a strange relationship that would only get stranger.

13

AIDS Awareness,
Mikhail Baryshnikov,
Liza Minnelli and Love

When the Indiana Jones–like rescue attempt at flying the hostages out of Iran by helicopter failed and eight American combat soldiers lost their lives, the egg on U.S. president Jimmy Carter's face was a stark contrast with the heroic presence presented by Ronald Reagan in his bid for the 1980 presidency. Americans were fed up with looking like fools around the world and being pushed around by Russia. Reagan stood up to the "evil empire" and taunted them to "tear down the wall," the Berlin Wall dividing East and West Germany since 1961—and the wall came tumbling down.

It was all posturing, of course, but Reagan believed his swaggering, John Wayne cowboy act and Americans began to feel better about themselves and their country again. Since Vietnam, we had felt guilty about our behavior. Reagan made no apology for it, and we liked it.

We were tired of approaching geopolitics with one hand tied behind our backs and our tails tucked between our legs. Whether posturing or not, Reagan made us, himself, and the world believe in America's might, both financially and militarily. Our testosterone was everywhere. In the years ahead, we would pay in American lives for this omnipotent, arrogant attitude with the invasion of Iraq on little more information than hearsay.

Even during Reagan's inauguration, Carter was still on the phone trying to solve the hostage crisis, which Reagan took credit for the following year when the hostages were freed after 444 days in captivity. Lucky Reagan, the posturing cowboy, superman king of testosterone had done it again—with a few sleight-of-hand tricks—and we liked our new worldly image.

As for New York City's financial problems—which recently elected mayor Ed Koch inherited from ex-mayor Abe Beame—Koch would manage to stabilize the city's coffers by drastic budget cuts that did nothing to provide the desperately needed police protection. When his successor, David Dinkins, took office in 1990 during a massive recession when one in four New Yorkers was classified as poor—a situation not seen since the Depression—he, in turn, would inherit a $1.8 billion budget deficit from Koch's three terms in office that would balloon to $2.2 billion by the end of Dinkins' one term.

Lack of funds to provide New York with proper police protection through three mayoral administrations translated to corruption and civil disobedience. Consequently, for two decades the city suffered the "Son of Sam" serial killings when David Berkowitz went on a year-long killing spree; the murder of musician John Lennon; the "subway vigilante" Bernhard Goetz, who took the law into his own hands and shot rampaging teenage boys on the subway; the jogger rape and the Zodiac shootings in Central Park; and the tax evasion convictions of Studio 54 owners Ian Schrager and Steve Rubell, who, after being hauled off to jail, would reappear a year later to reopen the disco for seven more outrageous years until it closed for good in 1988 at the height of the AIDS scare.

The St. Mark's Baths, too—renamed the New St. Mark's Baths to suggest that something new would transpire there besides sleazy doings with drugs and sex—would permanently close its doors two years later after a long fight to remain open, ending nearly a decade of wild living in New York as Koch left office in 1989 and George H. W. Bush took over the presidency from Ronald Reagan.

That same year, Steve Rubell would die of AIDS, like others around the world, with no end in sight, and few politicians were seemingly concerned. For many, it was considered a "gay disease," and for some, it was God's retribution for immoral conduct and nobody's business or fault but the gays.' The statistics of those dying in Africa and heterosexuals who also suffered were ignored or were somewhat vague.

Not until the AIDS quilt, a symbol of all those who had died from the disease, was first spread out in 1987 on the National Mall in Washington, D.C., covering an area larger than a football field, did it hit home that over 41,000 Americans had perished. It was apparent that one of the deadliest diseases ever to be introduced into society could be, and was, penetrating not only the gay community, but also the very heart of America: the American family.

In 1986, Reagan had prodded Congress to appropriate $126 million to fight the disease, but it was too late for many, and by no means enough. By 2004, the death rate for Americans would reach over a half million—20 million worldwide since the disease was first diagnosed in 1981—with 37.8 million people worldwide living with the disease, and still no cure.

Inadvertently, gays copied Reagan's posturing as the macho, tough guy and adopted the image for themselves. S & M black leather outfits were everywhere, as were clubs that catered to the fetish. Whether you were a true S & M–ite, black leather was in and everyone postured like the pseudo-macho man we had in office. It was cool to appear tough and dangerous. The world and everybody in the city of New York had better look out. If we didn't have cops to protect us, we'd, at least, look like we could do it ourselves.

The downtown gay bars on the Lower West Side became more and more jaded. One of them, the Anvil, started out during the week catering to a straight crowd, reserving weekends for gays. Realizing that it was more profitable, the bar soon became completely gay.

A friend told me they had a show down there where a man fist-fucked another man, a procedure where the fist was rammed completely up someone's anal track, at times nearly up to the elbow—how uncomfortable is that? I didn't believe it and went to the bar to see for myself. Sure enough, a big, muscular black man in a black leather-strapped outfit that crisscrossed his chest and exposed his black leather jockstrap and bare buttocks beneath his black leather chaps was shoving his hand—dipped in Crisco from a bucket—up a young white man's rear end that was raised invitingly to accommodate the intrusion.

As if that weren't enough, the black man then dripped hot tallow from a candle over the young man's back and buttocks. His moans of ecstasy momentarily convinced me that it might be a thrill, until he got up and I saw masses of welts, small mounds one on top of the other, all over his back and buttocks that had built up as protection from previous hot-tallow drippings.

Maiming the body was outside my range of sexual consideration, so I went about my simple routine that served me well enough, and supposedly my partners, without these kinds of dramatic antics. Many, however, were experimenting with everything, including poppers, which I detested the smell of, and angel dust, which was reputed to be derived from embalming fluid and left you feeling, if not looking, like a corpse. Then there were, of course, acid, mescaline, cocaine, heroin, uppers, and downers—used in various forms: swallowed, shot up, snorted, or smoked—and there was always marijuana and hashish to start things off. Everything was usually taken in combination to get you as far out, almost approaching death, as you could get without actually dying. That was the goal, but it didn't always work, and every day we heard of someone O D-ing, or overdosing, on some concoction. That would seem sufficient for a wake-up call, but no one I knew woke up.

Besides the Anvil, there was a notorious bar called the Mineshaft where, in a huge, black-as-hell space, bodies were lined up against the walls engaged in sex. A naked man would be lying in a black leather, hammock-like harness where passers-by would dip their hand in a vat of Crisco and give his rear—which protruded through the leather straps—a going over. Bathtubs were provided throughout the place to substitute as urinals, and men fought to climb inside them to be urinated on.

Then there was the dangerous activity in the parked trucks in vacant lots in the downtown meatpacking district, where sex was conducted in the back of a truck and any moment someone intent on killing gays could appear at the entrance and stab or shoot the occupants inside to death.

Before the city had the money to finally tear them down, for years vacant wooden warehouse shacks that stood on stilts extended out into the Hudson River on the Lower West Side. After hours, gays prowled these dangerous, rickety shacks looking for late-night sexual prey. In the dark, each step could be fatal if the rotting floorboards gave way and someone plunged into the water below, which could be seen through the cracks in the boards.

In the back of some of the shacks were small tool sheds where, in pitch-black darkness, sex was conducted nightly. The walls would be lined and the entire room filled to capacity with writhing male bodies engaged in sex. The hot, steamy air that saturated the room and the pungent smell of sex was so heavy that it could almost be sliced with a knife. A hand in the darkness could do just that and cut off someone's penis, stab them to death, or rob them, and no one could possibly have known who did it. It was the danger that some gays thrived on.

Sex in the back of a truck was also not in my range of possibility, or Michael's either, as far as I knew. A friend took me to a warehouse once, but the rickety condition and the activity in the tool shed ruled that out permanently. I didn't need to be that scared to have sex. I would stick to my old one-on-one activity, which was sufficient for me, and I felt no need to explore the bizarre. I experienced some of it moderately, the baths too, but

I would invariably hook up with someone who preferred one-on-one like me, and we'd go home together.

Someone pushed me down on the pool table at the Anvil once and started in on me just as I saw Michael coming around the other side of the table to have a look. I jumped up fast and squelched whatever he had in mind to look at. I was proud that I had shown at least that much discretion as we began to ponder coupling.

It never occurred to me to examine the absurdity of what we were about to do. With all our activity with other gay men, were we really expecting to settle down, give all that up? It had been easier, and even preferable, to have a vast turnover of sexual partners. Mother seemed to dictate nothing permanent for me but her, so coupling was always out of the question. With my pulling away from her, it now seemed possible. Then there was Michael's range of experience that I never considered. After all, he'd had a whole life in L.A. before coming to NYC. His knowledge of drugs alone far outdistanced anything I knew. By comparison, I was really green. Perhaps the word would be naïve—and I was seven years older than he was. Not all of my years in Paris, and whatever I had accomplished so far, prepared me for what was up ahead.

With Scavullo for *Harper's Bazaar* I was scheduled to do make-up on Mikhail Baryshnikov, the Russian ballet dancer who defected west in 1974 and became artistic director of the American Ballet Theatre in the early '80s, and on Dame Margot Fonteyn, the prima ballerina who danced so incredibly for years with Rudolf Nureyev.

In the morning I met first with Fonteyn to do her make-up at a rehearsal studio on the West Side of Manhattan, where she may have been rehearsing, and from there we would go by taxi to Scavullo's studio on the Eastside where I would do make-up on Baryshnikov.

I adored Fonteyn and adored being around her, even on our taxi ride to Scavullo's studio after her make-up. She was like an enchanting, delicate flower—lovely, poised, and charming, and, to me, a dead ringer for Vivian Leigh, one of my favorite actresses.

Baryshnikov, on the other hand, I found short-tempered, short on charm, short on manners, and just plain short—perhaps the root of it all. Like Avedon, he had a wiry, frenetic energy that grated on me like fingernails scraping over a blackboard—contrasted by my quiet, almost meditative time with Fonteyn—and it was a relief when the job was over.

But as fickle fate would have her quirky little ways, I would again be paired with Baryshnikov in 1982 to do make-up for him and all of the principal dancers of the American Ballet Theatre when he became artistic director there. It would be for a catalogue of the entire troupe, and one of those freebees for Scavullo, as well as for ABT, for which I would receive the customary inscribed book, or, in this case, a catalogue, while Scavullo spread his fame and kept his P.R. cooking.

As if Baryshnikov's frenetic energy weren't enough, fickle fate would abundantly supply more with Liza Minnelli for a make-up for the April 1980 cover of the *Sunday Daily News* magazine.

Minnelli rattled off non-stop every cliché I'd ever heard about her mother, Judy Garland ending with: "They want me to be like my mother, but I'm not like my mother ... I don't sing, I don't dance like her, I don't do anything like her ... do you think I'm like my mother?"

Before I could assemble my thoughts, she fast-forwarded to a pill that was prescribed for her.

Baryshnikov was a pain while Fonteyn was divine (courtesy Francesco Scavullo Foundation, as seen in U.S. *Harper's Bazaar.*

"I'm supposed to take this pill, but I don't know if I should take this pill—do you think I should take this pill?"

"Oh, God," I thought to myself, "give the son-of-a-bitch to me. I need it more than you do."

With Scavullo, I flew to Chicago to do the *Phil Donahue Show* where, on camera, Scavullo was to shoot a model while I completed another model's make-up and a hair stylist did his thing to demonstrate how a photo was taken in the studio. The model I was making up had several clothing changes backstage before returning to me for touch-ups, and every time she returned,

A very blabby Liza Minnelli wore me out (© Daily News, L.P. [New York]. Used with permission).

she had white powder on her nose, like David Bowie at the Grammys.

This time I knew what was happening, and before the cameras could swing back to us, I barely had time to wipe off the powder before we were discovered by thousands of viewers. I reprimanded her each time she did it, but she kept it up. It was the kind of nightmare Allen Purver created at the White House with his marijuana when we did Mondale and his wife. Illegal drugs were everywhere, even in government and on TV. My friends were seeing to it.

Before we left our Chicago hotel for the Donahue taping, Francesco had asked me to evaluate how he looked. He had plastered his face with a deep, sun-tanned color—more make-up than even Lucille Ball would have considered—but I answered him, "Fine," though I thought he looked like he had been dragged facedown over the bottom of the Mississippi Delta.

During the taping, some woman in the audience asked him about sunbathing and with a face as dark as a minstrel, he ranted about how destructive it was for the skin. The audience surely must have puzzled over his skin, which could have passed for charcoal.

Again with Scavullo, I flew to L.A. to do Victoria Principal's make-up for an ad for Jhirmack hair products. It was my first time with Principal, but I would make her up again back in New York at Scavullo's studio in the early '80s for a shot for *Harper's Bazaar*. In that shoot she sported a most provocative bathing suit with most of her rear exposed that prompted her to shoo away anyone behind her during the shoot.

I enjoyed being with Principal and found her sharp as a tack, quite witty, fun, and most delightful company. I could see any man wanting to be around her, as well as women, too. She sent a quote for my book that took thought and imagination, which I appreciated: "You are to make-up what Merlin was to magic."

We were to stay in L.A. at the Beverly Wilshire Hotel, and since I would have a suite large enough for two, I asked Michael to come along. Of course he knew the Beverly Wilshire, as well as the entire city. It was his hometown. We planned to visit his mother in Palm Springs, drive to his father's avocado and citrus fruit ranch in the hills of Encino, and then head up the Pacific Coast Highway to visit a woman friend of Michael's in San Francisco before returning to New York.

While I toiled at the studio during the day on Principal's make-up, Michael leisurely ordered his breakfast from room service, had a swim in the hotel's swimming pool, and made an appearance later at the studio.

In the evening, we took Francesco to Ma Maison, the trendy restaurant where Michael's father was part owner, and then Michael drove us back to the hotel in a car he'd rented for our trip to his parents' and to San Francisco. His driving was so erratic that it panicked Francesco and I had to insist that Michael slow down before Francesco had one of his famous breakdowns. It was an indication of what lay ahead.

The trip to Michael's parents' homes and the drive up the Pacific Coast Highway went without incident, but when we arrived at his woman friend's house in San Francisco, he insisted that we go look for some coke. I had no interest in coke because of its effect on me, but he and the woman wanted it, so we went to her dealer.

Her dealer turned out to be a woman's clothing shop with a large room in the back where the coke was dealt. With only a flimsy curtain hanging in the doorway separating the front room from the back, it was hardly the kind of fortress protection one might expect in that business, which led me to believe in the leniency of the cops there, or some kind of a payoff. In the back room was a long table where clear plastic bags of coke were lined up— presumably of various weights—with a large scale to weigh them.

I assumed that since I was a stranger it was only courteous, if not prudent, that I not go into the back room, but Michael motioned for me to come inside, and so I did. No one, apparently, was hiding anything. He chose a bag, paid a bundle, and we left. Throughout the day and into the night at a trendy bar the young woman took us to, she and Michael, and occasionally I, sniffed lines of coke from the bag as others around us were also doing. When we arrived late back at the woman's house, Michael said he had left me some coke in the bedroom where we would be sleeping. I went into the bedroom to inspect what was left and found that the entire bag, which had started out at about half the size of a man's fist, was completely gone except for a line he had left for me, which I didn't want anyhow.

The next day when we boarded our plane for New York, a red light had switched on in me. I tried to ignore it, but something was gnawing at me that I couldn't quite let go of.

Lovely Victoria Principal in her bathing suit with the rear missing (courtesy Francesco Scavullo Foundation, as seen in U.S. *Harper's Bazaar*).

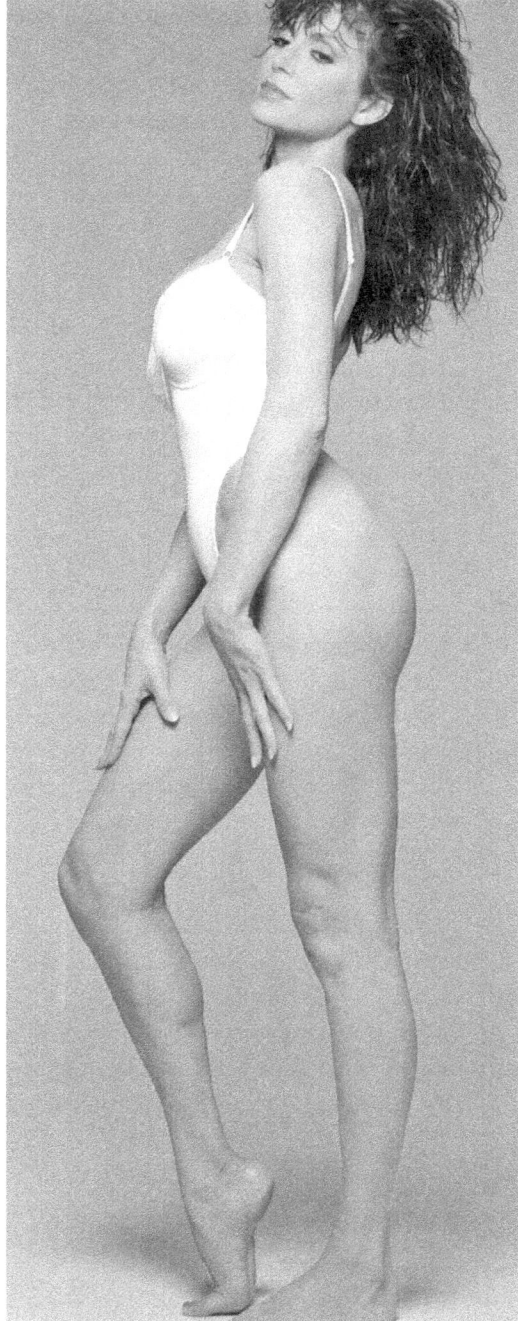

He and I had decided to rent a house for the summer and try out our new relationship as partners. We looked around Fire Island and in the Hamptons and found nothing that suited us. We decided to try Montauk, a community at the very tip of Long Island and a four-hour train ride from New York.

When our train finally chugged to the end of the track with no farther to go, the conductor came through and announced that we were indeed at the end. We picked up our gear and headed outside to a desolate, gravel parking area with nothing but a little train house surrounded by mountainous terrain and a road leading to what appeared to be civilization. It was the first of March and still cold, and the restaurants and motels that usually catered to summer tourists had not yet opened.

Montauk at the time was a wild, untouched wilderness with steep, chalk-white cliffs engulfed by a relentlessly pounding sea that further enhanced its wild, untamed quality. It was so far out on Long Island that few summer tourists wanted to go there, which was an attraction for us because we wanted to be away from the prying eyes of friends and others.

In the 1920s, some high rollers had had the idea of making the area into gambling casinos and hotels for wealthy Long Islanders. The Depression had swept all that away, and what was left were some ghostly shells of vacant hotels, which would have contained the gambling casinos, perched high on the mountainous terrain and a lonely statue, standing in a circular section of the road, that we trudged past to get to the center of the current Montauk village.

When we arrived in the village, in front of us was a motel right on the ocean. The early season guaranteed that there would be few but us there. Weary from our four- hour train ride and needing a bath and a change of clothing, we leaped inside and got a room in the middle of the others with a small terrace that faced the sea.

If heaven has a description, that little room facing that giant blue ocean, with an endless expanse of sand void of anyone, surrounded by chalk-white cliffs, the crystal clear, blue March sky, and the clean salt air of Montauk would suffice.

We showered, shaved, and walked up the road where we were told we'd find a roadside restaurant, one of the few that were open. There we had the most incredible fish dinner ever.

Fishermen from around there go out every day for their catch, and Montauk is the first served before the fish are shipped into Manhattan and points beyond. If you're lucky enough to have your skillet in Montauk, the fish hit your pan first.

After dinner, mellow from wine and filled with food, we strolled back to our motel room under that crystal clear sky, made even more radiant by a full moon and orchestrated by the endless waves heard everywhere. We smoked a joint and fell into bed next to each other, where our dreams were deep and spectacular.

In my dream, I saw Michael as a Viking warrior back from a battle. It was medieval times, we were in a stone castle with a roaring fireplace, and meat was cooking on the fire. With his long dark hair making him look even more authentic, he was dressed in a fur loincloth with leather lace-up boots, and the most bizarre thing of all: I was a beautiful maiden with long, long blonde tresses.

It was quite strange since I'd never envisioned myself being anyone's maiden, and certainly not with long, long blonde tresses.

I woke and stirred Michael.

I told him of my dream, and he said, "That's funny. I had the exact same dream."

The only difference was that in his dream he was the maiden with long, long dark tresses. I thought that this was no way to begin a romantic relationship, quibbling over who was to be the maiden with long, long tresses.

We fell back asleep, and the next thing I knew it was around six in the morning. I climbed out of bed, went to the small glass door that opened onto the terrace, threw back the curtains, and walked nude out onto the terrace.

Gently kissing the rim of the sky, the sea in front of me was a surreal mass of aquamarine-blue rippling waves that gracefully rolled like an accordion onto the shore. Everything was undisturbed and untainted by any living creature, not even a bird or insect. The sky was completely unblemished by a cloud—just this expanse of cobalt blue with a hint of pink, and a tiny, early morning star in the middle directly over my head—only that.

As far as I could see to the left of me was a fiery orange-red ball of an early morning sun that faced directly across the heavens; as far as I could see to the right of me, the pale yellow, full moon. Just these two gigantic, round heavenly bodies facing each other—with that tiny diamond of a morning star in the middle officiating the union. The scene was breathtaking.

I knew at that moment that there was unmistakably a God and that I was about to have the most meaningful experience of my life. It was frightening, yet, at the same time, exhilarating.

Later that day, a real estate agent took us to several summer rentals before he showed us a small, enchanting white-frame cottage tucked away on a hill off the main road and hidden by the masses of trees and bushes that surrounded it. It belonged to a family that had European plans for the summer, and it was apparent that it had received much love. The hill it rested on provided an excellent view of the sea beyond, and the sea breezes and foliage that lovingly cradled it kept it cool all day. We were home.

I set about to write the make-up book, for which I'd signed a contract with Times Books, and Michael located a piano in town at a bar-restaurant owned by two gay men, where he was allowed to practice his music each morning. The racket of continuous scales must have driven the owners mad, but they never complained, and this became our morning routine: him practicing his scales, and me writing my book.

At lunch, I'd pick up sandwiches from a deli in town, and he'd pick up fruit, or vice versa, and we'd rendezvous later at a given spot on the beach. We never conferred with one another about who would pick up what—the sandwiches, fruit, drinks, or dessert—but invariably it would work out that we'd pick up just the right thing for our lunch.

One chilly, overcast afternoon on the beach, we were cuddled close together for warmth under our blanket when, suddenly, standing over us, a man appeared who said he lived in a house on the hill above the beach. He and his wife had observed what we were doing, and they didn't like it. What we were doing was trying to keep warm, and whatever else was purely their own fabrication.

I was incensed. How dare these people presume they could butt in and judge us?

"You and your wife better take a look at yourselves," I struck back, "before coming down here and accusing us of something that's in your own sick minds!"

He was stunned and quite taken aback. It was obvious that he hadn't expected this.

"I didn't come down here for an argument," he said.

"Well, you got one," I replied. "I love this man, if that's any of your business, and we're doing no more under a blanket than you and your wife would do."

He stepped back. It never occurred to him that we were allowed to love too, that we could do what he and his wife could do.

He turned and went back up the wooden steps to where his wife was awaiting the results of his rude intrusion. She undoubtedly got an earful, and Michael and I covered up again, undisturbed.

There was prejudice in this world—there was no mistaking it. I had fought this as far back as when I was growing up in Kentucky, and I was damned if I was going to take it anymore. I felt that people should get a better understanding of what it was like to be gay, black, Jewish, or some other minority, and suffer the name-calling, hatred, and abuse that comes with it. Whether it would stop prejudice, I seriously doubted, but it would sure relieve those of us who had to put up with it to throw it back in their pompous, self-righteous faces.

There was no reality in what Michael and I were doing. We were living a dream, playing a part, and it was inevitable that we'd wake up and the dream would be over. When we had sex, I'd close my eyes. He asked me about this, and I made up some stupid explanation about the ecstasy I was feeling. The truth was that I didn't want to see that it was Michael there.

Every weekend he would bring along his coke. He said he needed it to keep up with the demands of his business, so why was he using it even on the weekends? Was it so he could play the part of a lover? And me? I was seeing other men in the city—as was Michael, I suspected—and then coming out to our enchanted cottage pretending to be lovers on the weekends.

It finally all hit home at the end of the summer when I observed him frolicking in the water with a young man. I was jealous, but there was more: it was obvious he wanted the young man—and why not? I had men in the city I wanted, and if it were I in the water, I would want this young man too. It was like trying to convert whores and make them domestic. Our lives were so out of hand that this was impossible.

When the time of our summer rental was up, we packed our belongings and left everything exactly as it was when we arrived, everything carefully back in its place as if nothing had transpired there—I even made sure of it—and we left our enchanted cottage for good.

When we got back to the city, I announced to Michael that it was over. Our experiment had failed because it never had a chance of success from the beginning. We were what we were: victims of our own promiscuity, and coupling was impossible. I wasn't sure, at this point, if it would ever be possible for me. We had become like those couples I always detested who united and then played around with everyone on the side. I hated myself, and in many ways, I hated Michael too.

I proposed that we be friends again, and he agreed, but I only half meant it because I sensed even that was unreal now. Humpty Dumpty had had a great fall, and the pieces might never fit together again.

We talked frequently, but I needed some space between us to get a handle on my life. From my lack of concentration, my make-up book had turned out badly, and Times Books wanted part of their advance back. I was drowning in my own life and couldn't stop it.

My work with photographers had also suffered until Scavullo was almost my sole client, an unpleasant place to be with his erratic and, at times, abusive behavior. Plagued by insecurity and doubts of self-worth—later diagnosed a manic depressive—he would abuse to protect himself from the world he feared.

The more pain I felt over Michael's and my failed relationship, the more sex I had to relieve it. Arms around me, any arms, were a momentary sedative that brought relief. When they left in the morning, the vacant place in my heart returned, and I needed my fix again to fill it. It was like free falling, downward, downward, and I was unable to pull out of it to save myself.

Unknown to me, Michael, too, was suffering. His antidote was also sex, and drugs to dull his senses. We had opened a can of emotions, like Pandora opening her dreaded box, and all of our pent-up pain from a lifetime of it had crawled out, and we couldn't get it to go away because we couldn't stop what we were doing.

At this time, Michael had a party to announce some new belts he was adding to his belt line, and besides the large fashion contingency he had invited, he also included me—and a new boyfriend. I didn't know this until I was leaving with the rest and the young man stayed behind with Michael.

I was sure that he had done this to pay me back for hurting him, something I hadn't intended to do; I'd simply wanted to save myself from hurt. I felt humiliated and betrayed. It was one thing to break up, but it was quite another to rub your previous partner's face in it. This was a mean streak in Michael that I was just now seeing.

I pulled away from him completely. I didn't read his letters and didn't return his phone calls. This went on for several months until we accidentally ran into each other and he asked to see me.

He came to my apartment and got down on his knees and said, "I want you back in my life."

He had humiliated me, and I intended to pay him back.

"I'm never coming back," I said cruelly, and untruthfully, because all I wanted was him back in my life too.

He got up, and we knew that there was no more trust between us. As a black widow spider has sex with her mate and then devours him, we intended to do the same.

14

Liz Taylor and Me

Elizabeth Taylor had been a fascination of mine since her days as a child actress at MGM. Totally smitten with the MGM studio, their big, splashy Technicolor musicals, and their impressive stable of stars—"more stars than there are in the heavens," as their slogan went—I was enthralled when Taylor visited Scavullo's studio to inspect a photograph he'd taken of her and I immediately told her that I had always wanted to do her make-up.

"Well, why don't you?" she responded.

Actually, I hadn't always wanted to do her make-up, but, rather, I wanted to get a close-up look at her. She was short, somewhat worn now, with rough skin from too much sunning, and portly—but not as fat as she had once been while married to her sixth husband, Senator John Warner from Virginia, whom she had helped put into office. Her hair was obviously dyed black—much too dark and harsh for a woman her age—and then there were those much-touted eyes that were reputed to be lavender—perhaps some press agent's myth that she perpetuated to separate herself from the masses. They looked plain old blue to me—a nice blue, but still blue.

I got my chance to do her make-up when Scavullo booked me for a *Good Housekeeping* cover with her and her adopted German daughter, Maria Burton. Maria had been physically damaged and left abandoned at birth, and Taylor and Richard Burton spent ten years restoring her to health. Perhaps Taylor identified with the damage of her own childhood by a ruthless studio determined to make money off her and by her own ambitions. She would later vow that she would never make another movie for MGM—a vow she wouldn't keep—but that was years after they had made her powerful enough to pick and choose.

The variation on the tale I got was that her father, an American art dealer working in London, had relocated his family to L.A. during World

192

War II and was out with other Air Raid Wardens during a blackout when a friend told him that MGM was looking for a young girl to play opposite Roddy McDowall in the movie *Lassie Come Home*. After a so-so beginning in films with a 1942 Universal Pictures film, *There's One Born Every Minute*, Taylor begged to do the Lassie movie. That ended her childhood as she had known it, and the rest, as they say, is history.

On the day of the *Good Housekeeping* shoot, I was to do Maria's make-up first before Taylor arrived, which turned out to be nearly two hours late. After applying Maria's make-up, there was nothing for the rest of us (Scavullo and his two assistants, a hair stylist, a clothing stylist, a writer from *Good Housekeeping*, the Art Director,

The *Good Housekeeping* shoot with Elizabeth Taylor was tame compared to my next shoot with her (courtesy Francesco Scavullo Foundation and Hearst magazines).

and his assistant) to do but sit around and wait for La Taylor.

Make-up photographs best soon after it's been applied—a consideration that never occurred to Taylor, had she even been prone to consider it. Consequently, after a nearly two-hour wait, most of Maria's make-up had to be reapplied—another consideration that Taylor didn't consider. But then, the rest of us weren't Elizabeth Taylor.

Maria at 19 was charming, quiet, and in a world of her own, which she revealed in her poetry that she read to me. Taylor, on the other hand, was a whole other kettle of fish—appropriately put with her being a Pisces like Gloria Vanderbilt, symbolized in the horoscope by two fish swimming in opposite directions: contrary, confusing, and provocative, at the least.

Arriving inebriated, Taylor proceeded to get even more so as what was

left of the day dragged by. I couldn't resist asking what she thought of Louis
B. Mayer, the tyrannical boss of the MGM studio for nearly three decades.
I read that he had been rude to her mother which, understandably, infuriated Taylor. Nevertheless, he made her one of the highest paid, most recognizable stars in the world—a trade-off she willingly accepted.

"He was a bastard," she answered my question in a broad, phony British
accent that, having been in America since she was a child, she could have
only acquired through association, probably with Richard Burton. By now,
she was far more American than British, though, at one time, she had taken
out British citizenship for tax purposes.

Before going on camera, she insisted on comparing the black around
her eyes with that around Maria's, which she was sure was more than her
own. The competition between mother and daughter over who got the most
black around their eyes was exhausting. To make her point, Taylor—still
caught up in her Cleopatra mode—grabbed the black pencil and carved the
black in around her eyes until they resembled the Pennsylvania coalfields.

As she was leaving, she wrote something illegible on the dressing room
mirror with one of my lipsticks, and I reminded her that she had already
done this in *Butterfield 8*, the 1960 film that had yielded her an Oscar.

"And well!" she brazenly shot back.

When the day ... er, evening ... finally ground to a halt and we could
go home, it was a relief to get away from all this ego fluffing. What was I
thinking with these MGM women—Lucille Ball with enough Max Factor
on her face to paint a house and now this one with the Pennsylvania coalfields? Who trained this bunch? I resolved to keep movie stars strictly for
the screen.

An overly zealous editor from *Rolling Stone* magazine later asked me
what I thought about an interview she had given *Women's Wear Daily*, where
she said I was one of the make-up artists she used.

"I'll be impressed when she says I'm the only one," I responded untruthfully, not at all anxious for a repeat.

Her "people" called sometime after this to ask me to come over to a
hotel where she was staying and do her make-up, and I declined. I wasn't
on call for this kind of thing that many stars took advantage of on a whim.
The rejection may have set her off for our next encounter.

Soon after the hotel thing, my agent called to tell me that I was booked
again with her for the *General Hospital* daytime soap in L.A. She was scheduled to appear in an episode when the show's characters Luke and Laura,

played by Anthony Geary and Genie Francis, were to marry. It was a big event for the show, and Taylor was to be their big attraction. She was a long-time fan of the show and had even encouraged it—getting far below her usual price, no doubt.

I was skeptical about this. During our time together, I was particularly bothered by her drinking, which reminded me of my father—always a bad factor for me. But my splurge in Montauk with Michael had cost more than I had anticipated, so I agreed. It would only be for two days—two, as it turned out, very *long-g-g* days.

I found out afterwards that she had tried to book Way Bandy first, but he had refused. He was well aware of the strain that two days with her would extract. When he and a hair stylist worked with her on another Scavullo shoot at John Warner's farm in Virginia, she decided, after all their preparation, to have a bath before going on camera. One can only imagine the damage hot steam would have on a freshly applied make-up and a hairdo. The lady liked things done her way, and since Way didn't need the money he didn't have to put himself through another episode. Unfortunately, I did.

Before I could make flight reservations to L.A., Lee had the bad timing to call to say that he was in town for a few days and wanted to stay with me. That this was a huge imposition wouldn't even begin to describe how I felt. I needed time alone to concentrate on the things I needed for my trip; I certainly didn't need to be entertaining someone at that moment. I was also in a fragile state about my deteriorating relationship with Michael and preferred not to have anyone around me. But Lee had given me so many things for my apartment when he and his boss, Howard, moved to Florida that I couldn't say no.

I reasoned that I still had possessions of his stored in my apartment that he couldn't take with him when he moved, and this would be a perfect opportunity to have him remove them while I was away. The night before my trip would be our only shared time together. I'd leave him my keys—he'd always been reliable—and when I returned he and his stuff would be cleared out and I'd have a lot more space in my apartment for my things. Sounded good, anyhow.

I spent the day of Lee's arrival packing, and when he got there, I agreed to have one drink with him at a local gay bar before returning home to fix us dinner. I had my drink and left him there, promising to be at my apartment shortly. He never showed. At 4:00 AM, I was awakened by a noise in my living room and, grumbling that the scamp was finally home, I turned over to get more sleep before I had to be up in three hours. Then I heard other noises that indicated he wasn't alone.

Putting a heavy crystal ashtray in the pocket of my bathrobe for protection, I cautiously opened my bedroom door and saw a strange man on top of Lee on the couch in my living room. Holding tightly onto the heavy ashtray, I went over to the tangled heap, shoved the man off, and demanded that he leave. Lee was so inebriated that he barely understood what was happening.

"He promised me cab fare home," the man griped, getting into his clothes while I stood menacingly beside him.

"That's not my problem," I said. "I didn't invite you here, and I'm not responsible for your fare home."

In his clothes now, he ambled over to the door, stalling for time, and reluctantly went out, obviously hoping I'd weaken and give him some money.

He was no doubt a hustler, and cab fare and payment were expected for whatever service he imagined he had performed, which, as far as I saw, having caught him in mid-air, was nothing.

However, a moment of compassion came over me for him having to hoof it home, and I offered, "I'm sorry about this."

"Well, you oughta be," he snarled, obliterating the benevolent feelings I had just had.

"But not that much!" I said, and slammed the door in his face.

"Now," I said, turning to Lee, who was nearly unconscious with no comprehension that he had recklessly and irresponsibly compromised both my life and his, "get your ass to sleep!"

When I got up at my appointed 7:00 AM, Lee was astonishingly already up, perhaps anticipating my anger and preparing for it.

"I don't know what to do about this key," I said, clutching it tightly in my hand while observing him combing his hair in front of a mirror in my living room. I could tell he was trying to retain his dignity and wasn't achieving it.

All the years of depraved, careless living had reduced him to what I had seen on my couch earlier that morning with a hustler pumping on top of him. This was the shell of a once golden god, the adulation of every gay man in New York, wasted and destroyed by years of booze and drugs, reduced to paying hustlers to service him.

"Do whatever you want," he answered arrogantly, continuing to arrange his hair.

Throwing down the key, I said, "I want you and your stuff out of here when I get back. Whatever's left is mine."

I went into the bathroom and heard him go out the door. When I returned from L.A., the key I had given him was on the couch where he'd had his fatal liaison with the hustler, nothing was removed, and I now considered his former possessions payment for his being an untrustworthy friend.

I didn't hear from him for years; perhaps he was ashamed to face me, or maybe he didn't care. We had one last go-around in the early '90s when he called to report that he had AIDS. I helped him in and out of hospitals for a time until he shriveled to a bald, fetus-like creature with a bloated stomach that resembled a pregnant woman's. After he died, his sister and I scattered his ashes in the Pines, the gay community on Fire Island he particularly liked. The place probably contributed to his condition as much as anywhere, with its promiscuous sex and drugs, which he had indulged in lavishly while taking care of friends' houses there.

Like his murdered friend, John Barrett, the antique dealer who was buried somewhere in a veteran's graveyard outside New York, Lee took his place in the Hall of Shame that was becoming the final tribute for most of my friends then.

Accompanying me on my flight to L.A. was a South African woman, Chen Sam, a onetime pharmacist who was now acting as Taylor's publicist and secretary. As far as I saw, she was mainly a gofer who ran interference and buffered her from undesirables. During our flight, Sam—made up like a Taylor look-alike, Pennsylvania coalfields and all—kept turning around to the people behind us and saying, "They're looking at me. They're looking at me."

Who wouldn't look at someone whose head kept bobbing around in their direction like one of those kewpie dolls on a dashboard? Maybe they were struck by her resemblance to a panda.

Sam warned me, "Don't say anything to Elizabeth about Kitty Kelley's book."

The author Kitty Kelley, who had written other biographies of famous people, had just come out with *Elizabeth Taylor: The Last Star*, in which she scathingly reported Taylor's greed, dissipation, and coarse, vulgar conduct of which even I didn't want to be reminded. Sam had already cautioned me not to call Elizabeth "Liz," the press's favorite name for her, and I had no intention of getting into more hot water by dredging up other matters. The information about Louis B. Mayer would be sufficient.

A stretch limousine met us at the airport and dropped me at the hotel Chateau Marmont, a playground for rock stars that Michael thought I'd get a kick out of. With its bizarre, ancient Spanish architecture, it resembled more a haunted house to me than a hotel. It was built in 1929 and would be where John Belushi died of a drug overdose in 1982—adding another notch to its notoriety.

It was now becoming clear that lateness was part of Taylor's routine. When she arrived the following day on the set of *General Hospital*—where the director's entire office had been transformed into her private dressing room—the cast, crew, and I had been waiting well over an hour for her. Suffering from jet lag, I was in no mood to put up with more of her drinking and other shenanigans as I had on the *Good Housekeeping* shoot.

Entering the director's office, she was presented by the executive staff of *General Hospital* with a gift that appeared to be a glass, odd-shaped holder thing for either candles or maybe plants. What its function was and what one would do or even want to do with it was mind-boggling, and I felt that Taylor felt the same way. She might possibly have expected a diamond ring— one of her favorite things to collect—but with a tightly budgeted show like this, that wouldn't be forthcoming.

Tossing the thing aside (while I stood waiting to be acknowledged at the makeshift dressing table, which must have normally been someone's desk), she strolled about the room with a male companion—some minor actor I vaguely recalled from TV—looking at the framed photos on the wall. She stopped at a banquet table piled a yard high with cold cuts, ham, chicken, cheese, fruit, and who knows what all, at the far end of the long room. Who was supposed to consume such a bounty was anyone's guess, but no one in Taylor's entourage, including herself, indulged—though I caught her several times eyeing the piled-up food like it was a fuzzy friend she would like to get closer to rather than merely ogling it from across the room.

Every so often her tag-along cohort would mumble something in her ear, and she'd giggle and respond with, "Oh, Robert. Oh, Robert!" but I had no idea who Robert was and what he could possibly be saying to provoke such a response, and I was too tired and growing impatient to care.

Finally, she sashayed over to the makeshift dressing table and greeted me with, "Oh, hello," like I was an afterthought and a stranger who didn't much matter anyhow.

I did matter, however. Based on my work with *Good Housekeeping*, and the fact that she couldn't get Way, I was hired to make her look her best at a time in her life when that wasn't so easy. This was years before the extensive plastic surgery she would later undergo; she was still somewhat obese, and her beauty days were ... shall we say ... well, in the rear.

And for a make-up artist that she had proclaimed by name in *Women's Wear Daily* to use for her photography, she certainly knew me better than: "Oh, hello." My feeling was that she was irked at my refusal to rush to a hotel to do her make-up when a member of her staff called me before I came out to do this job. I wasn't going to be one of her stooges, at her beck and call, since I knew from experience that her favor would only fade when another stooge came along. That was the case with the hairdresser who had done her hair for the *Good Housekeeping* cover, who had followed her everywhere doing her bidding, only to be dumped when a new hairdresser caught her fancy. I didn't want to be a victim of her stardom.

A woman in her entourage lined up on the dressing table quite a few bottles of Dom Pérignon, opened one, and poured a tumbler full. Taylor took a hefty gulp, gave her face a once-over in the mirror to reassure herself that it was ready for the oncoming assault, and sat. The make-up session had officially begun.

"Francesco sends his love," I said amiably, as I began.

"Who?" she coyly cooed.

She knew perfectly well who. It had only been a couple of weeks since the *Good Housekeeping* shoot in New York with Francesco, and she had worked with him before, as she had with me. She was purposely being rude for no reason. Or she was out of her mind, as may well have been the case considering the quantity of Dom Pérignon lined up on the dressing table.

Maybe the presence of her daughter Maria in New York had made her a tinge more civil. But trouble in her marriage to John Warner and the pressure of Lillian Helmann's play *The Little Foxes*, in which she had appeared in New York and now in L.A., may have been making her quite testy. Or perhaps this was the real Elizabeth Taylor fueled by booze that had finally gotten its nasty hold.

Whatever it was, it didn't take me long to dislike this woman, and the feeling was rapidly becoming mutual. Our professional relationship was deteriorating before we had even started, and this wasn't good for either of us at this most inconvenient moment.

As the day progressed, we finally declared all-out war, and it was obvious that neither of us was taking any shit. Who would win was yet to be determined.

To begin my work, she handed me the same tired Max Factor panstick that Lucille Ball had used, which must have been a big thing with these MGM women. I had declined it with Lucy and still made her look great and I made no exception with Taylor. This put her even further into a testy mood.

We haggled over every pencil, color of eye shadow, where to put the color on her cheeks, and even her eyebrows, which she insisted on beefing up herself until they resembled two jet-black mountain peaks looming over her eyes.

"Don't make them so...," I intended to say, "...roof-top looking."

Before I got it out, she snapped, "I'll make them exactly as I..."

"Damn well please," we responded in unison, and that didn't go over so well either.

After scraping throughout and slaving for what seemed centuries, I completed the make-up. Impressed with some of the pencils I had used, she pilfered from my make-up case a large selection that she had particularly taken a fancy to and shoved them into a ratty little make-up bag.

I explained that I needed them for a job I was booked for when I returned to New York and didn't have time to replace them. This fell on deaf ears. When La Taylor wanted something, you'd better fork it over or it meant you didn't love her. Since this wasn't even a consideration for me, I concluded that she never left a job—no matter how menial—empty handed. Way had confided to me that he had given her nearly half his make-up case. It wasn't that she needed anything or really even wanted it. It was a matter of principle: she was obsessed with getting something.

When she was dressed and had gone upstairs to the set, I got into that ratty little bag and cut all the pencils in half. I figured it was fair that she have half and I have the other half.

When she returned, sensing that I had been up to something, she immediately went into the bag and found the cut pencils. The scream she let out could have been heard in Culver City at the old MGM studio. They may have pampered the stars then, but, as far as I was concerned, her spoiling days were over.

"I told you I needed them," I said, unapologetically.

That was it! The war was in full gear. Not only had I refused to do her make-up at that New York hotel, I was again depriving her of something else she wanted. The day crept by like a nightmare caught in cobwebs.

When someone on the set yelled "make-up," I would race around trying to locate her bejewelled Cartier vanity—doubtlessly worth a fortune—that she insisted on using because it had a light in it, to reapply her lipstick that was constantly transferring to her champagne glass. By the time I located the thing and retrieved it from wherever one of her flunkies had hidden it for protection, she would be somewhere on the set fuming.

"You're late," she hissed after one of these marathon treasure hunts.

"Late for what?" I retaliated.

Taken aback because people didn't usually challenge her, she flustered, "Late, that's all. Just late."

What was the urgency? They hadn't even begun shooting. Was it that I again didn't give her what she wanted when she wanted it? Besides, I wasn't some stooge that stood around holding someone's bejewelled vanity while they smeared on more lipstick. I was a recognized artist in my field, the same as she, and I deserved the respect that she seemed to think was due only her.

When Anthony Geary—the Luke character who would marry the character Laura—poked his permed, frizzy blondish head in the dressing room door, I sensed that she found him attractive.

When he left, I said, "I think you like him."

"I do like him," she said immodestly.

I took this to mean more than we both had implied. She had been watching the show long enough to have built up an opinion. And it wouldn't have surprised me if she'd purposely taken this gig to get her mitts on him. Years later, both Taylor and Geary would confess to an affair, and I had clearly seen it coming.

A small dressing room tent was set up on the set to accommodate her so she wouldn't have to go downstairs to the director's office/dressing room each time she needed something. In fact, the entire studio was her movable dressing room that followed her everywhere. All of the actors on the show stood around the tent all day, gaping each time she entered or exited.

Parked in a chair outside the tent's entrance was a small woman; I instinctively knew her purpose.

"Are you her bodyguard?" I asked.

"Yes," she giggled in a tiny, girlish voice.

"I bet you could throw me right over your head."

"Yes," she giggled again.

There was no doubt.

When we wrapped for the day and I could at last return to my hotel, I ran into that Robert character, who had been with her earlier that day, roaming the corridors.

"What are you doing here?" he asked.

Funny, I was about to ask the same question.

"I'm staying here," I replied.

He gave no explanation for himself and quickly scooted around the corner of the hallway and disappeared.

I reasoned that with rock stars staying there, there might be businesses in the hotel that weren't exactly on the up and up for which he might be a client. He may have mistaken me for one, too.

My sleep that night was as deep as a coma. The following morning, having accepted Taylor's rude tardiness as habitual with her, I made no attempt to arrive at the studio as promptly as I had the day before. It was with a great effort that I went at all. Her arrival slightly improved from the previous day: not quite an hour late this time.

Seating herself at the makeshift dressing table, she announced that she would do her own make-up today and that I was to stand by for an emergency—whatever that might be. The emergency began for me the moment she started. I cringed every step of the way—and then there were those Pennsylvania coalfields again. Oy!

As she applied the final layer to her creation, with a few adjustments from me, her entourage, which consisted of a son from Michael Wilding, her son's wife, her publicist, Chen Sam, a hairdresser, and an assortment of other cronies, all dressed in suits and evening attire, gathered in the dressing room. When the vision was complete, she paraded out the door with her court trailing behind her, leaving me, the scullery maid, behind in my blue jeans.

I asked her son where they were going.

"To the party scene," he replied.

The party scene? What party scene? No one had told me there was to be a big party scene that day when Taylor, playing a rich benefactor, would give the hospital a check for a substantial amount of money. I had brought a suit with me that I could have worn. I felt it was deliberate because I hadn't let her trot off with those damn pencils.

As I went down the hall to check things out on the set upstairs, a woman from wardrobe came out and asked, "Aren't you going to be in the party scene?"

"No one told me," I lamented, with a hint of tragedy.

"Come in here and I'll fix you up."

She outfitted me with a suit, shirt, tie, and even shoes, and minutes later I was on the set anticipating my first Oscar. On the director's orders, I took my place beside Sam, who was stunned to see me. This had obviously been a plot, and she was in on it. I had done no more than refuse to allow Taylor to bully me around as Louis B. Mayer had doubtlessly done to her—so what was the difference? She hadn't liked it, and neither had I.

Sam wouldn't budge an inch to allow me in. She was stationed by the door where Taylor would make her grand entrance, and the camera had to swing past her as Taylor swept in. She was determined to be in the scene and thought I was upstaging her.

Fed up with the whole thing, I not only nudged my way in, but also demanded a champagne glass of ginger ale like everyone else, in spite of Sam's protests that my character didn't drink. I assured her that he most certainly did and settled in to wait for Taylor to sweep through the door and up to the podium where her character would announce her gift to the hospital.

When Taylor swept in, I immediately turned and faced her as she made her way up to the podium and fluffed her lines—for which I took credit—startled to encounter me at her entrance.

Moments later, I heard "Make-up!" I knew it was a call to get me off the set while they rearranged the group. Taylor mumbled something about needing some lipstick—God help us—and applied it herself. When I returned to the set, my place had been changed to somewhere in the back of the crowd—nowhere close to Taylor's entrance. It was no dishonor, and I even found it amusing. But my Oscar would have to wait for another time.

At the weary end of the day, everyone gathered downstairs in a large concrete basement for a cover shot for *People* magazine with Taylor, Geary, and Francis. Again Taylor screeched for her Cartier vanity, which sent me running in circles, and while she reapplied another layer of lipstick for the billionth time, I jokingly asked Geary if he would like some too.

"No!" he vigorously responded, as if his manhood required such strong defense.

(Unfortunately, *People* wouldn't allow me the cover of Taylor and her cohorts, but it showed a bloated Taylor, diluted that she could do professional work stewed to her Piscean gills on Dom Pérignon, with the accents of shadow that I had added at the ends of her eyes to balance the increased facial flesh since our last time together, her arm wrapped lustfully around Geary with her hand gripping his shoulder, claiming her territory, and Francis in front looking as though she had accidentally happened into the photo, oblivious to the cuddled-up couple behind her. It was hard to tell who was marrying whom here.)

When that last bit of business was thankfully over, I headed to the Paramount front gate to await my taxi back to the hotel when Taylor's limousine, with her and the publicist in the back seat, rolled past. She vaguely waved in my direction where I stood talking to the guard, and it was clear we had finally agreed on one thing: we never wanted to see each other ever again.

Before we left, all the champagne had been consumed, and every glass emptied. It was apparent to everyone that the lady had a problem. When I returned to New York, I reported my experience to a New York columnist. A short time later, Taylor checked herself into the Betty Ford Clinic where she met her seventh husband, Larry Fortensky, a construction worker.

I had long held the opinion that for a woman with such worldly power and stature in the public's eye, to be drinking and carrying on as she did was a total waste. Her finest hour—far more important than any performance she ever gave—would be her humanitarian work with AIDS. Her compassion for the downtrodden was a repeating theme in her life and if there was nothing else to her credit, for her AIDS work she deserved a standing ovation. Taylor would die at 79 in 2011.

15

Julie Andrews, Johnny Carson, Frank Sinatra; Michael Dies of AIDS

For the Oct. 1981 cover of the *Saturday Evening Post* magazine, Scavullo was contacted to photograph Mary Kay Ash of Mary Kay cosmetics. Aware of my particular make-up skill with older women, he chose me to do Ash's make-up for the *Post* cover. The photographs he took, and the make-up I did, turned out sensationally.

For my work on the *Post* cover, I opted for my personal collection of make-up—unimpressed with the Mary Kay make-up products, and with no objection from her—and created a most flattering make-up on Mary Kay. When the cover came out she sent me a copy inscribed with a note praising me for making her "look so beautiful" and promptly had one of the Scavullo photos put on plates, another blown up the size of a wall and placed in the lobby entrance of her Dallas office building, and another made into a large silk screen (which Scavullo was peddling at the time) for the living room of her home, which I saw when I was with her again in Dallas for another shoot.

To my shock, when I requested two of the Scavullo photos for my book, the Mary Kay Company raised a hullabaloo, threatening all kinds of legal action for all kinds of things—mostly imagined—and emphatically, unequivocally denied my request.

Well ... what can of beans had I unintentionally opened here? I immediately contacted them and assured them that I would gladly change any text that I had sent them which they may have found offensive, but to no avail. It appeared that the photos Scavullo had taken of Mary Kay had become sacred icons that the company zealously guarded and used for their own purposes. And their legal department even cautioned how I should write about Mary Kay or attribute things she'd said to me—in particular how she'd constructed her company—as if anyone from the company was there during our numerous make-up times together. When someone like Mary Kay—who had amassed a fortune in her lifetime—explains how she achieved success, wouldn't anyone pay attention and remember what had been said? And this they wanted to censor.

My experience with the Mary Kay Company remains a bizarre mystery, clouded by a lot of hostile threats, blustering, and wind-bagging—the kinds of things lawyers are prone to do—but no concrete, reasonable explanation for their denial of the photos. For me it is a tragic ending that diminishes the warmth and love of the woman herself whom I doubt that anyone that I dealt with about this matter knew in her lifetime. Without reservation, I am certain that Mary Kay would've gladly granted me permission to use the Scavullo photos in my book, and I further believe that she would've been appalled at her company's treatment.

I had been prepared to relate several wonderful and interesting stories in my book about my times and my association with Mary Kay: the several ads I did for the company at her request, and my sessions with her consultants on Long Island tutoring them in my method of make-up application, again at her request, and with no charge. I prefer to remember the woman she was rather than the symbol she has apparently become. (For a look at the make-up I did on Mary Kay you can always check the Oct. 1981 cover of the *Saturday Evening Post* magazine.) Her notes to me many times would include nickel crosses for me to give out to friends and others. It is my opinion that one might be considered for the lobby entrance of the Mary Kay Dallas office building as a reminder of their founder's kind and caring nature that may have been forgotten since her passing in 2001.

Having lost his *Vogue* account after insulting art director Alexander Liberman by sending him photographs in a garbage can, Scavullo wangled a new contract with *Harper's Bazaar*, and I began the bulk of my work with celebrities and models that would span the next decade.

Models had thankfully changed from the seventies bunch, like Lauren Hutton, Rene Russo, Margaux Hemingway, and the lot, replaced by Paulina Porizkova, Carol Alt, Iman, and Kim Alexis, who didn't take themselves so seriously, and working with them had become more fun. And though hanging with celebrities still didn't pay the bills, it helped soothe the struggle and made it somewhat seem worthwhile.

Scavullo was astute enough to recognize that I gravitated toward creative people, as I considered myself. Having found models in the past tedious, pampered, pretentious, and dull, I was booked more frequently with celebrities, far more than Way Bandy. While Francesco was impressed and frightened by a lot of celebrities, I had fun with them and liked them— most of them. In turn, the celebrities were in a better frame of mind to face his camera. Simply put, he got better photographs because I primed them first.

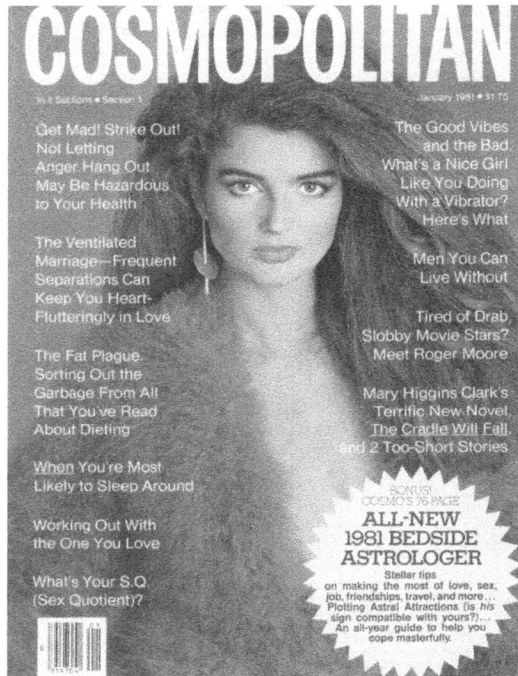

Cosmo cover of beautiful Czech supermodel Paulina Porizkova (courtesy Francesco Scavullo Foundation and Hearst magazines).

With Scavullo and an editor from *Ladies Home Journal* magazine, I went by limousine to Chambersburg, Pennsylvania, where Jean Stapleton's husband had a summer theatre, the Totem Pole Playhouse, at which she appeared in several plays each summer. She told me that after a summer there, before beginning the new season for her famous TV sitcom *All in the Family*, also starring Carroll O'Connor, she had to have reruns of the show shown to her to remember how she had played her character, Edith Bunker.

Diane Sawyer and Jane Pauley were becoming big newswomen on TV, taking some of the thunder from long-time reigning news diva Barbara Walters, and I did their make-up for *Harper's Bazaar*. I discovered that Sawyer was born in the same hospital as I was in my hometown, Glasgow, Kentucky, practically making us kissing cousins. Pauley was a hoot and quite regular, having come from the rebellious, long-haired sixties. She said that she and Sawyer often had lunch together, and I immediately told her a dirty joke, as I had Sawyer, and we all had a good time together.

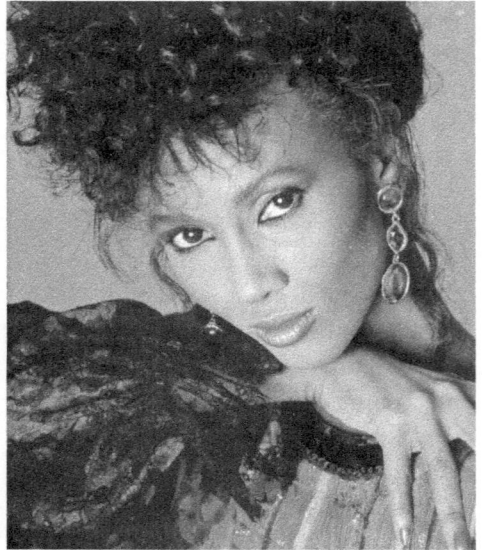

Left: Another beautiful '80s supermodel, Carol Alt, for Italian *Linea* cover (courtesy Francesco Scavullo Foundation). *Right:* Beautiful super-supermodel Iman, who would marry David Bowie (courtesy Francesco Scavullo Foundation, as seen in U.S. *Harper's Bazaar*).

In 1982, Julie Andrews appeared in the spicy movie *Victor/Victoria*, and I did a most sophisticated make-up on her for *Harper's Bazaar*. During the make-up, the hairdresser and I had the cheek to sing to Andrews the old song "Row, Row, Row," from the 1912 Ziegfeld Follies.

After lunch, as Andrews was returning to the dressing room, probably suffering from indigestion after our vocal rendition earlier, Michael called.

"Oh, Julie," I motioned to her before she could get into the dressing room, "would you say hello to my friend Michael?"

Her expression was both reluctance and exasperation, but she kindly granted the request.

"Hello, Michael," she graciously answered. "Yes, he's doing fine," supposedly about me, but I knew Michael was pleased.

I rarely asked favors of stars because I didn't want to impose, but Andrews was a truly special person that I wanted to share with Michael. I'm sure when the shoot was over she and her husband, writer-director Blake Edwards, who made an appearance at the studio that day, fled back to their Santa Monica, California, home, glad to be rid of all of us.

A young Michelle Pfeiffer was in *Grease 2* that year, co-staring Maxwell

Caulfield as the love interest. Pfeiffer was so beautiful that I hardly used any make-up on her. She was just naturally beautiful and needed nothing to make her that way. Observing the hunky Caulfield's impressive muscles, I teased him, asking, "Do you work out?" With a wry smile he answered, "Every so often I do a push up." Oh, sure. Like a billion times a day.

I also made up Helen Gurley Brown, editor-in-chief of *Cosmopolitan* magazine for 32 years—and Scavullo's most persistent client for 30 of them, until Brown left the magazine in 1997, taking with her the publicity and prestige that Scavullo heavily relied on.

Enchanting and sophisticated Julie Andrews (courtesy Francesco Scavullo Foundation, as seen in U.S. *Harper's Bazaar*).

Before I began Brown's make-up, Scavullo cautioned me to especially make her look beautiful, that I intended to anyhow, and I believe the results showed it—though at the party she threw for him at the Pierre Hotel in '97 to celebrate his book, and perhaps her departure from *Cosmopolitan*, she didn't remember me or the make-up.

Oh, well ... so much for impressions. She'd have my many *Cosmo* covers as a reminder.

Then there was Joan Collins, who at the time was in the TV series *Dynasty*. She preferred doing her own make-up—and lots of it. That was fine by me since it gave me time to read a magazine—or was it a book? When she was finished, she requested body make-up, and as I was applying it to her arms, she kept pulling away.

"You don't like being touched," I observed.

"I can't even stand to get a massage."

I wondered how she made love.

When the hairdresser finished with her hair—both strands of it—having ignored her vast collection of wigs, she checked her drowned-rat image in the mirror, thrust her fists on her hips in a huffy way to demonstrate her displeasure, and hissed, "This is it?"

She went immediately to Scavullo and complained, and out came her collection of wigs. The drowned-rat look was obviously not in vogue.

Later, upstairs in Scavullo's apartment over his studio, she was sitting next to me at the dining room table nibbling some food while a female reporter from *Harper's Bazaar* waited patiently at the other end of the long table to do an interview.

I don't know what got into me—perhaps the devil—but I'd heard about her memoir *Past Imperfect: An Autobiography* and wondered out loud, "Does it tell about everyone you slept with in Hollywood?"

Helen Gurley Brown didn't remember my make-up, but she sure looked good (courtesy Francesco Scavullo Foundation).

She dropped whatever she was eating onto her plate and snapped, "It tells about all the people in Hollywood that took advantage of me. I was a young, innocent girl. Why am I talking to you? I want to talk to that reporter," and she immediately got up and went to the reporter at the end of the table.

No time for cheap gossip, I guess.

In contrast, it was a delight making up her sister, Jackie Collins, who had recently published her very successful novel *Hollywood Wives* that would be turned into a TV miniseries in '85. I found Jackie charming, far more interesting—quite witty too—than Joan, who appeared to take herself rather seriously

Opposite: Naturally beautiful Michelle Pfeiffer (here with *Grease 2* co-star Maxwell Caulfield) required little make-up (courtesy Francesco Scavullo Foundation, as seen in U.S. *Harper's Bazaar*).

with the success of her TV show. Jackie and I agreed that Joan continued to play her character, Alexis Karrington, even off screen. Jackie sent a quote for my book: he "gives good make-up"—sexy, witty and real, exactly as she was.

Before sitting at the studio dressing table, Johnny Carson took off his shirt and in his white tee-shirt, puffed himself up and flexed his muscles like a bodybuilder. I didn't know if this was meant as intimidation or his way of saying "The man is here," but this exaggerated declaration of his manhood caused his then wife, Joanna—whom I had made up earlier that day—to cower as if a god had appeared.

By way of idle conversation, as I began Carson's make-up I said, "I made up Lucille Ball not long ago," knowing that he knew her.

"M-m," was his answer.

Not content with that, I pursued. "Must be tough doing that show every night."

"M-m," again came his answer.

"Do you like interviewing people?"

"M-m," it came again.

For someone who made his living talking, he sure didn't do much of it with me. The silence that prevailed throughout the rest of his make-up was deafening.

Frank Sinatra and Luciano Pavarotti were to be in concert together at Radio City Music Hall, and I made up both of them for a shot for *Harper's Bazaar*.

"Maestro," I said to Pavarotti, "do you sing bebop?"

"Bebop?" he questioned, in his rich tenor voice, never having heard of such a thing.

I told Sinatra about it later, and he laughed. He was charming, and we got along quite well, so well that his manager later called me to inquire about my availability for a film Sinatra was considering, which didn't happen. Being an excellent painter, he told me that he had studied with Marc Chagall, the Russian-born Jewish artist whose massive paintings—influenced by his life in Paris—hang in the lobby of the New York Metropolitan Opera. Sinatra denied, however, that he had studied singing—which I had heard wasn't true but didn't question it.

When Ian Schrager and Steve Rubell were released from jail, Studio 54 went back into full swing, and everyone returned to the party. Everyone I knew had never left it.

Michael and I regularly hurt each other with tales of our sexual exploits. Our parents had taught us that love hurts, and so we expressed our hurt and disappointment in our failed relationship by heaping on more hurt.

My latest conquest was a young man I had picked up at the Anvil and invited back to my apartment. We left the bar in the early morning; he took a taxi, while I rode my bike home. Arriving at my building before he did, I saw another man in front of the building walking his dog. He convinced me that the man I had picked up wouldn't show, and so with the philosophy that "a bird in the hand is worth two in the bush," I invited the second man up to my apartment.

Hip Frank Sinatra knew what bebop was but opera superstar Luciano Pavarotti didn't (courtesy Francesco Scavullo Foundation, as seen in U.S. *Harper's Bazaar*).

I had just poured us some wine—my customary beginning for these things—when the doorbell rang. I quickly grabbed the man's glass just as he was tilting it back for his first swallow, and he and his dog left, probably passing the other man on the stairs. When this one arrived, with me at the door holding two glasses of wine, he said, "Ah, you've already poured the wine."

Such was my fidelity and the reason a relationship was impossible.

Michael's current fascination was taxi drivers. Arriving home at some ungodly hour from wherever he had been, who else was around? He claimed he would pass them an erotic photo to arouse them, and they would follow him up to his apartment. More likely, the enticement was cocaine.

He'd had his rugs stolen—of all things—along with his clothing, and a silver bracelet and neck chain from Mexico that I had given him. He called one morning sounding groggy and said he thought he needed to go to a hospital to have his stomach pumped. Someone had slipped him something in his drink, and he had been asleep for two days.

All of this was painful, and I caught myself sometimes thinking that if Michael were only dead, life would be much simpler. Mother got the backlash of my frustration with my intolerance and indifference toward her. The message of love she had sent out had boomeranged and was now circling back at her—and at me, as well.

Then, as if my wish was granted, I saw an article in *Time* magazine—no more than three short paragraphs—that said there was a strange disease targeting gay men. I cut the article out and gave it to Michael. He paid no attention to it, but I took it seriously. The disease had not yet been named: AIDS.

When the disease received its official title, everyone who knew Michael said he looked like he had it. His thighs measured no more around than my arms. It was like a witch-hunt with everyone accusing everyone. The gay community was suddenly in a frenzy.

I had long believed that Michael's weight loss was due to his cocaine use. I thought these AIDS-mongers were ridiculous. There was no cure for this disease. That a young man like Michael—no more than 31 years old—should follow the horde of people dying was out of the question. I was ashamed I had ever even thought such a thing.

I begged him to go to a doctor for his weight loss, but he was going to a Chinese doctor in Chinatown and he would say, "I'm already going to a doctor."

I suspected he didn't want to go to a regular doctor because he was afraid his cocaine habit would be discovered and he would be hassled to give it up. By now, he guarded his cocaine as if it was a matter of life and death—and perhaps for him it was.

He came to my apartment one evening complaining that he had heard people's voices on his roof—his apartment was on the top floor of a brownstone like mine. He said he had also heard them in his fireplace, echoing from the chimney, I supposed. He had called the police, but no one was discovered on the roof.

He also insisted that the people across the street "know."

"Know what?" I inquired.

"They just know."

"Well, I'll tell you what I know. You've been doing coke, and that's why you think all this stuff."

"Okay, if you don't believe me," he said, completely ignoring my insight.

"You see," I reassured myself, "it's only his damn cocaine."

But AIDS was also about cocaine, the abuse of any substance that altered one's reality to the point of careless behavior. And so, this episode of our lives had begun.

We would have a plan to meet at his apartment—where he had a piano—to work on a musical I had written, and he wouldn't be there when I arrived. I would stand on the sidewalk outside his apartment screaming like a lunatic into the phone that I was moving to who-knows-where to get away from him—but there was still no answer, and no relief.

One summer when we'd had one of our plans to meet at my apartment to sunbathe on the roof, he never showed. After being with a friend later that afternoon, I was heading home on my bike when I stopped by a phone booth to call him again for the umpteenth time that day, and he answered.

"Where have you been?" I asked. "We were supposed to meet to sunbathe."

"I've been writing a song," he replied. "I've got the blinds pulled, and I'm writing this song."

"The blinds pulled? It's a beautiful sunny day. Why would you have the blinds pulled?"

"It's a nighttime song."

"Well then ... it's a nighttime song for a sunny day."

I knew at that moment I would use *Nighttime Song for a Sunny Day* as the title for a book I would write someday, and it was the title for this book before a wise agent advised me to change it for a more informative title, as it is now.

On a hot afternoon, I stopped in a West Side gay bar that had the coldest beer in town, and there was Michael coming out of the back room that was purposely kept dark for men to engage in sex.

"Would you like to go to dinner?" he asked.

"No," I said. "I'm going home."

"I don't blame you. I wouldn't want to be with me. I look horrible."

It broke my heart that he felt this way. That was not my reason at all. Had the war I declared on him done this much damage? Friends told me that it wasn't my fault, but I couldn't stop blaming myself.

I finally convinced him to go to a drug rehab at Gracie Square Hospital

on East Seventy-Sixth Street. He left for the rehab with an acupuncture needle stuck in his cap—a poor beginning, I thought. I called his psychiatrist
and told her that I had expected to feel better when I got Michael into a
rehab, but I didn't. She advised me to go to Al-Anon.

I knew of Al-Anon. It's the other side of AA for people who have been
affected by someone's drinking. Even though Michael's problem was mainly
cocaine, all the Twelve Step programs are basically the same. I had even
attended an Al-Anon meeting once with Michael, and he had waited outside
for me. A friend suggested it because of my alcoholic father. I had felt myself
coming apart for some time. I went to my second Al-Anon meeting in March
of '81 and eventually had 23 years in that program.

"I am a grateful member of Al-Anon," I heard a member say.

I could do nothing but cry. People kept passing me Kleenex, which I
didn't want because it called attention to my blubbering condition. I just
wanted to disappear into the wall, but that was impossible with the spectacle
I was making of myself. I couldn't even get up and leave because I couldn't
get to my feet. So I just sat there and blubbered.

At the end of the meeting, the chairperson said, "Is there anyone here
who needs to say something?"

Everyone turned and looked at me, which made me blubber even more.

Still, I was grateful to be there—to be anywhere, at that point. I felt so
destroyed. It wasn't only about Michael; it was a lifetime of my own careless
behavior, perhaps a backlash of my family, that had brought me there.

I went to a party around this time and there was a girl there—someone
I didn't know well—who I had heard was a very spiritual person. I told her
that besides the trouble with Michael, my landlord had me in court trying
to get my apartment away from me, I owed thousands of dollars in legal fees,
my work had drastically fallen off, and I was seriously in debt.

"I don't think you're grateful," the girl said.

I didn't fight it. I didn't say, "Grateful for what? Didn't you hear what
I just told you about my life?" I just took it in, and it became a part of me,
ringing around inside me like a precious chime.

Suddenly, I said, "I am grateful."

I had never thought of the word "grateful" before. I had never thought
to be grateful that I could see, that I had an education paid for by my parents,
that I could read—imagine that. I had two arms, two hands, two legs, and
I had grown up in a beautiful house with nice clothes, plenty to eat, and I
was an American. It had always been about what I hadn't had: the parents

I hadn't had, the circumstances of my childhood, maybe the lack of quality love. But what I had had, and still had, was plenty—a lot more than many people.

And I was grateful most of all that I was beginning a spiritual journey with God. I had heard in Al-Anon the slogan "Let go and let God"—and with nothing else to cling to, I did. At that moment of openness with this girl, I felt a warmth come over me and I again knew—as I had known that early morning in Montauk when I saw that full moon and blazing orange sun facing each other—that there was unmistakably a God and I was grateful to be beginning my journey with that.

Michael stayed in drug rehab for two months. His business fell off, and everyone there was constantly calling trying to persuade me to take care of his two cats of which they had inherited the care. I had told him when he got them—which I was strongly opposed to because he could barely take care of himself—that I would never take care of those cats.

"I'll just go home and take care of them myself," he arrogantly declared on one of my visits to his rehab.

"Suit yourself, but I don't care if they're two tiny skeletons on your living room floor when you get back—I will never take care of them."

I stuck to my guns, and the cats survived. When the two months was up, he came out. I was certain he was by no means recovered. He went to Coke-Anon, but soon he was right back on it. His father had sent him $30,000 to expand his business, but every bit of it went up his nose in seven months.

We would meet occasionally for dinner, but invariably we would get into a fight. It had become unbearable for both of us. We were too angry and disappointed about everything to be together.

Then his mother called. I thought it was odd that she should be in town all the way from California. She said she was taking the cats back to the animal shelter where he had gotten them. She also said he was in the hospital.

I had succeeded in getting him to drop his Chinese doctor, but a regular doctor he went to couldn't find anything neurologically wrong with the problems he constantly complained about, and I suspected he was becoming a hypochondriac. With him being in the hospital now, I was sure of it.

Then his mother dropped the bombshell.

"He's got AIDS," she said, nonchalantly.

She didn't know anything about AIDS any more than the rest of us. Few did at the time. We had heard it was fatal, but our denial translated that to mean fatal for some but not for others. It was the hope we wanted to cling to.

That evening I visited him at Beth Israel Hospital on East Sixteenth Street. I brought the article on AIDS from *Time* magazine that I had previously given him, but he again ignored it, more occupied with a TV show he was watching. His mother reprimanded me that it might upset him—as though, if we paid no attention, it might go away. I felt that if he had something life threatening, he should be aware of it.

He wanted me to steam seaweed and herbal concoctions that the Chinese doctor, who was again back in the picture, advised him to eat for his "condition," refusing to eat the food the hospital provided. I would spend all day steaming the brew, put it in plastic containers, and drag it down to him by bus—even in a snowstorm once.

When I arrived in the snowstorm, he announced, "You're late"—like Elizabeth Taylor's uppity attitude on the set of *General Hospital.*

The attendants at the hospital wouldn't touch anything that had touched him. I had to ask them to come into the room and clean it up. Even I eventually sat across the room from him, dressed in a facemask and doctor's gown, and never touched him. There was panic about how this disease was spread.

His doctor took me into the hall and casually said, as if writing out a routine prescription, "He's got one, maybe two years to live."

Just like that, so clinical, so de-humanized. Perhaps death was commonplace for him, but it wasn't for me—particularly this death. I had met Michael when he was 22; he was about to turn 32. He was supposed to bury me, not the other way around. That this young man should die was incomprehensible.

When I left the hospital that evening, it was beginning to drizzle, but I didn't feel a thing on my walk home—nearly 50 blocks to my apartment.

In my mind, I heard over and over the 23rd psalm: "The Lord is my shepherd, I shall not want."

With rain splattering my face, I knew that what I had learned in Al-Anon was true: that whatever was up ahead, there was a power that would watch over both Michael and me.

When he got out of the hospital, he talked of going back to California, buying a lot of new clothes, and driving up the Pacific Coast Highway, as we had done when we visited his woman friend in San Francisco. He would go straight to a hospital when he got there and stay another month.

We fought constantly before he left; it was our frustration and desperation. He told me that his father advised him not to have anything more to do with me, which, considering how we were fighting, may have been good advice for both of us.

I was incensed. I didn't like his father, and I believed he felt the same about me. To me, he was a cold, unfeeling, prudish man who had given Michael no more emotionally than my father had given me. For that, alone, I disliked him, and he knew it.

"Why don't you tell your father that I didn't shove $30,000 in cocaine up my nose, I'm not an addict, and I don't have AIDS!"

"Tell him yourself."

"I'm not telling him anything. When you go to California, I'll forget all about this." I told the biggest lie of my life, because all I did was think about it and talk about it in Al-Anon.

It was the most life-altering experience of my life. I loved this man, I cared about him deeply, and I was devastated that one day he would no longer be.

His last months in New York were trying for both of us while he wrapped up his business affairs and prepared to leave. We stopped speaking somewhere along the way, and it was a relief when he was finally gone and we couldn't run into one another. I had decided that the city wasn't big enough to accommodate both of us.

After a month in the hospital in L.A., he went to stay at his mother's house in Palm Springs. Soon he wore out his welcome there. When she wouldn't give him his dope—which was ridiculous considering his fatal condition—he called the fire department, the police, and an ambulance service. When they all came screeching up to her door with their sirens blaring, she threw his dope at him and told him she didn't care what he did. He then went to his father's house in the hills of Encino.

His father, incensed that Michael had blown the $30,000 on cocaine and that he now had AIDS, threw a sleeping bag on the floor and said, "This is where you sleep."

Eventually resigning himself to the inevitability of what was happening, his father became more compassionate. I, too, softened and made contact.

"I saw a shooting star tonight," Michael wrote me, having accepted his fate, "and I wished for the courage to go through what I must."

That was the last letter I had from him.

I called him a week before he died and said, "No matter what, Michael, you were always the best."

I heard him yell out the window by the bed where he lay, "You hear that, God? You hear what he says about me?"

His mother called a week later. I knew what it meant.

"Don't say it," I said. "I understand," and hung up.

I didn't want to hear "Michael is dead." I couldn't bear to hear that. Grieving, I went home, hoping to find solace.

Mother, only intending to help—though she had a way of sticking her foot in her mouth every time she tried—said, "Well, that's over. Now, go on."

"Go on?" I said, incredulously. As if you just go on after something as life shattering as that—as easily as getting over a scraped knee.

I recognized that this was how she had dealt with my father's death: denied her feelings, as she had always done with everything.

"You don't just go on," I said, "after ten years like that. I loved him."

"Love?" she said. "Love!" Like it was the most despicable thing she could think of between two men.

"Yes," I said. "I loved him. Like you did Daddy."

"That was different."

"No, it wasn't. And you're not going to take this away from me as you have before—not this time. I loved him, and I don't care what anyone thinks."

Mother and I grew up at that moment because there was nothing left to hide.

Michael made me feel alive when I thought I had lost the capacity to feel anything. Unlike Mother, he accepted me for what I was without question and never asked for more. I loved him just because he was, and I believe he felt the same way about me.

We were perfect for one another; even our flaws were perfect, just as we were. But we were trained to question and pick things apart, and so in pieces, we couldn't put Humpty Dumpty together again. We just separated, and we could never find the rest of us.

I have learned that when something is the real thing, bless it and accept it as the entire thing it is. In pieces, nothing looks the same as the whole and, after all, it was the whole we fell in love with.

16

Rose Kennedy, Shirley MacLaine and Al-Anon

One doesn't easily get over devastating events in life. Friends would remind me that it takes time—that old cure-all—but I knew there were some things in life that we may never get over, not completely. It felt like a part of me had permanently died—a part of me would always be sad.

A friend asked if I was over it, and I answered, "Do you ever really get over someone you have truly loved?" not to mention someone who has died.

And so, with the help of Al-Anon, I went on. To my gratitude list I added small, precious things like Mother's jams and jellies, her beautiful rose garden, my aunt's oyster dressing at Thanksgiving and Christmas, the tree my father and I chopped down in the forest each Christmas, the watermelon my cousin put in the creek to keep cool while we swam, my grandmother's wet kisses that I detested as a child but I wished for now, my childhood black cocker spaniel, Inky, and our family outings to the ocean each summer. These were the things I wanted to remember—the good things—and let the shadows and the bad fade like invisible ink.

I hadn't officially finished with all my cavorting, and a couple of times a year I would call a woman friend I knew who liked to frolic and we would get terribly drunk. The hangovers were excruciating and limited our activity to only infrequent get-togethers. I was still hurting and angry—I was aware of this—and I would take my anxiety out on myself and pay for it.

Drunk, I became involved with a black hustler at a bar one night, but I left alone. He followed me, and I stopped and gave him $20.

"You don't have to do anything for it," I established my reason. "Just do the same for someone else someday."

I turned and continued on home and he continued following, probably anticipating more where that came from. I took him up to my apartment, anyhow, and as we entered, I was aware of his attraction to my stereo. He climbed into my bed and got himself off, and as I went for a paper towel for him to wipe himself, I took a butcher knife from my kitchen cabinet.

When he finished with the paper towel, I pushed the knife against his throat and said, "This is for you if you touch anything in here. Understand?"

"Yes, sir," he said.

"Now, go to sleep."

"Yes, sir," he repeated.

I spent the night with the knife under my pillow and never slept.

In the morning, he got out of bed and I asked him where he was going.

"To the bathroom," he answered. "Are you going to get the butcher knife after me again?"

I had taken from his pants pocket the $20 I had given him the night before, and he discovered it missing as he was leaving.

"That was last night and this is now," I said, and gave it back. I had meant what I said: it was a gift to give someone else someday; it wasn't mine.

When he was gone, I recognized what a long way I had to go in Al-Anon to recover. I was so appalled at my behavior that I went in the opposite direction: I gave up sex and all gay men in my life and only cultivated straight people, particularly women. I was searching for the family nurturing that I hadn't had. I was terrified of repeating my past relations with gay men and felt untrustworthy and destructive with my philandering.

I even went so far as to try to convert myself to a heterosexual, as I had once been able to function. A straight friend from Al-Anon gave a party around this time where the men and women were looking to pair up. I was one of them. As a game, we were all expected to go into a room where a video was set up and tell a joke on camera that would later be shown to the group. When it was my turn I went in and told my joke, but when it was shown, I had the saddest face I had ever seen. Sadness was written all over it. I recognized that I was in no shape to have a relationship with anyone, heterosexual or otherwise. If I was to recover, I would have to be true to myself. Trying to be something I wasn't had caused me pain as far back as when Mother had tried to inflict her ideas on me. I was never dissatisfied with who I was. It was society's attitude about it that had made me unhappy, not my own. This self-examination and policing of my activities continued throughout the rest of the '80s.

I had bought a bill of goods when I was young from people like Tod in Paris, who had spewed his bromides—"You're a long time in the grave. Make hay while the sun shines"—like every available gay carnal intimacy was a duty to fulfill. The sun shined all right—over a thousand men I once calculated I'd had, and that might even be conservative considering three a week for years (at times, three a day), and that adds up after a while. The horrible result of that activity was that it took my friend away. I was one of the lucky ones.

What I had been trying to prove with all of those multiple partners was that I was wanted, worthy, necessary. I was looking for an outside source to validate me. I was told that Mother could do my life better than I could, and I was left with no sense of myself. For those moments with a stranger, or with booze and pot, I felt empowered—as if I had value. When the sedatives wore off, I was back to nothing and had to replenish myself. I discovered that not all the sex, booze, and pot in the world could give me self-worth. It was an inside job. I had to first learn to love and accept myself.

I had made Mother or Michael, or sex and substances, my God. When I stopped the chatter in my head that said, "Without us you're nothing," I heard a still, small voice inside say, "I am with you always. I will never desert you." This was the power greater than myself, greater than anyone or anything, that Al-Anon had promised. I chose to call that power God, and we have been partners ever since.

I began to understand that whatever had happened in my life, I ultimately had to take the responsibility. We can blame Mommy and Daddy, people, places, and things, but we must inevitably pick up the cards we were dealt and deal with them—or remain petulant children all of our lives, stomping our feet and insisting that things be done our way.

One night in Al-Anon, I was sharing that I felt like I was coming to a great precipice and I was going to go over.

Some woman who was one step away from being a homeless person came up to me after the meeting and said, "Oh, I don't want you to go over a precipice."

It was Christmas time, and I couldn't afford a trip home to visit my mother and sister, but this woman, the poorest of the poor, had reached out and given me the richest gift of all: caring. I left the meeting that night, and it was beginning to lightly snow. With snowflakes dancing all around me, I blessed that woman, Al-Anon, and all the people there. They were giving me another gift: the gift of hope. My life was truly blessed.

So, my slow recovery back to life began, breaking down the "me" I had hastily constructed in my youth for protection, the facade I had put up to fend off adversaries, and the foundation I had built on sand that had been crumbling for years. In its place, I was constructing my own building, my own self according to what I was learning, and this time Mother wasn't the master-builder.

I began not to respond as I once had to what she said. She would try to dictate, but it didn't feel as threatening and invasive as it once had. I took what I liked and left the rest behind, as Al-Anon instructed. I was learning a road map for my life. Without one, how can we tell where we're going and how will we know if we've even gotten there? I was designing a new me, and a new plan for my life. Most importantly, it was *my* design and *my* plan.

Through my encouragement, Mary, who had developed a drinking problem like so many then, went into AA. But it was short lived. She and her alcoholic boyfriend broke up, and she struggled with all of it for years. Too beguiled by the bottle to commit to giving it up, she was in and out of the program and in and out of other relationships, too. A sense of hopelessness overtook her. Unable to see any other way out, she took her life, adding another friend to the list of those who were in the Hall of Shame.

I was remorseful for whatever I had contributed with our past careless behavior, but as much as I would have wanted to save Mary, it was ultimately her responsibility. Alcohol had weakened her to the point that she couldn't do it, and as one friend pointed out, she may have even been bipolar. Perhaps the depression aggravated by alcohol was too much for her to handle—so I let go of another person that I had cared about deeply.

With the scare of AIDS, bars and baths were closing. St. Mark's Baths fought it for years, but finally closed in the '90s. The Anvil and the Mine Shaft also closed their doors, but not necessarily voluntarily. Everyone was terrified to go there. No one was looking for that kind of trouble anymore. This was a matter of life and death.

The straight world pointed the finger of blame at the gays for this, and the empowerment and freedom that were gained by the Stonewall Inn riot in 1969 evaporated overnight. If someone suspected that you were gay, there was fear that you might be carrying the virus, and they were cautious. The stigma continued throughout the decade.

Reaganomics and Reagan's optimistic outlook made the country feel that we were richer than we were. It was all done with mirrors and, in actuality, we were sinking further into debt. Still, we were on a spending spree with new building and construction everywhere, and we liked feeling richer than we had been in decades.

Since AIDS was widely considered a gay disease, only a small portion of Reagan's budget was appropriated toward it—relatively little compared with what his Star Wars program would have required. Gays were an unpopular group with the voters, and many secretly considered them second-class citizens. By the time the world accepted the disease as part of the entire culture, the hold it had gotten on society sent science scrambling to keep it under control throughout the following decades.

As the country prospered, so did my work. Then Scavullo got the job of his career that would also include me. *Harper's Bazaar* wanted a photo of the 93-year-old Rose Kennedy for an upcoming article about great living Americans, and they chose Francesco to shoot it. He had recently been hospitalized for gallstones and had to come out of the hospital to do it. Gallstones or not, he was not going to miss the opportunity to shoot with the Kennedy family. Still in excruciating pain and tanked up on extreme painkilling drugs, he willed himself to do this.

When I arrived at the studio, Francesco's two assistants were already loading the camera equipment into a large black limousine parked out front. Assisted by an unsuspecting, pretty young blonde nurse in a white uniform, Francesco dramatically came out of the door in a long white shirt—much too large for his diminutive frame—that trailed outside his flowing black pants, a pair of dainty black slippers that may have belonged to a ballerina, and a large white Panama hat that covered his jet-black toupee that he always carefully combed into his sparse, dyed black hair. He told us that his boyfriend, Sean, had dressed him—but for what was unclear.

His face was the face of a madman. I recognized that he was in no condition to shoot anyone, let alone a Kennedy at the Kennedy Compound. It would be a trip legends are made of.

Crammed uncomfortably inside the limousine with the camera equipment, the two assistants, a hairdresser, me, the nurse, a driver, and Francesco babbling a million miles a second every detail of our trip into a small recorder—deluded that he was preserving some important historical event that he would later have typed into text—we headed to the airport where we were to catch a small New England shuttle plane for Hyannis Port. I shuddered to think what would happen with Francesco hopped up on dope.

We were thankful, at least, to be inside the air-conditioned limousine and out of the oppressive July heat, but Francesco's incessant babbling into his recorder was wearing us down.

Uncomfortable with the condition inside himself and unable to do anything about it but pop another pill, he looked at me and loudly announced, "What would you do if I farted?"

"I guess we'd record it," I returned.

The humor made the trip slightly more bearable.

A Kennedy limousine met us at the airport in Hyannis Port, and the crew with the equipment all piled inside, while Francesco continued his ranting—this time that the Kennedys had had a hand in the demise of "poor Marilyn Monroe," as he put it.

"They just took a pillow, shoved it on her face, and sat on it," he declared repeatedly with great relish.

We tried to calm him down, but the pills were in control and doing the talking.

The recognizable limousine reached the compound, the guard waved it through, and in front of us on a rolling green lawn was a medium-sized, very New England white frame house with a grey shingled roof overlooking the bay and another house, almost an exact duplicate next door, which, we were told, belonged to the Bobby Kennedy family.

As the limousine cruised through the grounds, Francesco—not content with his indictment of the Kennedys over Marilyn Monroe—started another story. This time it concerned a woman who received a telegram and asked the man who delivered it to sing it to her.

"Oh, I don't think you want this sung, ma'am," he said.

"Oh, please," the woman pleaded. "I've never had a singing telegram."

After several more pleas, he finally relented.

"Okay. If that's what you want," and he began with a little musical introduction: "Ta-dum, ta dum, dum, dum. Your sister Rose is dead!"

"Por favor, Francesco," I said, as he gleefully shouted this out just as we pulled up in front of the main house where, on a large front porch overlooking the bay, Eunice Shriver came down the steps to greet us. On the porch, sitting in a rattan chair with her back turned away from the glare of the sea, was a frail Rose Kennedy in a large straw hat and a shawl over her shoulders in the near 90-degree temperature.

Francesco leaped from the limousine, briefly acknowledged Eunice, and, brushing past her, rushed onto the porch to meet his startled subject.

"Oh, Mrs. Kennedy," he gushed, "I've always wanted to meet you."

Mrs. Kennedy, with her worn, lined, world-weary face, looked up and said, "Why?"

Taken aback, Francesco continued, "Well, because of who you are."

"Why?" she responded again.

Recognizing the need to get the photo shoot over with before her mother was too weak to do it, Eunice broke in.

"Where do you want her?"

"Just leave her where she is," I answered the question, knowing that my job with make-up was first and not wanting to disorient the woman by transporting her about as if she were a potted plant.

As I got out my make-up and readied myself for the job ahead, Francesco complained that he needed to lie down and insisted on doing it in the bed where John Kennedy had slept. Eunice graciously obliged and took him inside the house while the rest of us busied ourselves with our tasks.

I approached Mrs. Kennedy and introduced myself.

"Who's this for?" she asked, as I began my work.

"*Harper's Bazaar*, Mrs. Kennedy."

"Oh, yes. I know these things are important. My husband was an ambassador and they were always important."

"I know, Mrs. Kennedy," I said, continuing.

Suddenly, water began pouring from her mouth like a spigot had been turned on, and I stepped back to keep from being splattered.

A hefty nurse in a white uniform—who had obviously seen it from inside the house—shot out the screen door with a bucket and pushed it under the woman's mouth. What was left of the water poured into it.

"Because of the heat she's been drinking a lot of water," the nurse explained, "but she can't keep it down."

It totally washed off all the make-up I had just applied, and I had to begin again. During the next round, Mrs. Kennedy repeatedly asked Eunice how old she was.

"Ninety-three, Mother," Eunice patiently and lovingly answered the question each time it was asked, only to answer it several more times before the make-up was complete. It was evident the love Eunice had for the matriarch of the Kennedy clan who had known unfathomable tragedies with her oldest son killed in a plane crash, two others murdered for political reasons, a daughter in an institution, and her husband crippled by a stroke and confined to a wheelchair for years.

When I was finished, I gave Mrs. Kennedy a mirror to view what I had done.

"The mouth." She pointed to the small V-shape in the middle of her upper lip that I had rounded off and ignored because it was now absent in a woman this age. She remembered it, however, and wanted it back, so I immediately restored it. Eunice then took her inside the house to choose her clothing for the shoot as Francesco, assisted by his nurse, made his appearance refreshed from his nap in John Kennedy's bed.

He and his nurse hobbled out to the site that had been chosen for the shoot, where his assistants had set up the camera equipment by the bay with the house in the background. Soon Mrs. Kennedy, in a sparkling white sweater ensemble, assisted by her nurse and Eunice—with one of Francesco's assistants holding an umbrella over her head to shield her from the sun— hobbled out to the site. Each step of the way, she complained that she wasn't sure she could do this, and was constantly encouraged by Eunice and the nurse that she could.

In the meantime, Francesco, steadied by his nurse and an assistant, resumed mumbling about Marilyn Monroe and how the Kennedys allegedly shoved a pillow over her face and sat on it. When he wasn't mumbling that, he was mumbling how mean his father had been to him. Everyone was mumbling something about something.

When the group arrived at the site, with Mrs. Kennedy complaining that she wasn't sure she could do this, or that she didn't want to do this, and everyone assuring her that she could, and Francesco rattling on about Marilyn Monroe and his mean father, Eunice, like a drill sergeant from hell, suddenly bellowed out, "All right, Mother!"

Out of astonishment, or maybe fear at hearing such a determined, I-damn-well-mean-it voice bellow out, everyone, for that moment, straightened up.

"One, two, three!" Eunice counted, and Mrs. Kennedy dropped the arm that had been clinging to Francesco's assistant holding the umbrella over her head, snapped her hand to her hip, threw back her head like she didn't have a care in the world, and beamed a radiant smile that would have beguiled the angels. Francesco clicked his shutter.

Immediately following, everything fell apart, with Mrs. Kennedy continuing her complaint that she couldn't do another, Eunice insisting that she could, while the nurse held her up and the assistant kept the umbrella over her head, and Francesco rattled on about the Kennedys and Marilyn

Monroe and how brutal his father had been, when again Eunice bellowed out, "All right, Mother!"

Everyone snapped to attention; all dissension ceased.

"One, two, three!"

Mrs. Kennedy again snapped her hand to her hip, threw back her head like she didn't have a care in the world, and beamed that radiant smile. Click went Francesco's shutter.

That was it. Mrs. Kennedy hobbled back to the house with Eunice and the nurse and went to bed. Francesco, assisted by his nurse, followed and did the same. That was the last we saw of either of them for the rest of the afternoon.

Eunice graciously and

No one would have suspected the chaos behind the scene at this shoot of 93-year-old Rose Kennedy (courtesy Francesco Scavullo Foundation, as seen in U.S. *Harper's Bazaar*).

unexpectedly served the crew lunch. What else could she do with all these people at her house and unable to go anywhere with Francesco in one of her beds? Her husband, Sargent Shriver, also joined us in the dining room. Afterwards, I walked through the living room viewing the private photos on the walls of the family and John and Bobby. I couldn't help but think that perhaps someday this might be a museum open to the public that I was privileged to view alone.

Later, Mrs. Kennedy's nurse took me to see the indoor pool with a ramp in the water to accommodate Joe Kennedy's wheelchair that allowed him to exercise. With Eunice and her youngest son, Anthony, and one of Francesco's assistants, I went for a sail around the bay in their boat. It was a glorious day—one for the memory books.

In spite of the fact that there were only two tries, the photo of Rose

Kennedy turned out fabulously. Who would have known all the tension behind the scene? She really looked like she didn't have a care in the world. This was truly a great living American.

It seemed that the 1980s floated past like a dream from one job to the next: a model one day, a celebrity the following. Other than Scavullo's camera, there were always cameras everywhere: on the set or in your face while you were doing a make-up, catching everything short of your going to the bathroom. And even there I wouldn't have been surprised if there'd been a camera. Scavullo was obsessed with recording everything for something he believed he would write or photograph for a book. The books he'd produced so far only whetted his appetite for more, and needing the money, or wanting it, he fantasized he was continually involved in his next big hit. Everything he did, every celebrity he photographed, was geared to it. It was like existing and participating in storybook land.

He even somehow got involved photographing baseball players in their locker room with little clothing on or naked in the shower. It wasn't a bad idea, recording players in degrees of nudity, and there certainly would've been a curiosity about such a book, but the players were having none of it and Scavullo and his crew were eighty-sixed from the locker room.

So much for jockstrap athletes.

For me personally it was an era of getting my life together in Al-Anon. I had been introduced to a power greater than myself, and I was grateful. Gratitude had become an important word in my life. I had stopped all sexual activity, not only because of the AIDS scare, but because I wanted to. Michael's death had taken away all incentive. It'd had a sobering effect.

I began seeing a therapist, and she would say, "Well, you're gay. What about meeting other gay men?"

I really didn't have a need. For years, I had met men for sex only and never got to know any of them. This was, unfortunately, how most of the gay community operated. There was no dating as straights had been doing since they were kids. Gays had no experience at that, and, consequently, most that I met had emotions that were immature and unformed. Forget about social skills. Many times, you didn't even know their name. When sex is the objective, names are unimportant; talking is unimportant. I had gotten burned by the men I did get to know, and I wasn't so willing to venture out again.

I was content with the Al-Anon meetings where I met straight men and women who were forming the family I never had and I was happy with that. Who needed more? The truth was that I didn't want to face my feelings and the disappointment that was bottled up inside. I had never really grieved Michael; I had just gotten on with my life. I was even surprised by how easy it had been.

I joined a church group called Unity, a metaphysical interpretation of the Bible, and it was on one of their retreats that one day, during a discussion about love, I broke down and wept deep sobs from a depth I didn't know I had. I realized how much I had loved Michael, how sad I was over the loss, and how much I missed him in my life. Mother's love, which was the only love I had ever experienced other than Michael's, was so conditional, based on her set of rules: if you did things her way, she gave love; if you didn't, she withdrew it. It was such a wonderful revelation to realize that, at least, one time someone had loved me unconditionally. But what a bittersweet memory that it was gone forever. How grateful I was, though, that I had had it once. Better to have loved and lost than never to have loved—and been loved—at all.

As the '80s rolled on, with the years passed my deepest sorrow. I was discovering new possibilities and understandings. Someone at Al-Anon one evening remarked that death brought with it fringe benefits. Though I would never have chosen that route to bring it, my emotions were maturing, and I felt an expansion of spiritual growth—perhaps partly from growing older.

Even the make-ups I did had become easier and more fun because I wasn't as self-conscious and concerned about the outcome as I once was. With my creative juices going into my writing it freed me, an experience I had never really had. I now knew that make-up wouldn't be forever; I now had alternatives.

For *Harper's Bazaar*, I made up Anne Bancroft and Mel Brooks after their film *To Be or Not to Be*, a forgettable rehash not to be compared with the brilliant 1942 Ernst Lubitsch film by the same name starring Jack Benny and Carole Lombard. Bancroft complained that she would rather be tending her flower garden than having a make-up and ridiculed Brooks for wearing false eyelashes—whatever for? After a tussle with me over her lipstick, she swore—jokingly, I hope—that she'd never forget me. Brooks reported that every time the limousine they arrived in came to a stop, the doors flew open. I doubted that I should take him seriously, and decided the same was true of his wife.

The Thorn Birds was a blockbuster TV miniseries spanning several weeks and starring Richard Chamberlain and Rachel Ward, a previous model—with an impressive performance by Barbara Stanwyck—and I did Ward's make-up for the second time for *Harper's Bazaar*. After this, Shirley MacLaine—who was in the film *Terms of Endearment*, for which she won an Oscar—came into my make-up life.

MacLaine was bright but tedious with her endless prattle about Martians, something one might expect from her after her 1983 book *Out on a Limb*. MacLaine was definitely out on a limb. When she asked me who had the greatest face I ever worked on—a question that had been asked me a zillion times and always bored me—I replied that it was Bella Abzug, the New York politician who ran for the Senate in '76 and a friend of MacLaine's. Abzug was by no means a beautiful woman—some might even say she was downright homely—but her face was dynamic, strong, and angular. Besides, it threw people off when I said that. Who was I going to single out as the greatest face? All of them had some redeeming quality. Some were more tiresome than others, however—a point of fact in this case.

At first MacLaine accepted my evaluation until she considered my sincerity and quickly added, "Are you kidding?"

I considered her disbelief and returned, "Why do you ask?"

There must have been some question in her mind one way or the other. At any rate, neither of us broached the subject again.

To illustrate a scene that had been cut from *Terms of Endearment*—which she obviously relished doing and was sorry it was gone—she used me as a stand-in actor for the maid in the film. MacLaine's character, Aurora, was a ranting, raving, barely controlled harpy who was overbearing in the film and totally unbearable doing this scene with me. I decided that the real reason she insisted on displaying the scene was to have another chance to rant and rave, which she unmistakably enjoyed, but which was as unpalatable to me as it was in the film.

MacLaine came into my make-up life again when she did her 1984 Broadway show titled *Shirley MacLaine on Broadway*. She had been discovered on Broadway in the 1954 show *Pajama Game* by Hollywood producer Hal B. Wallis, who happened to be in the audience the evening she replaced the injured dancer Carol Haney.

This time around, I got word that MacLaine wanted body make-up, too, and I made a special trip to a theatrical store on Broadway to purchase it for the shoot. She was not one to tolerate much time on make-up, so I was rushed putting all the make-up on her face and body—a lot of territory to cover that requires patience, of which she had very little.

She scolded me as I carefully outlined her receding lips.

"This is silly," she said, pulling away.

Maybe she thought it made her more of a trouper not caring about her lips, but it would have been sillier for her to appear on camera with smeared lips. It may not have threatened her career, but it did reflect on me. No matter how many successes an artist has had, you're still considered just as good as your last make-up. It was the same impatience that Anne Bancroft had showed with her lips.

Shirley MacLaine endlessly prattled about aliens (courtesy Francesco Scavullo Foundation, as seen in U.S. *Harper's Bazaar*).

Glenn Close, too, became impatient when I outlined her lips and left them that way while the hairdresser did her hair. An outline around the lips is merely a guide to where the final lip color will go, and she mistook it for the finished design.

Lips aren't easy to do. One slip of the red outlining pencil in the wrong direction and a woman can look like a clown. It is necessary that they remain still and quiet and have patience. Judith Krantz, the writer of such women's fiction as *Princess Daisy* and *Scruples*, talked so incessantly throughout the lining of her lips that I could hardly land the pencil on her face. It was evident why her books were so thick: she had plenty to say.

MacLaine's face had been lifted, and her lips were stretched, as well as receding. At a certain age, every woman's lips recede, and this requires even more careful drawing to make them look plump and youthful. Many aren't aware what is required and how hard the artist must work to restore things that are altered or disappearing on their face. They only remember how easy it was when they were young and think that it should still be this way, but those features took a walk—a long walk—down memory lane ages ago.

After the shoot, MacLaine wanted me to wipe her down with a damp washcloth to remove the body make-up. Instead of going upstairs to Francesco's private bathroom that was offered her and washing it off herself, she crammed us both into the small studio bathroom, folded her arms tightly across her bosom like a pretzel to cover herself, and then expected me to rub off what I couldn't even get to. I complained until, in exasperation, she released her arms, out came her boobs, and she grabbed the washcloth and got the stuff off herself as she should have done in the first place.

Stars can ask the strangest things of artists and then make the job impossible to do. It is with great relief when an artist has few like that in their career. Unfortunately, mine was littered with neurotics.

17

Fear in the Streets,
Drew Barrymore, Madonna;
My Mother Dies

In 1984, Reagan won his second term against Walter Mondale, only to have it marred by the Iran-Contra affair in 1987, for which others would get the blame, leaving the resilient Reagan unscathed. Even his 1987 challenge to Gorbachev—"Mr. Gorbachev, tear down this wall!—was probably a matter of good timing and economically beneficial for both Russia and Germany, but lucky Reagan still got credit for the Berlin Wall's destruction in '89.

In the late '80s, the real estate market that had begun with such a boom—due, in part, to Reagan's rosy outlook that promised more money than there was—collapsed. Prestigious stores along Fifth Avenue, like Bonwit Teller's, closed from lack of revenue and lack of tourists. With the crime in New York, no one wanted to come to the city anymore. Walking down Fifth Avenue was like being in a ghost town. Broadway shows, too, were in jeopardy; vacant apartments were everywhere from the extensive construction, and all business in the city was threatened.

Not until 1994, when Rudy Giuliani, a tough former U.S. Attorney with the Narcotics Unit, took over the Mayor's office from David Dinkins would the city truly get back on its feet again. With desperately needed cops added to the force, "zero tolerance" for crime, a crackdown on the mob, and the resurrection of Times Square and 42nd Street to their former glory to attract tourists, Giuliani made New York City thrive again and even made it the safest city in America. Until then, however, the AIDS epidemic raged on, and throughout all of the '80s, the battered city limped along.

In '84 I did a make-up on nine-year-old Drew Barrymore. One might ask why a child that age would need make-up. Drew had deep circles under her eyes, perhaps from stress and overwork, and needed coverage to hide that and a bit of blush to brighten her tired, drawn face. She was precocious and quite determined, even bossed her mother around, and when she wanted something, she got it. She knew exactly how she wanted to look and recognized quality in the make-up she got. She wasn't unfriendly, but she was not particularly friendly either. She was somewhat reserved and basically used her amiability when it was required.

During the make-up, she wanted a Coca-Cola. I reminded her mother that the caffeine and sugar in a coke were stimulants like alcohol and with the Barrymores' weakness to that, it might be prudent to skip the Cokes. Drew got it anyhow because she wanted it. She would later have addiction problems that her strong, determined will would overcome.

She was curious about night life in New York City—it seemed she couldn't grow up fast enough. In spite of her young age she was occasionally taken to clubs. I wasn't surprised when, sometime later, a photo of her, still an adolescent, appeared in a publication that looked as though she was inebriated. For one so young, it was shocking. I was glad when she overcame her addiction and became the responsible young adult and accomplished actor she is today. In fact, I still have the tooth she lost on that shoot when she was nine and would gladly return it to her, if I ever see her again.

In '85 Rock Hudson died of AIDS, bringing Elizabeth Taylor into the fight and giving her a purpose she had never had before. GMHC, the Gay Men's Health Crisis organization that was set up to deal with the disease in the gay community, kept saying that it wasn't just the problem of gay males but one of humanity, but the heterosexual community didn't hear it. By 2004, the "gay disease" would claim women as a third of its victims.

In '85, I did what I considered a beautiful cover for *Harper's Bazaar* of model Kim Alexis, and I also made up Madonna, who was appearing in her first film, *Desperately Seeking Susan*, which she stole—as they say in film language—from the intended star, Rosanna Arquette. It was probably Madonna's best film effort even today because the character she played was the closest to who she was at the time.

She wore tons of bracelets on her wrists and had scruffy hair that looked as though it had never been washed, thick, heavy eyebrows, and a Lower East Side rebellious attitude of a young woman on a quest. I had no idea who this oddball was, but I instantly recognized that she knew exactly what she wanted and how to get it, and intended to be a star. It was practically

Left: Harper's Bazaar cover of beautiful '80s supermodel Kim Alexis (courtesy Francesco Scavullo Foundation, as seen in U.S. *Harper's Bazaar*). *Right:* Madonna knew exactly what she wanted and how to get it (courtesy Francesco Scavullo Foundation, as seen in U.S. *Harper's Bazaar*).

written all over her face—which, by the way, wasn't a bad face: a little dirty-looking, but okay.

I did a make-up that enhanced the dark quality around her eyes, which were naturally shaded by her overbearing eyebrows. The eye shadow I used—a moss-greenish concoction I mixed up—swept her eyebrows into the darkness around her eyes and made her eyes even more intense. She was great in front of the camera—not so great when she had to speak and move, but great sitting still looking intensely into the camera lens. When she had to move or speak, it was strained, unless she was posing, and then she came alive from one pose to the next, which created a movement that was distinctly Madonna.

I came into the studio dressing room to get something and found her standing in front of a full-length mirror looking at the outfit she had just gotten into. It was a black, nun-like, wrap-around thing that was hooded, silhouetting her face against the black, with masses of crosses hanging around her neck. With only her face showing, she looked luminous, like a vision. I wasn't sure if I should worship this vision or put it on a runway and claim it as the newest fashion.

"Oh, my God," I gasped, as I entered the dressing room.

She turned and looked at me, not knowing if I approved or disapproved. Either way, she was up for the challenge. I did approve, and it instantly became apparent.

"You like?" she smiled.

"Yes," I managed, but I was in shock.

I had never seen anything with such a twist on religion, in a rock and roll sort of way, with a blend of blasphemy and irony. It was quite distinct and even amusing, and uniquely Madonna. I recognized that she was one of a kind. She was going somewhere; I had no idea where—perhaps hell—but she was sure to get there.

My agent booked me for a job with the outspoken, gnome-like sexologist Dr. Ruth Westheimer, known to TV audiences as Dr. Ruth. She was famous for her TV appearances, where from the mouth of this innocent-looking older woman with tiny, twinkling eyes and a scratchy, mouse-like voice with a German accent would come the most outrageous sexual information—more than any talk show host wanted to hear, but which they always encouraged because the public loved it and the ratings shot up every time she uttered "dildo," "penis," or "anus."

Unable to resist, when I finished the make-up and she was waiting for the photographer to complete his lighting arrangement, I said, "Whatever you do today, Dr. Ruth, just don't say 'penis.'"

With that familiar twinkle in her eyes, she pointed her finger at me and said, "You want to say penis."

She was right. I just did.

Some time after Ruth, Valerie called from Boston to report her lung cancer.

I had repeatedly warned her for years about her heavy smoking, and she now said, "Tell everyone not to smoke"—ironic and a little late.

Her two daughters on Martha's Vineyard would now have to witness their mother's slow agonizing death from starvation—lying on a couch day and night, consuming no food—until she died. In what could have been her finest hour making amends and helping heal the scars her daughters had suffered from her five marriages, Valerie chose, instead, to end her life as she had lived it: strictly for herself.

I called her at the end and offered to come visit her before she went, but she refused. She didn't want anyone to see her in that condition, which

I understood. When it was over, her youngest daughter called and asked me to come up for the funeral. I was on my way home to visit my own mother for Christmas, and this time I refused. There was nothing more to be done for Valerie, and it was now time for the rest of us to do what was best for us and get on with our lives.

Paraphrasing Henry David Thoreau's *Walden*, perhaps we all live lives of quiet desperation. Valerie lived hers in a desperate search for something she never found, and selfishness was the legacy she left behind.

"This is the way the world ends," T.S. Eliot wrote in his 1925 poem "The Hollow Men." "Not with a bang but a whimper."

When I went home that Christmas to visit Mother, she was at the Louisville airport to meet me, as she always was when I flew in. As usual, she had forgotten where she left the car in the parking lot, and it took a bit of looking to locate it. I had told her to tie a scarf around the radio aerial to help locate the car in the future, but she never did. She was frail, and I told her that she looked "feeble," at which she bristled.

She could never accept anything but that she always looked beautiful all of her life. And after being with her at home for a day, all signs of age or anything negative magically vanished and she only looked beautiful to me again. It was the most amazing feat and I could never figure out how she did it. Her identity was beauty, and she intended to keep it that way. My sister once told me that Mother didn't look well, which concerned me, and I made the mistake of repeating it to Mother.

"She must have been drunk," was her response.

My sister doesn't drink.

Our Christmas and New Year's together went by so swiftly that it seemed I had hardly gotten there before it was time to return to New York. On Christmas morning, we had exchanged our presents in front of the fireplace in the living room. Because of her frail constitution, she was unable anymore to purchase gifts from the closest large city, Louisville, and had to settle for what she could find in our small rural town—not exactly what I might have bought for myself in New York. I tried to appear enthusiastic and thought I had achieved it until one of them forced me to confess that she really should return it and get her money back because I was sure I'd never wear it. I tried to be tactful, but perhaps my distaste showed, and it came out hurtful. Her revenge came when she opened one of my presents to her: a beautiful wig of real hair that I had made up in New York especially for her in a becoming red color that would have been quite flattering on her.

"I'll never wear it," she quickly responded, somewhat defiantly.

Her hair was now quite sparse, and she had been ordering wigs from the Eva Gabor Company. They were quite attractive on her in a perfect red color like her own natural hair used to be, but they were synthetic hair and permanently styled. The one I had brought could be styled in many different ways, but, being real hair, would have required maintenance. No, the ones she had been buying suited her fine because they required nothing, and that's the way she liked it. I saw her point, but it burned me up—perhaps the same as my negativity toward her gift.

During my trip there, I asked her several times to put on the wig I had given her.

"No," was her curt reply.

I could have smacked her for her contrariness. Finally, one evening she put it on and let me see it. It looked wonderful on her, but she immediately took it off and returned it to its box, which she put in her closet. I accepted it, but it still burned me. There's an old saying: "What goes around comes around." We'd attend to this later.

The morning I was leaving, she insisted on preparing my breakfast. It was unnecessary, but I accepted her kindness. Her maid—who was almost as old as Mother—had been out ill for some time. The two of them could barely hold themselves up, much less each other.

The maid finally succumbed, but when my sister and I advised her to get another one, Mother stubbornly insisted, "I want my Mamie"—her cook's name.

I felt that part of her problem was her diet, which, without "her Mamie," might only be a bowl of cereal and a cup of coffee for the day. Her health, her life, really depended on Mamie, or some cook, being there. She was too spoiled to do it for herself.

In her bathrobe, she shuffled across the kitchen floor with a small pot of boiled water to make instant coffee in a cup which she had placed on a tray on a cabinet opposite the stove. Suddenly, she stopped midway across the room and complained of feeling faint. Instead of putting the pot of scalding water down on the cabinet, she shuffled back across the floor to the stove—while I held my breath—put it down, and then sat.

"I must have gotten out of bed too soon this morning," she justified her condition, sitting at the dining room table.

I sat with her observing her until she finally got up and went upstairs to lie down in her bed. I completed preparing the breakfast she had started, and, as I was finishing, a friend's car that would return me to the Louisville airport pulled into the driveway. I yelled to Mother and ran to get my packed bag. She met me at the front door, and as we embraced, there were tears in her eyes—something I had never seen before when I departed.

"I'll be back in June for my birthday," I comforted her. "It won't be long."

We continued embracing, but the tears never went away, as if she might never see me again.

She was right: at least not this way—ever again.

She told me once of a little white poodle named Fluffy Ruffles she'd had when she first married. While she was away one time visiting her ailing father in Pennsylvania, Fluffy died. She always said she believed Fluffy died of a broken heart because she went away and left her. I wondered if our separation now could bring the same heartbreak to her.

It continued to concern me—all of it: her frail appearance, lack of a maid, and lack of a proper diet—for which I had no proof, but which I suspected was true.

In April, I got a call from Mother telling me she was going to my sister's in Lexington, Kentucky, for Easter. This was quite a distance away, and I had noticed at Christmas that her driving was erratic. It seemed that she was having problems with her peripheral vision; she kept veering off the road. I'd have to tell her that she was driving on the side of the road. I was concerned about this, and when she called, I asked her to be careful with her driving.

"I will, dear," she said, somewhat condescendingly.

I was perplexed that my sister had invited her for a visit. She knew Mother's eyesight wasn't good; she shouldn't be in a car. My sister said that she had tried to arrange Easter at Mother's house, but Mother insisted on coming to Lexington. She loved the excitement of going places, like the anticipation of a child opening a new present. She had traveled all over the world since my father's death, and she particularly loved the freedom her car gave her. Still, she was a menace on the road to everyone, including herself.

I worried the entire Easter, and then I got the call I had always dreaded getting.

The voice on my answering machine when I arrived home late one night was that of my sister's oldest son. I knew that if she or her husband couldn't call, they must be someplace they couldn't leave, perhaps a hospital, and it was serious.

"Nana has been in an accident," my nephew said. "She's at…"

He gave the name of the hospital, but I couldn't reach her room. I couldn't get any information from the hospital, I couldn't reach my nephew, or my sister or her husband, and so I got down on my hands and knees in my living room, under the disco ball of John Barrett's—Lee's murdered friend from years ago—and prayed.

"Dear God," I said, "I know you've always taken care of Mother and me, and I know you'll take care of us now."

The light from the streetlights outside mixed with the shadows of my darkened living room and created the appearance of a cross on one of the walls. I took it as a sign and got up. I remembered an image of Jesus on a stained glass arched window in our church in my hometown—with his arm raised triumphantly—and I visualized Him standing at the foot of Mother's bed taking care of her.

There was nothing more I could do. When I reached my sister, she said she had arranged for the hospital and doctors and advised me to sit tight until something developed. She suggested that I come home when they knew more about Mother's condition.

The following morning, I was scheduled to audition as a make-up artist for a new line of cosmetics—that never got off the ground—at a TV studio on the West Side. The cosmetic company was looking for a charismatic spokesperson for their new line, and they had contacted several agencies trying to find just the right artist to represent them. I was known, so I was chosen, along with others from other agencies.

As I sat in the waiting area waiting to go on camera to be interviewed by the producers, my heart was so heavy I wasn't sure that I had the strength to do this. How could I smile, be personable and chatty at a time like this?

"My mother's been in an automobile accident," my insides repeatedly drummed the fact into my brain. "What am I doing here? I should be there with her."

I had contemplated canceling this, but I heard Mother's show business voice boom out, "The show must go on! Life goes on."

This was what I knew she would want. This was what I was expected to do. My career had always been even more important to her than it was to me. So, I willed it—or perhaps she willed it—but we did it together.

Conflicted and confused by the chatter in my head, I waited while another artist was being interviewed and some actor I had seen in TV commercials—whom they had gotten in case none of the real make-up artists worked out—nervously paced the floor in a most annoying way that made things even more complicated for me.

Finally, it was my turn and I went in with the "show must go on" attitude, sat in the spotlight, smiled like Rose Kennedy as if I didn't have a care in the world, and delivered the goods, amiable and chatty as I could be, while my heart broke in a million pieces inside.

Unable to wait any longer, in May I made arrangements to fly to Lexington, Kentucky, where my sister picked me up and we immediately went to the hospital where Mother had been transferred from the first hospital she was in after the accident.

Mother was in a single occupancy room, for which I was thankful in case I made a public display of the emotional state I was in. When I came through the door, her face lit up and a tiny smile crossed her face—briefly— then vanished as quickly as it had emerged. It was as though her memory circuit had snapped off and her recollection of someone she had given birth to and known all her life had crumpled inside her like a wadded up piece of paper.

"It's John, Mother," my sister announced, as if I needed to be introduced to the woman with whom I was once attached by an umbilical cord.

There was no recognition. I could've been introduced as Donald Duck and had as much impact. Mother was simply no longer there. She was more present in the beginning few days after her accident, I was told, but she had since been deteriorating rapidly. She relayed to my sister once when she came to visit her that she was on the ceiling with the angels.

"Wait a minute, I'll come down," she had said.

"What's it like up there?" my sister quizzed her.

"Well, it's this big dome, and there are all these people, but you won't let me go there."

"I'm not keeping you, Mother. It's in God's hands."

One day she had asked, "Why did God do this?"

"God wasn't driving the car, Mother," my sister answered her.

Both of her legs had been broken, her insides badly damaged, and her jaw broken from crashing through the windshield and being hurled to the ground when her car had rammed head-on into a parked trailer along the side of the road. This was the result of her habit of veering off to the side that I had witnessed when I had driven with her during my Christmas visit. I was afraid that something like this could happen.

I spent the day holding Mother's hand, with my head bowed and praying by her bed. Her legs were in casts, her jaw was wired shut, and her hands were tied to the bed to keep her from pulling out the feeding tubes that were keeping her alive. She was heavily sedated—the only way she could have endured this situation—but I was sure she was still uncomfortable. It broke my heart to see her so frail, small, and helpless. Every decision regarding her from here on in would be made by someone else—and this for a strong woman who had always controlled her own destiny.

When it was time to go to make my flight back to New York, I called the airlines and re-booked my reservations for a later hour. It was all I could do to pull myself away and leave her like this. I took consolation that I would return in June for my birthday, as I had promised her.

In June when I returned, I was sure that she would be waiting for me, in spirit, for our last and final goodbye. She had miraculously survived for two months and was now in a nursing home, the last place she ever wanted to be. My sister had been making all the arrangements, and it was frustrating for me, being so far away, to receive information about a decision that had already been made. With no alternative other than giving up my life in New York and going there, I was still thankful my sister was there overseeing things. My visit now to the nursing home was to be brief before we drove to our old hometown to settle some of Mother's affairs, and a longer visit was planned when we returned the following day.

As we entered the bare, white, antiseptic room in which Mother and other old women in wheelchairs were dispersed about watching TV, my sister said, "Mother, this is your son," another of those introductions that made me cringe.

Mother looked up with no recognition this time, and her head quickly returned to the TV.

"Your son," my sister repeated to emphasize it, and encouraged me into the room.

I took Mother's hand and kissed her on the cheek as I always had. Her brow furrowed, puzzled at what was happening, and she ignored the intrusion.

I sat next to her, and my sister whispered, "I'll be outside in the car," and left.

I had no idea how much time I had and what I was going to do with it since conversation seemed a futile, one-way street. I mentioned something about tomorrow being my birthday and got merely a nod from someone who had played such a big part in my beginning—as if to say, what was that to her in her situation?

My sister had found the nursing home when the hospital informed her that Mother was no longer in intensive care and had to leave. It seemed cruel to kick someone out just because they were a little less close to death. Mother still needed help, but a nursing home was the last place where I, too, wanted her to be.

I had mentioned to my sister that I was considering coming home to take care of Mother, but she said that I would need around-the-clock nurses, machines to feed and help Mother breathe, constant attention to soiled bed sheets, and I would have to haul her in and out of bed to keep her from getting bed sores and keep her limbs in some working condition. It all sounded so dismal and impossible that I reneged in my head and accepted that I probably wouldn't be good at it anyhow.

I settled in to watch TV with Mother when she turned to me and said, "Have you met my son?"

"I am your son, Mother," I said compassionately, understanding that the Mother I had known all my life no longer existed, that she was only here because there was no place left to go.

I held her hand, and she wiggled her thumb against the palm of my hand in an affectionate way, which was the only way she could communicate. This frail, helpless woman, who, at times, I had been so frightened of, was now so pitifully in need that it was difficult to resign myself. Gone was the fire that had inflamed me, infuriated me, and driven me with such intense fury all of my life. Gone, too, was the ravishing beauty who had beguiled me, gnawed away by time and the destruction of a head-on collision. It was a phenomenon that this 88-year-old woman, hurled through a windshield, had survived this long. A lesser person would have succumbed on the highway.

She had looked up as they were carting her away on the stretcher and yelled to one of the medics who had retrieved her wig, "Don't throw that away. I want that!"

But that was two months ago, and things had grown steadily dimmer since then, and the light was nearly out.

Her thumb continued exploring my palm, and in a weak, high voice—not at all like her own—she said, "I'm all washed up."

Without hesitation, I responded, "Well, you may be washed up here, but you're not washed up up there. Why don't you go on?"

Her thumb stopped twitching, and she looked at me like a prisoner who had just been given a reprise.

"Yeah, go on. I'll be there soon enough. You don't have to worry about me anymore," I boldly declared, but in truth I wasn't sure if I could survive without her.

No more words were spoken, and she began to comfort herself with a little song, no doubt of her own creation, in her strange, high-pitched voice. The only words I could decipher, which she repeated over and over were: "Strength and courage. Strength and courage."

It was like something Michael had said about the courage he had wished for on a star, and here it was again being summoned up to see Mother through her ordeal. It was a lesson in the strength and courage that I, too, would need to recover from the destruction I had imposed on my life.

When my time seemed comfortably up and I had soaked up all the TV I could stand, I got up, kissed Mother on her cheek, and said, "I'll see you tomorrow"—but my instinct was to pick her up, carry her to the car, and take her home, something she had repeatedly begged my sister for.

"I just want to go home and get in my bed and go to sleep," she had begged. But this, of course, was impossible due to the seriousness of her condition.

In a suddenly strong, assertive voice, she said, "I won't be here when you get back."

Startled by the abrupt change, I said, "Where are you going, Mother? Out there?"

I pointed to an outside garden beyond the TV set. She said nothing more.

The following morning, when I awakened in Mother's house in our old hometown to prepare to return to the nursing home, I went to close the window in my bedroom when I saw in the corner of the windowsill a firefly caught in a cobweb struggling to get out. I gingerly lifted the firefly from the web with the tip of a candle I removed from a candleholder, took it to the door, and set it free. The firefly reminded me of Mother, caught in her web, and I prayed that if she could never have quality in her life again, that she, too, would be set free.

While my sister waited in the car, I entered the nursing home a few hours later, and a doctor took me aside and gave me the news: Mother had died that morning.

It was Sunday, and they had asked her if she wanted to go to a small chapel that had been set up in a section of the nursing home. She had said yes.

After chapel, they wheeled her back to her room, and an orderly told me he had heard her say, "God take me."

He turned and saw her bow her head. That was it.

I asked to see her.

In one of their sterile rooms, with an old woman with her back turned lying in a bed across the room, unaware or uninterested that a corpse was in the bed opposite her behind a screen that had been pulled around the bed to hide it, Mother lay peacefully with a white sheet draped over her.

I pulled back the sheet and looked at her radiant face, pearly, dewy eyelids, soft, clear, still moist skin with no make-up. She was young again, and the look on her face was of someone who had seen something wonderful. I believed I knew what it was.

"Mother," I said, "you look better lying there than I do up here walking around."

I meant it. She was beautiful, and I was happy for her.

She was right. She had not been there when I came back. Like the firefly, she had flown away. She was free now.

18

The Funeral, Studio 54
Closes, the Wind Down

It rained the day of Mother's funeral as if the angels in heaven knew the weeping below and joined in with sympathetic tears. Deep in my thoughts, I sat in front of the casket under a tent over the gravesite with other family members while a windbag preacher went on and on ad nauseum with some flowery eulogy that even Mother would've found too boring to listen to. Aware that some family members were already on shaky emotional ground, I had requested that things be kept simple, but the preacher obviously couldn't help himself. Near me, I heard whimpering from one member who wasn't that mentally stable to begin with, and I pulled myself further into my thoughts to steady my own emotions.

In front of me passed a firefly. It lit up and went on. My eyes followed it as it deftly circled the tent and sailed outside into the rain. I smiled and pondered the possibility of it being the firefly I had freed. Whether it was or not, I was sure it was Mother saying goodbye.

When my sister and I had returned to Mother's house to begin arrangements for her burial, the antique clock on the mantel in her living room had stopped exactly at the hour of her death: ten minutes past eleven in the morning—as mysterious and unbelievable as that might be. They had given us the exact time at the nursing home when we were there. I had wound the clock, as Mother always did, before we left for the nursing home the day she died. Fireflies and clocks that stop were all too spooky and improbable for my sister, but I knew that there were some things that could never be explained, and I sometimes wondered myself if they had really happened.

When we were searching in Mother's closet for the clothing to bury her in, we deliberated which of her wigs to put on her head, since the wreck had damaged her favorite one. Then I spied the box with the wig I had given her our last Christmas together—the one she had contrarily refused to wear.

"Aha," I said, "I have just the one. She said she'd never wear this ... she'll be going through eternity in it."

And that was the wig she was buried in. It was a kind joke, one that even Mother would have thought funny and ironic. At a time like this, humor is a soothing sedative. Sharing in a harmless joke of this kind, as if the deceased were still there participating, was a way of staying connected.

While settling Mother's estate and paying her bills, my sister and I had a dispute. I felt she was still being the bossy older sister that she'd been as we were growing up, and I balked at her continuous directions. This caused her to threaten to leave and let me deal with matters myself. I retaliated that I, too, was hurting, and that she had no right to boss me around. I left the house to cool off.

I walked down the street to another section of expensive residential houses, like Mother's, with their manicured lawns, elaborate flower beds, and meticulously trimmed hedges, until I came to a familiar brook I had known as a child that trickled its contents eventually into the Barren River. I sat down by the brook on the soft, young grass dotted with small, colorful flowers, where the cool crystal water bubbled tenderly over rocks and moss on its way to join a tremendous flow.

In someone's yard behind me was a mass—perhaps a hundred or more—of purple irises grouped in a large bed. The brazen purple color against the fresh, bright green grass all around was breathtaking. The smell of young, clean, tender grass mixed with the sparkling early summer sunlight filled my nostrils and revitalized and refreshed me.

Close by, through tall young thistles and grass, strolled a tall bird—perhaps a crane—its head peeking up over the top of the thicket. It threw back its head and trilled a bright melody into the crisp, sunlit air—then again—and then spread its long wings and took flight. Up, up it went, sailing nonchalantly back and forth like a kite, until it was out of sight.

God was here; God was everywhere—there was no mistaking it. He was in the brook, the flowers, the sunlight, the fresh green grass, and all the living things before me. He had never forsaken me, nor had he forsaken Mother. I recognized that it was impossible to be separate from God because here it was all around me. The anger I had felt for my sister and she for me was our grief and frustration. Everything was insignificant compared to the magnificence surrounding me and throughout the universe. My anger left me and was replaced by the love I felt everywhere. It was all created in love, and I, too, was loved. I was at peace.

I returned to Mother's house and my sister had gone, but her belongings were still there so I knew she hadn't gone for good. I sat down at the desk in the library and resumed doing Mother's bills. Soon my sister's car drove into the driveway, and she came inside. She had gone to town, she said, to take care of some errands.

"Do you want to do the bills?" I asked.

"No, you're fine," came the acknowledgment I had wanted.

"Let's have a hug," I said, and got up.

"Yes," she said, and we did, and the pain left us both.

We spent the next two days dividing the silverware and other household things, sorting through all of Mother's personal things like jewelry and clothing, and doing a little decorating to hide all the junk she had collected in her worldly travels to get the house ready for a real estate agent to sell it. When our work was complete, my sister waited in the car while I did one last inspection before we drove to the airport for me to return to New York.

I knew that I would never again see my old home like this with everything in place as I had always remembered it. My sister would return soon to empty it out completely when it was sold.

I went around checking every item in every room: a lamp, a table, a chair, or some knick-knack I'd always loved. Suddenly, everything became precious and important, and I couldn't bear to leave any of it. I went to Mother's closet and smelled her clothing, opened a drawer and looked at her neat pile of lingerie, and touched her bed that she had left that fatal morning when she went to my sister's for Easter—the bed that she had repeatedly begged my sister to bring her back to; the bed to which she had never returned. She had intended to begin plans to paint her house when she got back. How fragile and impermanent life is, I thought.

When I finished my tour, I went out the front door, closed and locked it, got into the waiting car, and left the house I had grown up in forever.

It was where the tomboy girl next door with the angelic, golden ringlets used to beat me up daily—when the class bully wasn't doing it. It was where my grandmother lived in the house on the other side of us after my grandfather died. Summer afternoons, she'd stroll through our yard observing Mother's flower beds, her hands behind her back, humming a tune we sang in church. She'd enter our house and call out to Mother, who would be hiding upstairs, not wanting to be disturbed at that moment. Mother would motion for me to be quiet and I would, but I felt badly because I knew Grandmother was lonely.

When Mother was an old woman, she, too, would stroll through the yard observing the flowers, and then return to her house, but this time there was no one to call out to. We had all gone, and she, too, was lonely.

This was the town where in my uncle's drugstore as a boy I had seen the ad in *Seventeen* magazine for an art school named Pratt Institute in Brooklyn, New York, that would be my ticket out of there. The town was named after Glasgow, Scotland, and that was how Glasgow, Kentucky got its name— though I never met a Scotsman there except the preacher of our church, and he was imported there from someplace else.

A statue of a Confederate soldier stood in the courthouse front yard in the middle of the town square. With its segregated drinking fountains and bathrooms, the courthouse was where my father and his father had tried their legal cases. They had expected that I, too, would be a lawyer, but I had other ideas that didn't include living my life there at Mother's disposal. On Saturdays, farmers would come to town to sell their tobacco and spit tobacco juice on the sidewalk. Only the agile could maneuver through town on Saturday without being spat on.

The town had one train that went back and forth to Louisville—our closest, largest city—carrying produce. That was as far as it went—just back and forth to Louisville. At night I'd lie in my bed listening to the lonely whistle of that train getting an early start, and I'd fantasize about the places it was going to see—not that spectacular, but I'd embellish it. It was more than I was seeing, and I yearned to go with it.

Mother and I rode that train to Louisville once. We both got motion sickness, but Mother was the only one caught with her head out the window upchucking when the train pulled up to a small town along the way. The farmers outside laughed and shouted, "Look at that," like it was the most exciting thing they'd seen in their ornery lives. Mother pulled her head in and daintily dabbed her mouth with her handkerchief, and nothing further was said.

This was where I was always the last chosen when my boyhood chums picked a team to play football or baseball in one of our backyards. I couldn't throw or catch a ball for beans. My first sexual encounter there was at 16 with a 13-year-old girl who was reputed to have taken on the entire high school football team, so my infringement wasn't that bad. Late one night, we began our tryst in the backseat of my father's Packard limousine parked on a dirt road by a farmer's cornfield, but we were interrupted in the middle of it when the farmer showed up with a shotgun. I drove that old Packard through that cornfield—with cornhusks slapping against the windshield and the girl yelling bloody murder in the backseat, jumped like a jackrabbit onto the highway, and sped away. Needless to say, it was a short affair.

I had been humiliated and called names there like "sissy" and "queer" because I was different from others. It was where every gossip in town had condemned me for drawing a nude woman—the place I hated the most which, ironically, I still called home. I had gotten myself a tombstone when I got Mother's, and this was where I, too, would be buried. I was leaving it for now, but someday I would return to spend forever here.

The AIDS issue in New York had become a serious city matter. The Health Department had begun shutting down the gay bathhouses in 1985. But Mayor Koch signed a gay rights ordinance in 1986, following several failed attempts to get it passed by the City Council, who probably didn't think the gays deserved it under the circumstances. This created a double standard for the city that gay sex clubs had to close while heterosexual clubs—most notably Plato's Retreat in the Ansonia Hotel on Broadway—could remain open. With Koch's approval, the Health Department then went after the heterosexual clubs, and Plato's Retreat relocated to Fort Lauderdale, Florida, to reopen as Plato's Repeat—as if repeating the setup in a hetero-sexual way didn't spread the disease.

For me, New York had become a lonely place of sad memories. Like many at the time, my life was completely altered by AIDS and the deaths of loved ones and friends. Way Bandy, my biggest competitor, had died of the disease in '86, and others I knew had also perished. Valerie was gone; Lee would soon follow with AIDS, and Mary, too, from suicide. My two cham-pions, my mentors, my cheering section, and, at times, my adversaries, Mother and Michael—the greatest loves of all—were also gone. What was all that hullabaloo about, all that noise, those arguments all those years, to end up alone like this? I would now have to clean up the mess that all of it had left behind.

Part of the grieving process is anger. I was angry that Mother had bel-ligerently driven that car without a seatbelt, though I had repeatedly warned her. Her driving, at best, had become erratic, and death was the result of all of it. And I was angry that Michael had gotten so far out of control with drugs and sex that he had gotten AIDS. Didn't these people have any sense? It was hypocrisy on my part, of course, considering my past behavior. Perhaps I was more disappointed that life had turned out the way it had, and I was left to remember it all.

My greatest mourning was, of course, for Mother and Michael, but I also mourned the life I'd once had. Though I would never have considered returning to the risky, careless behavior, it felt like my life had ended—at least that part of it, for sure. Now all I did was work and go to Al-Anon meetings. At one Al-Anon meeting, I shared that all I did was go to meetings, and I saw all these heads nodding in agreement. Perhaps many there did nothing but go to meetings, which indicated how serious the damage of addiction and all the destruction had been to our lives.

Curtailing all sexual activity seemed prudent in the climate of AIDS that now prevailed. Though AZT, the first anti-viral drug that slowed down the replication of the AIDS virus, would be FDA approved in '87—with more potent drugs, the protease inhibiters, to follow in the '90s—it was still no incentive for me to resume sex. These were only temporary fixes and by no means a cure. I had literally been scared out of all of it.

When all the new drugs did finally come into existence in the '90s, they provided a "cocktail" of pills to help ward off the disease, which many younger gays—who had not gone through the terrible beginning of AIDS with no help and seeing loved ones die—decided it was "cool" to be positive. There would even be Pos Parties where those who tested positive for the disease would attend to participate in group sex, erroneously assuming that if they were already positive it wouldn't make a difference, never considering—or wanting to consider—that the constantly mutating AIDS virus could further infect them.

I attended a gay symposium in 2004 called "Gay Sex in the City," paraphrased from the TV show *Sex and the City*, and the originator of Pos Parties spoke. He was asked if gays who were not positive showed up at his parties.

"Yes," he answered. "We tell them that almost everyone there is positive, but they want to join in anyhow."

I also knew someone at that time who was positive, and he was having public sex in bars that had begun catering to that sort of thing again. He never told his partners he was positive, and, therefore, they didn't have the option to say no. It was selfishness on his part: withholding information in order to get what he wanted. On the other hand, his partners were there willingly accepting whatever they got.

All of this behavior was irresponsible to me, and only indicated that many had learned really nothing from this disaster. However, it had left an indelible mark of horror in my life that I could never ignore. The memory of Lee—a once incredibly handsome, virile man—curled up in bed like a fetus, bald, with his stomach swollen like a pregnant woman, skinny arms and legs with skin shriveled like a prune, and a hollow skull for a face, was an image I could never forget. This was the disease in all of its hideous, gory reality, and there was nothing "cool" about it.

Lee once showed me a photo taken on Fire Island, the preferred gay resort for New York City gays, where sex and drugs were the lifestyle. In the photo with Lee were eight other handsome, smiling, tanned men, their drinks held high in anticipation of the summer ahead, with the sun picturesquely setting over the ocean behind the porch where they stood, all in seemingly exuberant health.

One by one, Lee picked them out: "This one has AIDS, this one died last year, this one is in the hospital, this one is dead..."

One by one, each had succumbed to the disease, and Lee would soon follow.

The therapist I had been seeing since Michael died suggested that I might one day consider another partner. This I immediately squelched.

"Let's just talk about my career," I answered, with that being the only panacea I would consider to get my life back on track.

It was the only remedy I knew—that I had always used—to give my life purpose. My "fabulous career" would silence the shrill scream in my head that I couldn't escape. Many times when I wasn't working, I'd lie in bed until it was evening before I'd get up. I allowed myself this luxury; in fact, I couldn't avoid it. Life—the life I had chosen—had devastated me, and whatever it took, I had no choice but to accept it.

Barbara Taylor Bradford, previously a syndicated British journalist, had become a superb and popular writer of women's fiction with A Woman of Substance, continuing the story with Hold the Dream, which her husband, Robert Bradford, co-produced for TV. I was booked by Scavullo to do her make-up for the back cover of her newest book, To Be the Best, which completed the saga trilogy.

Barbara had a beautiful face with a flawless alabaster complexion that only the British can have. Her hair was a lovely shade of blonde, shiny and quite luxurious. In fact, her entire demeanor was that of a woman who was well cared for and pampered, not unlike the women she wrote about.

I totally related to all she presented. She knew exactly how she wanted to look and exactly how she wanted her hair to look and directed it all—either verbally or willed it so with her strong presence. It was not hard to see why her books were so successful. She was writing about a subject she knew well: herself, or her alter ego. Barbara was the best and a woman of substance rolled into one. Some time after the make-up, she sent me a note praising me for being the best—a class act that only a thoroughbred possesses.

Contrasting that pleasant experience, I then had Arianna Stassinopolous Huffington, a Greek writer who married Michael Huffington, an oil-rich Texas billionaire and California congressman who ran for the senate—or was it Arianna who ran?—in 1994 and lost. With a wife as headstrong and determined as Arianna behind him, how could that have been? After their divorce in '98—and after he declared himself gay and a Democrat—she herself made a bid for governor in 2003, but bailed out against the stronger Republican candidate, Arnold Schwarzenegger. Public service—or might it be called power?—knew where not to go.

We knocked ourselves out with Arianna's make-up and hair and when we finished, what had been intended as a photo for *Harper's Bazaar*—which *Bazaar* paid for—Arianna decided she wanted for the back cover of her latest book, *Picasso: Creator and Destroyer*.

Not intending to further compensate the artists responsible for the creation of a photo that *Bazaar* had paid for enraged me and I complained to Scavullo, who always kowtowed to anyone who might bring him future money. He rebuked me for wanting to be paid extra by Arianna or the publisher for a photo that I had agreed to at *Bazaar*'s rate—which was minimal at best. But the photo had now grown into something quite different from my original agreement. To me, it was taking advantage of all the artists: the stylist, the hairdresser, and myself, who had contributed considerably to the success of the photo. And considering all the freebees all of us had done for Scavullo over the years, he should have been on our side. Even a small gesture of gratitude would have been adequate compensation.

I took the fight to my agent, who also made a complaint to Scavullo, which was ignored. This entire bunch of affluent people had conspired to get something for nothing from the smaller artists who were an essential part of it. If Huffington's mantra was: "it's more blessed to get than to give," I vowed never to vote for or buy a book with Huffington or Stassinopolous attached to it.

Biloxi Blues, one of a trilogy of plays about playwright Neil Simon's life, opened on Broadway in '85, starring Matthew Broderick, and he reprised his role for the film version in '88, directed by Mike Nichols. When I made up Broderick for a photo for *Harper's Bazaar*, he cautioned me not to use too much make-up, astutely recognizing that his face had a tendency to appear pretty and make-up might make it even prettier. For *Harper's Bazaar* I also made up Marlee Matlin, the deaf actress who won a Tony for her stage performance in *Children of a Lesser God* and an Academy Award for the film version in '86. Again for *Harper's Bazaar* I made up Sting, the lead singer–bassist for the British rock group The Police, who was appearing that year in the romantic thriller film *Stormy Monday*.

Sting had a most handsome face and a strong, attractive body that presented clothing well. Whatever the stylist put on him hung perfectly and he had a casual, unstudied way of carrying it that made the clothing look appealing. If it were a song, it would be that he nailed it and sold it well.

Scavullo had acquired the Fortunoff jewelry account for a series of ads using famous women as the models. The women were no longer that famous in that most of them had reached their peak some time ago, and that's why they were available at a reasonable price. We had already done Hermione Gingold, best known as Gigi's grandmother in Lerner and Loewe's classic 1958 film musical *Gigi* when she sang with the great Maurice Chevalier the song "I Remember It

I had to get permission to put shadow around Sting's eyes (courtesy Francesco Scavullo Foundation, as seen in U.S. *Harper's Bazaar*).

Well." Now we were doing Imogene Coca, best known as Sid Caesar's comedienne side-kick in *Your Show of Shows*" in the early days of TV from '50 to
'54.

While I was doing Coca's make-up, the pencil slipped as I was outlining
her eyes—which had never happened before—and it hit her eyeball with a
dull thud.

Horrified, I quickly withdrew the pencil, and she said calmly, "That's
okay. It's glass."

That was why the pencil had slipped: the territory around her eye had
been altered in a way that was unfamiliar to me.

Scavullo had numerous advertising accounts offered him, but his arrogance and that of his companion and studio manager, Sean, caused advertisers to search for more compatible studios. Francesco and Sean had the
art director for Oil of Olay—a young woman in her 20s—in tears when they
told her she knew nothing about advertising, though it was her account
they were doing, and they literally dismissed her from the shoot. I had to
console her in the bathroom
while the photograph was being
taken without her presence. It
was the same arrogance and dis-
respect that cost Scavullo his
Vogue account when he offended
art director Alexander Liberman
by sending him photographs in a
garbage can. Incidents like that
were ruining their business, and
mine too. With the little that
magazines paid, advertising was
where the artists finally made
some money, and these two were
ruining it for all of us.

Francesco tried to make up
the difference peddling silk-
screen portrait blowups of people he had shot. Some, like Mary
Kay with the photos he had
taken of her for the *Saturday Evening Post*, had bought, but the

A glamorous jewelry shot with beautiful lighting on the model's face (courtesy Francesco Scavullo Foundation, as
seen in U.S. *Harper's Bazaar*).

Strong '80s clothing design required strong make-up on supermodel Paulina Porizkova (courtesy Francesco Scavullo Foundation, as seen in U.S. *Harper's Bazaar*).

enormous five-figure price he unreasonably asked for the portraits—another example of his arrogance—put people off, and few could afford it. The books he had published weren't that successful and he was always scrambling to invent ways to make money from a career that was rapidly winding down—and I was forced to do the same.

With Scavullo's career beginning to wane at age 66—and with the untimely deaths of photographers Chris Von Wangenheim and Bill King who used me frequently—I sensed it would be only a matter of time before my career went with Scavullo's, particularly with him being one of my few remaining photographers. Nevertheless, I continued doing some of my best work during this period, both in fashion and in beauty, and with Way Bandy's untimely death in '86, more work had been extended me—though I would never have chosen it that way.

But as it goes sometimes in life, a new hotshot make-up artist had come on the scene, Kevyn Aucoin, and he was creating the same kind of make-up excitement that Way and I had created when we first began. Aucoin was in the same make-up vein as Way—even buying one of Way's books to emulate his style—in that he liked exaggerated make-ups, very stylized. He made women look glamorous, but in a very made-up way—not at all the style I preferred, which was softer, more real, and vulnerable. Like Way, Aucoin's make-ups were well suited for models and women who wanted a more exaggerated look like Liza Minnelli, Sharon Stone, Cher, and Mary Tyler Moore.

As Way's make-ups had always been for me, Aucoin's had a hard edge that I tried to avoid. I hated make-ups that looked like make-up, in a drag queen, stereotype-of-women sort of way. Many make-up artists who are gay resort to stereotypes because that's all they know of women, or it's how they might turn themselves into one. Scavullo did a photo of Way painted to the hilt with black for days around his eyes and wearing black lace gloves. It was the kind of male/female thing that rockers Marilyn Manson and Keith Richards might do, but Way took himself quite seriously.

The occupational hazard of an industry that celebrates perfection can be that the artists who create the perfection on women can become obsessed with it in themselves. Way had a handsome face to begin with, but he'd had massive plastic surgery and wore make-up all the time. It was as if nothing could make him perfect enough.

On a 1997 Oprah Winfrey TV show, Aucoin turned several women into alleged celebrity look-alikes, and Oprah, herself, supposedly into a Diana Ross Supreme look-alike. It was a curiosity and an artistic achievement on one level, but of little value past that to the general public. Anyone who wanted to look like someone else—and an exaggeration at that—was psychologically suspicious in my book and someone I wanted to avoid.

The make-ups I did were perhaps best suited for a public where I felt women wanted to look like themselves—not some exaggeration of womanhood or looking like someone else. Many had been told all their lives that they should be someone else, and this was exactly what I didn't want to encourage. Women need to accept themselves exactly as they are. They need practical information like what products to buy, where to buy them inexpensively, and how to apply them. They need to learn a technique of application that looking at someone made up like Marilyn Monroe or Elizabeth Taylor can never teach them, and which is intimidating at that. This was why I didn't belong in the fashion world, which encouraged fantasy and the extreme. I was searching for truth in my life, and camouflage wasn't the way to achieve it.

My roots were in acting, which I probably would have pursued had it not been for my persistent demons. This was what had always attracted me to the actors I made up and people like Tallulah Bankhead. They embodied the world in which I wanted to live—a world that searched for truth, honored it, and never denied it. Years of the phoniness I had encountered in the fashion world had left me hungry for that. Tallulah brought theatre and entertainment alive for me. I had just never pursued it except with Michael. Now that he was gone, I needed to pick up the pieces of what we had begun.

I could expect a small inheritance when Mother's house was sold and her estate was settled. With that money, I resolved to record the music for a musical I'd written, which Michael and I had started, and move out of the make-up and fashion field once and for all to pursue my original dream. With Scavullo's career declining and Aucoin's appearance on the scene, it seemed the appropriate time to do it. As I had done with Way, I would leave the make-up field to Aucoin with no encumbrances from me.

Sadly, like Way, Aucoin would die in 2002, leaving the field empty, perhaps forever, of a superstar make-up artist. Perhaps the days of the great fashion make-up artists were over. At any rate, by then I intended to be well on my way to another life. But I had no idea of the mountains I would have to climb.

19

Paul Newman,
L.A. Revisited, the Kiss-Off

In '89 the Reagan era ended, Ed Koch left office as Mayor of New York City, and his replacement, David Dinkins, took on a $1.2 billion deficit as the country sank into a deep recession. Reagan, the fairy godfather of make-believe, had left behind a trail of financial fairy dust, and we weren't as well off as he had made us believe we were.

Reagan's vice president, George H. W. Bush, became president for one lackluster term that barely kept the government creaking along with enormous economic hardships while the country entered a quick war with Iraq in '91 that his son, George W. Bush, would resume when he became president in 2001.

As for Reagan's part in exchanging arms for hostages with Iran—known as the Iran-Contra affair—he would plead that he didn't remember anything, which may have been true considering his revelation in '94 that he had Alzheimer's, from which he would die in 2004. It was no consolation for the country, however—given Reagan's reckless cowboy posturing, one twitchy, trigger-happy finger away from the World War III button—that he may have suffered from the disease throughout his two presidential terms.

Oliver North would take the fall for the Reagan administration's wrong-doings in the Iran-Contra mess with massive charges, fines, and community service leveled against him that would eventually be dropped and, in the final analysis, amount to little more than a slap on the wrists. He would benefit tremendously from his notoriety with book deals, a TV show, and other TV appearances, and even make an unsuccessful run for the Senate in '94—leaving one to ponder that lying to Congress, destroying evidence, and attempting to obstruct justice has its rewards. When the whole hoopla ended in '91, many speculated that it had been a put-up deal to begin with, much like the pardon from Gerald Ford that Richard Nixon doubtlessly arranged for himself before he left office.

The Berlin Wall that Reagan had goaded Gorbachev to tear down, fell in November, ten months after Bush took office. Reagan's prophecy had come true, so he may have been the fairy godfather after all. At least, for a few blissful moments, he made us believe in one—perhaps his real legacy.

With Dinkins as Mayor, New York wasn't any better off financially than it had been with Koch, or Beame before him. Witnessing the rapid disappearance of here-before raunchy places and situations in town was like watching a magic act. Studio 54 was gone, Steve Rubell was dead from AIDS, and fashion designer Halston would soon follow. Bars were dropping like flies from a flyswatter, and gay bathhouses and sex clubs would become relics of the past when the St. Mark's Baths gave up its fight to remain open the following year. Out of guilt and necessity, the city, and the gays themselves, were policing the city to death.

My own change was as dramatic and miraculous as the rest. No one escaped the terrible effect that AIDS had had on them. It was as if a war was being fought, with no victory in sight.

A recession was in full swing, and I was afraid that it would affect the amount of my inheritance. The lawyers were taking forever settling Mother's estate, and I felt helpless to guard what I was to receive—had I even known what to do. It wouldn't be a lot of money, but it was more than I had ever had.

I was equally concerned that when I got it, I wouldn't be able to handle it. No one in my family had ever discussed money; it was always a taboo subject with a kind of mystique about it that was alarming. In fact, I had always been told that I knew nothing about money—which was probably true—so I wasn't that comfortable with it and couldn't get rid of it fast enough, not a good attitude if you wanted to prosper.

Also, Mother had always been so frugal (sometimes to a fault) that I didn't want anyone—the government or myself—to squander what she had struggled to save all those years. I just wanted to act responsibly, but, given my track record and naiveté regarding money, I didn't feel that secure. It felt kind of scary.

When I received my first check for a rather substantial amount, to make sure I didn't misplace it, I nervously carried it in my hand up the street to the bank to deposit it. Not until the transaction was complete did I calm down. I got a financial planner, recommended by a friend of substantial means, and the planner directed me where to make sound investments. I also took a class in investing, given by a broker from a respected investment firm, and invested with her company, but that was a mistake. I learned that brokers are glorified sales people, and this one wanted to sell me the moon— not a good person to do business with.

I was learning to stand on my own feet without the help of Mother or Michael or anyone but myself to rely on, and it felt good. Mother had always rushed in and declared that I didn't know what I was doing and that she did, and I let her run the show. Now it was only me; but as good as it felt, it still felt scary.

As it had always been, work was the nourishment that helped me through troubling and uncertain times.

Donna Mills had played the character Abby Fairgate-Cunningham-Ewing-Sumner on the TV show *Knots Landing* since 1980. She left the show in '89—she told me, having never seen the show—driving down the road merrily singing "Don't worry, be happy," ironic in that her character had apparently caused a lot of trouble.

In making up Mills, Scavullo asked me to make sure that she didn't end up resembling a raccoon with her excessive, trademark black around her eyes, as she was used to doing. She was a delightful person, quite bright and certainly pretty, but I, too, agreed that the excessive black only hardened her lovely, delicate features. This may have been what her character in *Knots Landing* might have done, but Mills herself had beau-

Controlling the black around Donna Mills' eyes was an all-day job (courtesy Francesco Scavullo Foundation).

tifully shaped sky-blue eyes. All that black may have brought out their beauty, but it also made her look rather otherworldly, as if from another planet.

As anyone knows who has ever tried to control another person's habit, it was impossible to control the black around Mills' eyes. I did them, and every time I looked at her, more and more black appeared, like she was baptizing herself behind my back in that black pencil, as Elizabeth Taylor had done throughout her make-up. These girls liked it black. In the end, raccoon was back in town big time.

As I passed Scavullo on our way into the studio to do the photograph, he mumbled, "What did I tell you?"

"If you want to control her, you go and control her," I said.

Mills knew how she wanted to look, and if it meant looking other-worldly—so be it.

Another delightful TV star was Susan Lucci. On TV she was daytime soap bitch Erica Kane on *All My Children*, but in person she was sweet, bubbly, witty, funny, certainly beautiful, and altogether pleasant company. I wondered why someone didn't write this talented comedienne a comedy role instead of the dark, dramatic, villainous character she played.

On *All My Children*, Lucci was always excessively painted like the harlot she portrayed. I wanted to go into the opposite direction and have Lucci show through as pure and lovely as her dark beauty is. The make-up I did was subtle and definitely far

Susan Lucci was so much fun that I thought a TV sitcom should be written for her (courtesy Francesco Scavullo Foundation).

less than her character would have used—and this time, Lucci permitted me. The resulting photograph almost didn't resemble her as the public is used to seeing her. Without a mound of paint on her face, she looked younger, more vulnerable, and with a wistful hint of virginity—not at all Erica Kane, but probably more like Lucci herself.

Around this time, Christopher Reeve came to the studio to have a photograph taken for an article in *Harper's Bazaar*. As much as I admired Reeve's courage following his tragic accident in '95 when he fell from a horse and was paralyzed and in a wheelchair for nine agonizing years before his death in 2004, when I made him up several years earlier I found him arrogant, self-centered, not that pleasant, and in perpetual motion throughout the make-up. He simply never sat still and talked incessantly about his choices of future films, even asking my opinion. It felt as insecure as Avedon asking my opinion about his photography. If the experts didn't know, how should I? Everything seemed to be geared to Reeve's ego.

Of course, in such a short meeting, no one can really be sure exactly what a person is like, but I found that when many people were with a hairdresser or a make-up artist, they could be quite revealing at this most vulnerable time. We are working on an intimate area that few touch—their face and head—and many give it all up, like going to a psychiatrist. One would be surprised what people will tell or ask you, even when you

Long before his tragic accident, Christopher Reeve (here with Annette O'Toole) seemed in turmoil (courtesy Francesco Scavullo Foundation, as seen in U.S. *Harper's Bazaar*).

would rather they not. Many become obsessed with getting a load off while paint is being slathered on or when they're head-down in a sink having their hair washed. It's such a relaxing moment that Pandora's box can fly open and out scurries the pack of pests they harbor inside.

As with tragedies in many people's lives, Reeve's accident would change the course of his life forever. Whatever he may or may not have been before, he will always be remembered for his courage and as a crusader for spinal cord and stem cell research. The legacy he left behind would be far greater than any of his choices of films.

I had a dream soon after this in which I saw Mother walking a large white dog, perhaps Big Boy, an Afghan hound the family had had when I was a baby that I didn't remember except from photos. Mother's hair—and Big Boy's too—was blowing in the wind. She looked to be around 30, and she had a beautiful make-up with bright red lips, and her long legs and slim figure glided along as if on air.

I was sitting on our front porch in Glasgow with several people that I was sure were dead, and everyone was smiling and chatting.

I looked over at Mother and yelled, "Mother!"

She looked back and waved, and her bright red lips broke into the most brilliant smile. I knew from that moment that she was fine.

I had heard her say many times, "Go on with your life. I'm fine."

All the sorrow I had carried began to melt away.

It was something Scavullo had said when Michael died that started me thinking differently about death. He was not a deep man, in fact quite superficial, and rarely said anything that didn't directly pertain to him. This time, however, he was profound.

I was sitting at his dining room table having my lunch during a break when he started down the stairs and observed me having a quiet cry.

Apparently, he understood and came back up the stairs, walked over to me and said, "I had a woman friend once. We went out together several times a week, always on the phone together, and then she died of cancer. I read her letters today and I cry. But that's life."

Then he turned and went back down the stairs. This superficial man had delivered the most profound statement: "That's life." Perhaps I didn't know Francesco at all. Few did, really. He hid behind so many facades that it was hard to get in, but perhaps I had been wrong.

This began a change in my thinking. "Go on," I had heard Mother say. She had gone on to the end, and so must I.

I decided to invest a portion of the money I had inherited in me. The financial planner I had gotten advised differently, but I knew that if I didn't do what I'd always wanted to do—which was all things theatrical—I might never do them, and I didn't want to leave this world with regrets. As long as I had some money, this was the time to pursue the dream that I'd put off all these years.

When I wasn't working at make-up, I went to a recording studio and recorded the music for the musical I'd written that Michael and I had begun many years earlier. It was the most satisfying and creative time of my life: sitting with musicians and working on the music. The best part was that I sang most of the songs for the recording—something I knew I could do, having sung in church as a child and having been in bands throughout high school—but something I might not have permitted myself to do before. I even sought male singers to do it, but when it finally boiled down to me, I gratefully accepted the challenge. With the new money in my life, I had a new confidence that I had never had. I knew that if the make-up part of my life went under, I now had the resources—and I was creating a backup with the musical and two screenplays by now—that I hoped would carry me along.

The '90s arrived somewhat unceremoniously, which was more a gratitude that the '80s were blessedly over. I hoped and I prayed for a better future, and whereas better may not always be happier or even easier, it can mean growth—and growth may not always be that pleasant. At least, that's what the '90s turned out to be for me.

It was significant in that my therapist talked me into attending a gay Al-Anon meeting, a switch from the straight meetings I had been attending where the straight people I had made friends with were no threat. They had been a refuge for me, but now I had to put myself on the line.

I was terrified that I might fall into my old trap of picking up men. I was equally terrified that I might hear someone mention AIDS. Sure enough, at my first meeting someone said he had AIDS, and I sank into my seat and finally ran out of there and back to my safe straight meetings. I wasn't ready to tackle anything gay but myself.

Even in the straight rooms, when I knew someone was gay, they immediately became the enemy. I was still angry and blamed gays for the bill of goods I perceived I had bought that had taken away someone I loved. I was really angry at myself for being unable to communicate with other human beings like me without using sex. In truth, I was as backward and guilty as those I blamed. I would have to learn to love, respect, and accept myself before I could include others like me. I was still too angry.

In 1990, the couture designer Halston died of AIDS, New York versus the New St. Mark's Baths was in court to close the bathhouse, and I had a photo run-in with the willful Yoko Ono, the Asian widow of murdered ex–Beatle John Lennon.

To begin with, Ono never stopped talking about her husband's death or his assailant, Mark Chapman, as if the incident had just happened. It appeared that she had been traumatized for 10 years and hadn't come out of it.

As if that tension wasn't enough, she never stopped bossing everyone around. She wanted to wear the overbearing goggle sunglasses that covered most of her face and had been her trademark since they were designed 20 years ago. This meant that if her small eyes were to even remotely peek through all that glass and darkness, they would have to be made strong with plenty of outlining and shadowing.

Scavullo requested that I make sure her eyes showed through, and she, trying to hide behind goggles the size of a billboard, didn't want it. Talk about being caught between a rock and a hard place. In the end, Scavullo and I won, and she was not pleased. She simply didn't want to be seen, so why was she there having a photo taken?

Ono wasn't the most attractive woman to begin with, but she had at least gotten her hair styled from her previous straggly-haired hippie look, and if she had allowed the artists to give her their very best effort, she could have been far more appealing. But she was too controlling for that and did herself a disservice by not allowing skilled artists to teach her what they knew. I could only wonder how Lennon had fared with it all.

Later, BBC Television was doing a documentary on Ono, and we were all asked to assemble on the set to participate. I had to put the tops back on the make-up I had used before it dried up and arrived on the set a moment after the rest. She screeched at me as if I had committed the cardinal sin, and there was no redemption between us after that.

I saw her on the street with two men some time after the shoot and called to her as they passed. She stopped, stood her distance to make sure it was safe, and then slowly approached me when she recognized me. The trauma of Lennon's murder would probably always remain with her. Her people called me at another time to again do her make-up at the Ansonia

Hotel where she lived, but I declined. The tension and energy inside her was more than I wanted to cope with again.

Make-up was becoming a chore and putting up with clients' eccentricities was a bore. And so, the biggest bore—and probably the most difficult client I'd ever had in my career—came into my make-up life.

Paul Newman and Joanne Woodward had appeared in nine films together, and they were teamed again for their tenth one, a Merchant Ivory film about a boring Kansas City couple, circa 1930s–1940s, based on Evan S. Connell's novel *Mr. & Mrs. Bridge.* I was scheduled to do their make-up for *Harper's Bazaar.* The point to this episode in my career was that *Harper's Bazaar* had hired me and paid me, and they, therefore, owned the rights to the finished photo, not the Newmans, as it appeared to have been presumed. But I am getting ahead of myself.

The Newmans arrived at the studio and were quite congenial—certainly Woodward was. Newman was harder to connect with, but men usually were. I did an adequate make-up on both of them—particularly bringing out Woodward's eyes, which needed definition. Her hair had been colored an ashen color, neither blonde nor grey, just lifeless ashen—not even a real hair color. The photo was to be black and white, so that didn't matter, and the result was quite pleasant, with Newman leaning on Woodward's shoulder for support—perhaps as in real life.

At that time, I was in the process of making a new card to send out to magazines, ad agencies, and photography studios to display my current make-up work, and I had held off until the photo of the Newmans came out in *Harper's Bazaar,* thinking that I might use it on my new card. Artists regularly send out cards to display their work, and in this way they get jobs—like an actor sending out a resume.

At any rate, before the photo came out, I was again scheduled to do a make-up on Woodward for an interview with the film critic Gene Shalit that was to be taped in the Newmans' office in the same building on Fifth Avenue in the East Nineties where they also had an apartment. I arrived at the appointed time to find Woodward darting out of the front entrance into a limousine that was to take her to her hairdresser—rather odd in that it was the same time we had agreed to begin.

"I'll be right back," she yelled, hopping into the limo—a gross exaggeration considering the time hair usually takes.

It seemed rude that someone would be trotting off to a hairdresser the same time we were scheduled to begin. But many stars did as they pleased,

Difficult and problematic was all I could say for the Paul Newman–Joanne Woodward shoot (courtesy Francesco Scavullo Foundation, as seen in U.S. *Harper's Bazaar*).

rarely considering others' time or adhering to their agreements—the ones, that is, that thought they had the right to get away with it, like Elizabeth Taylor who had no compunctions about keeping masses of people waiting for hours while she diddled around before she made her appearance. It was the kind of arrogance that I detested.

Unless I wanted to cancel the job and go home, I had no alternative but to wait until Woodward returned. I took my make-up case into the Newmans' office on the ground floor where I saw Newman sitting in a chair next to a secretary's desk, his spectacles perched on the end of his nose, reading a newspaper. I told the secretary that I'd be back shortly, asked if I might leave my make-up case there—I could—and departed. Newman never looked up from the newspaper or said anything—not even a small acknowledgment that we'd ever met—suggesting that artists were considered workers who were necessary to the craft of actors, but nothing further.

I went out for a cup of coffee, took it into Central Park to soak up the marvelous, sunny spring weather, and when I calculated that it was time for Woodward to reappear—well over an hour later—I went back to the office. Yes, Woodward was in their penthouse, and I could go up. After receiving instructions from the secretary on where to locate the penthouse, I picked up my make-up case and left. Newman, with his spectacles still perched on the end of his nose, again said nothing.

A maid let me into the penthouse apartment and quickly disappeared, allowing me a moment to look around. Leading from the hallway entrance, overlooking Central Park, was a modest terrace with lawn furniture that was much too large for the dimensions of the small terrace, and reeked of Connecticut, where I understood they had a home. I concluded that the terrace might, in essence, have been an exact duplicate of their terrace in Connecticut, only smaller. The entire apartment had the look of country living—very folksy and homey—with plush couches and pillows with country-design fabric, and other furniture and objects everywhere that signified country living. I could only imagine Hud, Cool Hand Luke, or Butch Cassidy—some of Newman's macho film characters—living here with the gingham, lace, and calico cats. It must be true that actors are really acting.

The maid reappeared and directed me to where Woodward was waiting. I passed through a small hallway containing a gallery of framed photos of the Newmans together and alone—at functions, with dignitaries, or receiving awards—and emerged in their bedroom, which contained a canopy bed trimmed in ruffles of country fabric over the top with a fringe of ruffles around the bottom. I envisioned Cool Hand Luke, his specs perched on the end of his nose, decked out in a long flannel nightshirt topped with a nightcap with a tassel, propped up in this fussy, fluffy, ruffled bed.

Woodward was stationed on a high stool in front of the bathroom basin with barely enough room surrounding it on which to place my make-up. In a studio, I had the luxury of a large counter to place things I was using, as well as the proper lighting, with lights all around a mirror. This bathroom's light source was on the ceiling and, perhaps, a light over the basin, which created shadows everywhere. This was why I disliked doing make-up in private homes. There was never proper lighting, which made the work much harder, and the outcome was rarely my best. Lighting had to be evenly distributed, with no shadows, and there needed to be counter space on which to place make-up. It was difficult to concentrate having to return everything I was using to the make-up case because of the lack of space and then having to take it out again when I needed it.

Trying to deal with the inadequate space, I straddled my make-up case across the basin to leave open space on the right side of the counter for the make-up I would be using. This meant that I couldn't run the water to wash make-up from my hands or use it in my work.

It was most awkward, and Woodward's constant chatter didn't help matters. Whether it was a result of nerves from having to do a TV interview following the make-up or from the hairdresser having screwed her hair too tight, she never shut up. It was most distracting, but I did learn a bit from her about the old Hollywood system with both Woodward and Newman being at the end of the era of studio contract players when they began with 20th Century–Fox.

After a stressful, difficult time that left me depleted, I finally managed a so-so make-up—by no means my best and not as good as at the studio when I first did Woodward. She then took over the bedroom to dress while I waited outside and resumed my perusal of the framed photos in the hall-way.

When she was dressed, we went down in the elevator where Shalit waited in their office for the interview. While in the elevator, I reviewed the make-up I had just done, and she, recognizing that she was being scrutinized, quickly lowered her eyes to deflect my gaze. Perhaps we mortals were not supposed to gaze at stars, but my purpose was purely academic and part of my job, not from admiration. I concluded that it must take a certain conceit being a star. Did they really believe everyone was looking at them because they were one? To me they were like everyone else and by no means deities.

This was the main problem for me with Elizabeth Taylor, who seemed to feel that she deserved some kind of adulation and unreasonable respect because she was considered a star. This cut no ice with me because I felt that people had to earn respect by being respectful of others, and keeping an entire crew waiting for well over an hour—and I had heard she had kept others waiting far longer than that—started things off disrespectfully from the beginning. Woodward had done the same, which created a shaky beginning with us.

When we reached the office, Woodward ducked into the next room, where Shalit and the camera crew awaited her, and I seated myself next to Newman by the secretary's desk in full view of the activity in the adjoining room in case Woodward needed a make-up touch-up during the interview.

I picked up a newspaper, which made a crinkling noise, and Newman, peering menacingly over the specs that were perched precariously on the end of his nose, immediately shushed me. From then on, everything I did seemed to require a severe shushing until the only solution was to sit dead still—barely breathing, with no movement at all, not even a blink of an eye.

Agonizing time passed—perhaps nearly an hour that I couldn't swear to because I was barely conscious from lack of air and close to lapsing into a coma. I was then informed that Newman himself would require a make-up—not at all in the agreement between his office and my agent. He got up, and his concave butt and skinny legs got lost in the fabric of his jeans.

Did Hud have a concave butt? Good Lord. Disillusions were mounting on top of fables like barnacles on the back of a whale.

Along with a writer doing a story on the couple, we adjourned to another room in the office. By a floor-to-ceiling window, Newman seated himself in a low chair—much too low for my tall frame—and informed me that he didn't like make-up, didn't want it to look like he was wearing any, and then directed me to begin. It was not the most secure beginning. As I began my work, he and the writer broke into a loud song, making it hard to apply anything on his constantly moving face, but it was somewhat amusing.

Outside in the street, a group of three young girls had spied Newman in the window, and they were yelling. He waved back and seemed pleased that young people recognized him. When I finished the make-up—which was quite light, only covering small defects in his skin while leaving his own skin showing through—he went to a mirror to inspect the work, approved it, and left to become part of Woodward's interview. My services were no longer needed, so I packed up and left.

A short time later, the photo that was done with Scavullo came out in *Harper's Bazaar*. I included it on the new card that I was intending to do, along with photos of other stars and models I had made up, and sent it out to prospective clients, as was common practice with artists like me to show our work. I also sent a card to the Newmans since it had their photo on it, and never thought further about it until I received a letter from their lawyer, with a Xerox copy of the card. The letter said something about suing me for using their photo. Since this was a representation of my work and how I earned my living, I also felt that I had a share in the photo, which *Harper's Bazaar*, owning the rights to it, had given me permission to use. (Because of this incident, I made extra-sure this time around to have written, legal permission to use an image of my work that had appeared in a magazine before I used it in this book. I'm not taking any chances this time.)

Immediately, I contacted a lawyer, and he agreed with me that I had a right to display my work and search for jobs by sending out a card to advertise what I did. However, since the Newmans had far more money than I and could keep up quite an impressive legal fight that I might even win but would drain me financially, he suggested that I eat "humble pie." I disliked that. It was against my principles, but I decided he was right and called their office.

"Paul only wanted you to request from him the use of the photo," his secretary informed me.

I was sure that he was sitting right next to her prompting her about what to say, his specs traveling farther down his nose as we spoke. He didn't own the photo, so why would I request from him the use of it? However, his image and his wife's were on it, so maybe they had a point. But I, too, had a point in that my make-up was on it, and how could I get work if I couldn't display what I did? I felt that a judge would side with me, but it could've been the other way around and it wasn't worth a fight—especially if I lost, and lost a lot of money I didn't have.

"I won't use the photo further," I said.

It appeased them, and they let it go, but I had spent over $1,000 for that card and that was gone, too. All of this seemed so unnecessary since the cards were only going to photographers, ad agencies, and other clients in my industry, as I had explained to the secretary—hardly a massive media campaign using a star's image to promote a product, as they seemed to imply. And the secretary's conversation with me also seemed to imply that if I'd only asked Newan for permission all of this could've been avoided. It reeked of ego and pettiness to me. The other stars on the card didn't utter a peep, and this only showed how some could behave.

I was becoming disenchanted and bored with incidents like this from stars, and the entire fashion industry. I had been bored for years with spoiled, pampered models, and now it was all becoming unbearable. The new make-up artist Kevyn Aucoin had begun working in Scavullo's studio, and I was being compared with him, as I had been with Way Bandy. I continued to work, and of course receive those nifty little thank-you notes from Francesco for freebees, but that, and schmoozing with celebrities as payment, had grown very old and was no longer acceptable. It was time—in fact, past time—to be proactive.

I contacted a well-known agency in Los Angeles and began making plans to spend a few months out there exploring the possibility of working in that area. The agency, in turn, sent me one of their top clients, Kathy Smith, an exercise guru who made videos of her workouts, like Jane Fonda. The videos were made and distributed by the Guthy-Renker Corporation, with which Smith had a contract. On late night TV, Guthy-Renker's infomercials regularly touted an array of products they claimed were marvels that no one should live without. Smith's videos were among them.

Smith was a tall, quite attractive, extremely fit young woman, but suspicious of everything I put on her face. We met in her hotel suite when she came to New York on business, and as I was putting make-up on her, she kept pulling away. It's almost impossible to apply something on someone's face when they're pulling away from where you're applying it. You never really land on their face and end up in mid-air making a lunge for the spot where you want it. It's awkward, and the result is always a clumsy effort.

Recognizing that she might not be comfortable relinquishing her control to someone or that she simply didn't like being touched, as Joan Collins had confessed to me about her pulling away, I devised a plan whereby I would tutor Smith in doing her own make-up. I would stand by, handing her pencils, brushes, sponges, and different colors, while carefully explaining where to put them, how to hold them in her hand, and the results she was trying to achieve—much like her instructions in her exercise videos. Every time, she turned in dazzling results that had my touch and were expertly applied. She was the best student I could ever have imagined. The results were always perfect, and she seemed pleased with the method I was using. But I was only doing what she herself did in her videos.

Throughout my two-month stay in Los Angeles, Smith was my number one client. She did commentary for sports events for a local TV station, and I routinely worked with her make-up on these, and she had regular photo shoots that she did for her exercise videos. I would be at her house at 7:00

AM, driving in over the back roads from the valley where I was staying in a friend's apartment while he was in New York—refusing to trust my luck on the hectic L.A. freeway. That I made it to Smith's house on time every morning was a miracle, but I was never late. However, I never got any sleep either, remaining awake most of the night anticipating my early rise.

From Smith, I got information on where to contact Guthy-Renker and set up an appointment to discuss doing a teaching make-up video. It was one thing to have good make-up products, but quite another knowing how to apply them like an expert. I even envisioned Smith being an ideal spokesperson, having experienced my make-up training firsthand. It never occurred to me that she was quite content demonstrating exercise without venturing into anything to do with make-up.

I met with a representative from the company in a restaurant on Rodeo Drive, and it was decided that I should get in touch with their lawyer in New York when I got back. I even got in touch with people interested in the musical and screenplays I'd written. When I was sure that I had successfully set myself up to begin a new life, I said goodbye to Smith, the other clients I had worked with, the L.A. agency, and friends that I had made there, and headed back to New York.

I began negotiating with their New York lawyer and proposed that he also handle the screenplays and the musical with the people who had shown an interest. As it turned out, Los Angeles was far less sincere than New York. In New York, you knew where you stood. They'd tell you the truth, no matter how brutal. In Los Angeles, they tell you what you want to hear. It's all make-believe. They paint pretty pictures, talk out of each corner of their mouths, and mean nothing they say. Everything I had set up fell through.

After I trusted Guthy-Renker with a sample make-up video that I had made in New York before I left, they claimed to have lost it. Soon after, an infomercial promoting make-up products by an unknown L.A. make-up artist, Victoria Jackson—the wife of Bill Guthy of Guthy-Renker, as it turned out—began to run on late night TV. I suspected that I had simply supplied them with the idea. The people interested in my screenplays and musical turned out to be phonies who were only interested in ideas, as Guthy-Renker seemed to be. It appeared that no one in L.A. had an original idea. There was something kind of desperate and pathetic about all of it. I resolved in the future to remember that promises are like musical chords that are struck often, but are often out of tune. L.A. was over for me.

It was where Lucille Ball had also promised the moon and had given nothing, a celluloid fantasyland of make-believe and let's-pretend, where dreams fizzled and turned as brown as the petrol-polluted palm trees that lined the boulevards, where nothing was beautiful past Rodeo Drive and Beverly Hills—a meaningless blast of gas that diffused in the hot, hazy western sunlight.

Kathy Smith, too, on a trip to New York became convinced that a pair of false lashes that I put on her had been previously used by someone else, even though I explained that if they had been on anyone they wouldn't have been in my make-up case. When they went on someone—as with Smith—they were never returned. Her suspicious nature finally did us in, and we parted company.

All of it was a dismal experience, but it did confirm that I would never live in L.A. and made me even more determined to succeed with my writing. With the money I had inherited from Mother, I no longer had to be so dependent on make-up for my financial resources. Along with the other investments I had made, I decided to invest in learning the craft of writing.

I took courses in music, playwriting, and even novel writing at some of New York's best institutions for those kinds of things. The education I was getting was like going back to college. And I took them at night after a hard day of make-up at a studio. I was determined to become the best writer I could be.

Still, I had to work during all of this. Agnes de Mille, the niece of famed film producer Cecil B. de Mille, and legendary choreographer for some of Rodgers and Hammerstein's most memorable musicals like *Oklahoma!* and *Carousel*, was now 86, and Scavullo was to shoot her for *Harper's Bazaar*. Since I was especially good with older women's make-up, I was asked to do de Mille. But with such a distinct face that had grown old gracefully without surgical help (unlike many others I had worked on), de Mille was what she was, and at her advanced age, with her once-striking face years behind her, what more could I contribute? Besides, de Mille wasn't about being beautiful, anyhow.

This was why I regularly turned down Martha Graham, the legendary dancer, with her face so extremely lifted that it had become frozen and cadaver-like. There was nothing I could do to enhance it other than soften her scary, starey features—and I was never up for the challenge. Still, it's the challenges that make us strong, so I tackled de Mille, perhaps to make amends for my lack of interest in Graham.

I did very little with DeMille, recognizing that she had little tolerance being touched and fussed with. I felt that it was best to leave her as natural-looking as possible—salt of the earth sort of thing—and allow her strong features to speak for themselves. To try to glamorize her, as with Helen Hayes, would have been absurd. She, like Hayes, was no glamour puss—quite the opposite of Lucille Ball, who was all (with the emphasis on all) about make-up. Without it, she simply wouldn't have looked like herself. For some people, like some models, their faces demand make-up, while others would look foolish, even clown-like with it. It's a thin line that a make-up artist has to determine beforehand.

While I was working on de Mille, to ease the tension of working with this persistently pious, stoic, older woman whose emotions were all inward with little expression outside, I told her about another elderly woman who was the grandmother of a friend of mine.

"Life is just a dream, she once said."

"Just a dream," de Mille repeated, and mused philosophically about it.

Not content with leaving it there, I added, "But then ... there was this old man in a film I saw who was dying, and as his family gathered around his bed to hear his last words of wisdom, he said, 'It's all shit.' Depends on how you look at it."

She was not at all amused or interested in hearing this and the conversation ended there.

Though I was through with L.A., the agents I'd had there were still working with me. It behooved them to have someone in New York to provide make-up for their clients when they came through town. Rosemary Clooney was one such client, and it was arranged that I would meet with her at an East Side hotel to do her make-up for an early morning talk show intended to crank up her career after years of dormancy.

When I arrived at her suite at 7:00 AM, she had just gotten out of bed—probably to answer the door—having arrived late the night before and still on L.A. time, three hours behind New York time. The lights were mostly off in the suite as she staggered to a dressing table mirror, propped herself up with pillows in a chair, yawned, and said, "This okay?"

Well, not really. First—as with Joanne Woodward's bathroom—we needed proper lighting. The lights we had turned on only cast shadows. Make-up is best done in flat lighting that has no shadows. Since it was so early, there was no help from the light outside either. Never mind that she no longer resembled the girl in the 1954 movie *White Christmas* in which she starred with her old friend Bing Crosby. She had put on a lot of weight, for one thing. But Clooney obviously had a generous heart that would transcend any make-up I put on her face. Still, I was uncertain what to do with her: leave her looking like the fat lady next door or try to glamorize her.

With all the elements necessary to do a good make-up missing—particularly the light—I needed space to ponder my next move and began to stall for time, which we didn't have much of before she had to be downstairs to meet with people to go to the TV studio. It was one of those uncomfortable situations when you're expected to make miracles and you're not sure if you can. And she hadn't even washed her face.

While I fiddled around trying to find some inspiration, we talked about whatever came up. "Do you ever think of Bing Crosby?" I asked.

"Sometimes," was her answer.

"You're from my state, Kentucky."

"Maysville," she affirmed.

It was "Joe did this" and "Joe did that." (José Ferrer, whom she married in 1953.)

Finally we got into the comedienne Martha Raye (I have no idea how). I remarked about how much energy she had, having observed the manic Raye playing the maid in a version of *No, No, Nanette* when I worked with that show.

"Whatever she's on," returned Clooney, "...gimme some, gimme some."

"I don't think I want what Martha Raye is on," I said, innocently.

Clooney immediately shut up. Unwittingly, I had evoked the scary shadow of drugs that she had written about in her 1977 book *This for Remembrance*, in which she confessed to being institutionalized and to years of struggle to get off tranquilizers and sleeping pills.

The make-up I did was adequate—adequate, that is, had she intended to remain in this interminably dark room—but in the scrutiny of harsh studio lights, I wasn't so sure. Then she put the icing on the cake of ineptitude.

"I want false lashes," she insisted.

"Oh, you don't want those," I tried to dissuade her, knowing that I didn't have any with me that were suitable because I hadn't been told to bring them. "They're so old-fashioned."

"I want them!" She practically hit me over the head with her demand.

I scrambled in my make-up case and located a pair of lashes that resembled shoeshine brushes. They were thick and perfectly straight, with no curve at all. I had no idea where they came from or why they were so straight, but with her dogmatic determination, I had no choice but to glue them onto her eyelids. When I was finished, I observed the lashes sticking straight out over her eyes like awnings—a horrifying déjà vu of the woman years before at the Revlon Salon. I felt faint.

Because they were so straight, they appeared far too long to be believable. With no time to remove them, and with no more lashes in my case anyhow, I now had the dilemma of trimming them while they were on her face. Instructing her to keep her eyelids lowered so as not to get the tiny trimmed hairs in her eyes, I made a few careful, strategic snips, terrified that I might snip her real lashes. I dusted off the small hairs that fell onto her cheeks, gave her a bit more eye shadow and blush and, mercifully for both of us, ended the make-up.

On my way out, I passed her downstairs with the TV people; she smiled and waved, and the lashes seemed to take a bow all by themselves. I prayed that someone at the TV studio would replace them before she came out on camera resembling a broom.

For an artist who was a perfectionist, working under such adverse circumstances like bathrooms, hotel rooms, and private homes, with poor lighting and inadequate conditions, was wearing me down. I wondered how many stars could do their best work in any circumstance that was thrown at them without their air-conditioned trailer and food catered by a first-class chef.

It felt like they were saying, "Oh, just come over and do that little thing you do. We'll do it in the bathroom."

For me, make-up was an intricate art that requires skill, precision, and patience and should be given the same respect that an actor and photographer receive for their work. I had long been concerned that it was the last thing thought of when a Broadway show was being put together, which seemed to indicate that it was considered a lesser art, if it was considered an art at all.

Elizabeth Taylor taking a bath after a make-up artist and hair stylist had spent a lot of time getting her together for a Scavullo shoot only reflected her arrogance and disregard for the other artists' work. It was as if she were all that mattered. Another example of disregard was Shirley MacLaine's reaction that it was "silly" when I tried to perfect her lips, instead of being grateful that the artist was seeing to it she looked her best.

The younger stars today know the importance of it all and allow the time necessary to perfect their make-up, hair, and attire. They recognize that is how they will be remembered, while older stars many times look frumpy and foolish.

No longer content to rely on make-up as my means of support—particularly since it was becoming so unfulfilling—I explored other avenues of making a living. I knew that I had a lot more to offer, and I wanted the chance to offer it.

I taught a make-up course at the Learning Annex, but few attended, and I made very little money. As Guthy-Renker had done with the video tape I lent them, the Annex, too, lost a photo of me I lent them for publicity—so the experience was similar and dismal. I tried marketing my own teaching make-up video, but ran into trouble with a gluttonous partner. The same was true of a company that backed a cosmetic line I designed, but wanted all the profits while I did all the work.

Many were willing to make money from me, but none wanted to share it fairly. I didn't have the resources to do it by myself, but I did have enough to sustain me while I wrote. Writing, therefore, became my primary occupation. In time, I was sure it would be successful. Besides, it seemed that the universe was telling me to get out of the make-up business.

Susan Sarandon had just made the box office hit film *Thelma & Louise* with Geena Davis, and I was scheduled to do her make-up for *Harper's Bazaar*. I had done Sarandon once before and found her politics a bit tiresome. She always seemed to have her cause célèbre, like a war or some injustice—for which I basically admired her—but it was still heavy to be around.

This time—perhaps sensing that I was gay—she was on a jag about the gay group *Act Up*

Susan Sarandon had many causes with which she vigorously took issue (courtesy Francesco Scavullo Foundation, as seen in U.S. *Harper's Bazaar*).

that she applauded for standing up to the Catholic Church and demanding their religious rights. I, too, felt that gays deserved religious rights and everything that was extended to heterosexuals, but I disliked *Act Up* throwing feces on the altar of a Catholic Church, as I had heard they had done. That certainly didn't represent me as a gay man—as I chose to be represented—and I didn't condone it.

For several years, I had marched with the Al-Anon group in the New York gay pride parade the last Sunday in the month of June. As we passed St. Patrick's Cathedral on Fifth Avenue each year, there was always a group of people waving large banners that told the gays they were going to hell. They were unaware of how spiritually devout many gays are. The ones I knew were God-loving, good people, good parents, kind and loving to their partners. To me, disallowing anyone who loved another human being the right to marry did far more harm than the alternative of marriage because it encouraged multiple partners and, therefore, promiscuity. My past promiscuous behavior, for which I was greatly sorry, had gravely affected my life, and Michael's too, and I recognized the harm these people did with their bigotry. As far as I was concerned, anything that God created was good and intentional and should be respected as everything else on earth—which was probably what Sarandon was saying, though her version was not quite as palatable.

Throughout the make-up, Sarandon hammered away about the right of *Act Up* to act up. She wanted me to agree with her, but, regardless of the fact that I was gay, they didn't represent me with their tactics, and her determination for me to accept her viewpoint was wearing. Being pent up for a period of time with stars like Sarandon and MacLaine, who had strong opinions and political agendas, was exhausting, and I yearned to be out of my predicament. Make-up was becoming an infringement on my right to my personal privacy.

Then the invader of all personal privacy and crosser of boundaries hit my make-up life: Dyan Cannon. Other than being a sometimes-good comic actress, for which she twice received Best Supporting Oscar nominations, Cannon was most noted for somehow managing to have a three-year marriage with actor Cary Grant, with whom she had a child. Past that, her screen performances were mostly unmemorable, including a current autobiographical, self-indulgent, psycho-swill she wrote, directed, and starred in titled *The End of Innocence*, in which she relayed her nervous breakdown and psychiatric treatment supposedly back to mental health—though I couldn't have personally vouched for it.

She was one of those clients, like Rosemary Clooney, who came to New York and was referred to me by the agency in California. I was scheduled to make her up for an interview with *New York Post* columnist Cindy Adams, who had an apartment on Fifth Avenue with her husband, columnist and comedian Joey Adams. My job, as far as I was informed, was to meet with Cannon that morning before her interview with Adams, do her make-up, and leave.

I arrived at Cannon's hotel suite, was ushered inside by some young woman, and finally a much-disheveled Cannon made her appearance with her characteristic freaky-curly, long blonde hair—that hadn't made a transition since the 1960s. We adjourned to another room, and as I prepared to begin, I said something that struck her as funny and she shrieked a high-pitched, shrill laugh that sounded like it was feeding time at the zoo. It so jarred me and put me off that it was a relief when the make-up was completed and I could make a beeline for the door and return home before the vampires struck.

As I entered my apartment, the phone was ringing. It was the agency in California wanting to know why I had left Cannon's suite. Apparently, she was under the impression that I was to be her prisoner for the entire day. The notion that I'd be pent up with her all day both horrified and per-plexed me—and I'd never negotiated a fee for it. To add further insult, I wouldn't be getting my usual daily rate because Cannon's company wouldn't pay it.

Under any other circumstance, I would have bailed out. It was the fault of the agency that I was unaware the job was to be all day and that a daily fee had never been discussed. I also didn't particularly like whom I was work-ing with—she simply grated on my nerves—and for that alone, I deserved to be paid more for the day, or certainly not less. However, being a profes-sional who had never left a job undone, and feeling that the California agency had been especially kind and loyal to me and I didn't want to let them down or embarrass them, I reluctantly accepted what was offered—but I was royally pissed off.

I returned to Cannon's suite to find her done up in a plaid mini-skirt outfit with a halter top and white blouse that looked as though she had ripped it off some young Catholic schoolgirl—and this from a woman then in her mid-fifties. The end of innocence, indeed. With a couple of young women she continually bullied around, we climbed into a limousine and began an arduous journey to Adams' apartment for the interview.

While in transit—with New York traffic stalling us at every stop sign—

Cannon yakked ad nauseum on a phone with someone on the West Coast while we, her captive audience, endured her tirade.

It was an enormous relief to finally arrive at Adams' apartment, which was charmingly decorated in a Chinese motif with a collection of Chinese objects against a wall of red—my favorite color. Cindy was also charming, and I would have preferred to be working with her. We were directed into another room, where Cannon showed me her implanted teeth that did create a great smile, I had to admit—but without the accompaniment of the laugh. After the cameras were set up in the living room, the interview with Adams began while we watched.

I expected to be going home after this, but I was informed that I would be needed for a photo shoot that was to follow with *People* magazine. My heart sank. I was desperate to get away from this woman. Even without the hyena laugh, she had no appeal for me, and I wondered what Grant had seen in her—but then, he was an old man when he saw it.

A painted horse from an old merry-go-round that represented something from the movie had been placed in the photographer's studio, and she was supposed to be photographed on it. A whole disagreement now erupted with Cannon not sure she wanted to be photographed on the horse and the photographer insisting that it would make a great photo.

It was late by this time, I was exhausted, hungry, and fed up, and I wanted out. I told them I had a ticket to a Broadway play and would have to be going soon in time to make it there—a small white lie that was intended to free me and get me the hell home. They could argue all they wanted about the frigging horse, but I'd had enough.

Now Cannon insisted that a union make-up artist be summoned to see her through whatever she might need after I left. A poor, unsuspecting soul from the union arrived and I quickly tutored him as to what he might expect in the way of make-up patch-ups during the shoot, hurriedly packed up, and left before she could think up something else.

Whether that California agency ever again sent me another client from there made no difference at this point.

As I had been pulling away from make-up, Scavullo, too, had been pulling away from me and others who had worked with him over the years. He hoped that the new crop of artists like Kevyn Aucoin would revitalize his photography. His work had been stale, predictable, and unexciting for years, but whenever he ran into trouble, the artists were to blame and they were immediately replaced.

The phenomenal success of brilliant new photographers like Patrick Demarchelier, Steven Meisel, Herb Ritts, Bruce Weber, and his old nemesis Richard Avedon gnawed at him. He would be devastated to lose his much-coveted *Cosmopolitan* magazine covers to Demarchelier—after more than 30 years working on them—when editor-in-chief Helen Gurley Brown left the magazine in '97.

"Thank you for all your beautiful make-ups all these years," his voice announced on my answering machine.

Click. That was it: my dismissal—not in person or even a gold watch.

"I called you all the way from Florida," he said later in a ridiculous attempt to put a more valuable spin on it, but only after a German cosmetic company, owned by a wealthy friend of mine, was considering using him for a series of ads—at my suggestion—and they insisted on me.

It was a small triumph that he would now have to eat crow and include me after his rude, unkind brush-off. However, the price he wanted for the ads scared the company away, and they decided to do them in Germany, ending my triumph. As quickly as my make-up career had begun, it was now officially over.

20

Empty Pockets, Helen Gurley Brown's Party, Finding Myself

The best thing about the 1990s was that they weren't the 1980s. The '80s for me—as for many others in the country—were a period of uncertainty in that we thought we had more money than we did, our leaders weren't that trustworthy, and unemployment, budget deficits, and a recession flamed out of control past our capacity to handle them.

As the '90s rolled in, I was sure that they would bring with them better times. Each year since Michael's death, I felt that there would be a renewal, a fresh new start, but each year only seemed to get worse. Now that I had lost my job with Scavullo, it only seemed to point to more of the same.

Luckily, I was fortified with some money from Mother to see me through. I believed that I could sell a screenplay or the musical and everything would be all right. I spent lavishly on some new clothes—I certainly deserved them—and I redid my apartment. It wouldn't be long, I told myself, until something sold, so I didn't worry about expenditures.

In '91, George H. W. Bush led the country into a war with Iraq for invading their small neighbor Kuwait. The war that Iraq's ominous leader Saddam Hussein titled "The mother of all wars" was titled by America "Operation Desert Storm." Directed by General Norman Schwarzkopff, it lasted about a month and might have been more appropriately titled "The wuss of all wars." As it turned out, it was only a preliminary rehearsal for a more aggressive invasion in 2003, authorized by George W. Bush, and this time titled by America "The 2nd Persian Gulf War." The conflict would again last about a month, and nine months after it officially ended, Saddam Hussein would be captured and held accountable for his atrocities against his people.

286

In '93, a bomb was detonated by radical Islamic terrorists in the underground garage of the first tower of the World Trade Center in New York, killing six people and injuring 1,000 more. Sadly, this, too, was a preliminary rehearsal for what was to follow when on the morning of September 11, 2001, the terrorists again struck more aggressively at both the Pentagon and the World Trade Center—this time demolishing both of the Center's towers. The combined attacks would kill 3,030 people and injure 2,337 others, the most devastating mass murder in American history.

Also in '93, after a 51-day standoff with federal agents over illegal possession of firearms and explosives, the Branch Davidians, a radical religious group in Waco, Texas, led by David Koresh, burned their compound to the ground, killing 80 people inside, while injuring scores of others. In '95, Timothy McVeigh, a white extremist suspected of al Qaeda ties, with his cohort Terry Nichols, bombed the Murrah Federal Building in Oklahoma City, Oklahoma, killing 169 people, which was then considered the largest mass murder in American history until the 2001 bombing of the World Trade Center. Rounding out the violence of the '90s, on Hitler's 110th birthday in '99, two deranged schoolboys shot and killed 12 of their classmates and a teacher at Columbine High School in Jefferson County, Colorado, before turning their guns on themselves.

It seemed the terror that AIDS had introduced into society at the beginning of the '80s signaled the same terror the world would one day face everywhere, right into the new millennium. The lawlessness I had seen creeping into New York society nearly two decades earlier was the same that would spread worldwide. Where it had its beginning roots was impossible to say, but if it was true that man is how he thinks, hate, bigotry, and the lack of love and caring for others would surely encourage more of the same.

I wondered if man had brought all this on himself by his own thinking. If we cared so little for one another, why not take a gun and shoot everyone, bomb everything? This seemed the same kind of thinking that was becoming prevalent throughout the world. Had we forgotten the strength of love, that a lack of it can crumble mountains? Was society doomed to its own destruction merely by a lack of love? Was this what promoted lawlessness and issued a license to kill? It had happened in New York with all the murders in the '80s—why not everywhere now? Hate and violence was the new fashion, and those who practiced it were our new media stars.

New York still had ineffectual Mayor Dinkins until Rudy Giuliani took over in '94 and provided better police protection and restored stability to the city. Bill Clinton would take over the presidential helm from George H. W. Bush in '93 and—in between sexual liaisons with Monica Lewinsky—manage to balance the government's budget that would be sent askew when George W. Bush became president in 2001 and once more got the country entangled with Iraq with no end in sight.

By the mid '90s, my money ran out. I had invested it, even wisely, but I also spent it quicker than I could make it, which could be classified as foolish. My plan to have a screenplay or my musical produced by then and living off the proceeds didn't pan out. It was obvious that I would have to return to work. It had felt good to arrogantly give the finger to the fashion and cosmetic worlds for several years, but now I needed them.

After an eight-year absence, they didn't need me. In fact, no one even remembered me. Everyone was new and had never even heard of me. My portfolio was dismally out of date, and the models that were represented in it were over the hill or no longer in the business. I had a book of relics of the past.

I was sure the photographers, ad agencies, and agents that I showed it to would at least be impressed with the celebrities I was presenting—and surely the make-up too—but they were also out of date. A few years out of an industry that caters to and thrives on the latest makes anything that was yesterday obsolete.

They were impressed to the extent that it was all a curiosity, but the business had changed. The agents now had their stable of photographers, make-up, hair, and stylists, and agents now controlled the business and said who was in and who was out. If they didn't need you, you were out. The business was saturated with everyone who had any talent at all, and they were all young, in their twenties.

Fashion was a young industry, as it had always been even when I started. But there was no one doing what I was doing at the time—and I was young then, too. The numbers of creative people who wanted into the industry now were staggering, and age played a big part in who got in. A man who was—shall we say—mature wasn't what they were looking for. They were looking for youth. They believed that youth would bring vitality to the art, and perhaps they were right because after years of drudgery in the industry—having seen it all—perhaps all I was really willing to bring to it was a cynical view.

I knew that I could still cut it, and with the knowledge that only experience can bring to one's art, I could dance rings around these young upstarts and show them how make-up should supremely be applied. But they were only interested in youthful types like Kevyn Aucoin, who had taken over the make-up business since I left, and others who had funneled through the golden gates of fashion until their swelling numbers had rendered the industry filled to capacity and overflowing. I was literally out of fashion.

I had half-seriously told myself that when the money I had inherited ran out I would commit suicide. Mary had recently committed suicide, and, stunned and morosely reflecting on the act, I concluded that it would be a quick fix for my dilemma, too. It had been her way out of her addictions and the pain they must have caused her, and now I would have to make my choice.

I chose not to even consider it. I recognized that Mother—no matter how painful it must have been living alone all those years without her partner—still saw life through to the end, and the last part couldn't have been that pleasant after a debilitating accident left her infirm and in a nursing home. She couldn't have done anything about her situation had she even wanted to, but I was certain, no matter what, that she would never have chosen suicide. If she could stick it out to the end, so could I. I was even repulsed that Mary had chosen that route out of her predicament. It seemed weak to me and definitely out of the question. There was nothing to do about life but accept it on its own terms. Fighting it made no sense.

Still, I was in a quandary as to what to do. I was down to my last thousand dollars, and with time having rendered me obsolete in my old industry, I couldn't expect help there. The rent was now due, and to make matters worse, I had foolishly maxed out several credit cards for which I had insufficient funds to pay the monthly charges. As Job in the Bible said: "The thing which I greatly feared has come upon me." As I thought, so I had become.

I had been fearful about money from the beginning of my inheritance and, in spite of myself, had bought what Mother had said about me not knowing anything about it. Though I thought I was trying, I was really afraid to hold onto it for fear of losing it, so I got rid of it so I wouldn't have to worry anymore. Now I had the worry of paying my rent with no money to do it. I couldn't lose my apartment. Like many people seeing the homeless on the streets today, my biggest fear was becoming one of them. That just wasn't an option. I had hated camping out since I was a child, and I certainly wasn't going to make it a lifestyle. I doubted that I could survive on the street, anyhow, after years of creature comforts that I had no intention of giving up.

I couldn't expect immediate money from any work I might do—whatever that might be I had no idea at the moment—but I did have things to sell. My sister had sent me several things from Mother's house that I had asked for, and part of them was a considerable amount of silver. I'd had a taste of polishing the silver I was using in my apartment, and the exhausting monthly chore made that an easy choice of things to give up. I loved how the silver sparkled around my apartment for a time before it turned a dismal shade of soot and was no longer attractive. Then it was back to the polishing routine to make it shine before the cycle had to be repeated all over again. It was a big, big drag. So the silver was easy to let go of.

Then I had Mother's and my father's diamond rings. Though I had particularly wanted Mother's ring because it reminded me of her, it had become a burden to figure out whom to leave it to when I was gone. I didn't want to be put in the position of playing favorites with the females in my family if I left it to one but neglected the others. It didn't look right on the hands of any of my female friends, so I decided to let go of both rings. I wasn't interested in keeping my father's, anyhow. Diamonds weren't really my best friends, and I didn't need anything to remind me of him. Some things in life are best left buried, so to speak.

Each day for several weeks I loaded a bag with silver things—terrified that a thug on the subway might grab the bag and run—and pounced on antique shops all over Manhattan that bought such things. I also had an antique clock—the one that had stopped at the exact time Mother died, which had belonged to my grandmother—and, not wishing it to tick away my life too, I took it, along with two matching candelabras, and sold the entire set for over $1,000. Mother's and my father's rings brought nearly $2,000. For that month the rent was paid, but I still had credit card debt that was eating away everything I could scrape together.

After sternly reprimanding me for spending all of my inherited money, my sister suggested bankruptcy as a way out of part of my situation, but not wishing to incur bad credit, I held off. Now it had become clear that I could no longer make the credit card payments and stay afloat. I visited a lawyer and arranged to file for bankruptcy. There was simply no alternative.

The small bankruptcy court in downtown Manhattan had about 20 people there to file, as I was. I met the lawyer outside the room at our appointed time, went inside, and waited our turn. When my name was called, my lawyer got up and motioned for me to follow him to the judge's desk. The judge, or maybe arbitrator, a no-nonsense, grim man, asked me if I knew what I was doing. I didn't, but I answered "yes," signed a paper, and that was it. My creditors would get no more money from me, and I would be issued no more credit cards from them. Instead, I'd have to pay enormous interest rates in the future if I wanted a card from anyone—Capital One would be the first to make the offer—and I'd have a bad credit rating for seven or maybe ten years, with no store allowing me a credit card in the foreseeable future. Bad credit doesn't speak highly of one and isn't something to be entered into lightly, but with no other solution, I was forced to suffer it.

This solved only some of my problems. Until I found a means of support, I still needed financial help. I was told about food stamps and immediately applied for them. Downtown on East Sixteenth Street, I entered a large room filled with people, poor people who had never had any of the advantages that I'd had. It was unlikely any of them had attended college—most probably hadn't even finished high school or perhaps gotten farther than grade school—and certainly their education hadn't been paid for by their parents, as mine was. I recognized how lucky I had been that I hadn't had to work my way through college to get my education, that I hadn't graduated with a huge debt from the money I'd had to borrow to get it.

After hours of waiting as each person in the room filed through the door in front of us into another room filled with rows and rows of desks behind which city employees—some probably not that financially stable themselves—decided who qualified for food stamps, my name was called, and I entered the room behind the rest. A black woman, who had inherited my number that we had queued up by, gruffly went over my financial situation from my monthly bank statements, rent, phone, and utility bills, which we had been instructed to bring as proof of our need. When it was determined that I qualified for food stamps, a photo of me was taken, more forms were filled out and signed, and the amount of food stamps I would be getting a month—the maximum the government then allowed—was a whopping $130.

"I don't think I can get by on that a month," I complained, not realizing that was it and there wasn't any more regardless whether I could get by or not.

The black woman, frazzled from having to do this job in the first place and weary from complaints she could do nothing about, looked at me with disgust. I didn't look like the usual person who trundled through here. I didn't look poor—though I was; I was clean and well-dressed, and I didn't speak like I didn't have at least some education. She was putting up with no shit from me.

"Honey," she said, "I could feed my whole family on that and still have some left over at the end of the month."

I looked at her worn, lined face, a face that had history, hard history, and I said, "I bet you could, too."

Like Ebenezer Scrooge in Dickens' A Christmas Carol viewing his past, present, and future through three visiting ghosts, she was one I would be blessed to meet on this miraculous journey I was taking on a road I had never been on before.

I still needed more help. The money from what I could sell was small, didn't last long, and eventually didn't pay the rent. I spent a day in a long hallway corridor at Bellevue Hospital on East Twenty-Sixth Street waiting to apply for financial aid. Sitting against the wall with me in this narrow, sterile hallway with cold marble floors and stone walls were families with children, women and men who were at the end of their rope like me, all poor and disheveled, with worried looks on their faces—desperate. They were the people I had passed on the streets for years, no-name people that I didn't care to know, shadows that float past us daily that we take no notice of because their plight doesn't pertain to us. I was now one of them.

I never thought I would ever be. I had gotten a B.F.A. degree at the University of Kentucky and had advanced training at Pratt Institute after that. This poverty I was experiencing was not the promise I had been told to expect after all of that. I had been an acclaimed artist in two fields: make-up and fashion illustration. Surely, this couldn't be happening after having achieved that much. But it was, and I waited like the rest of them lined up in chairs along this corridor while the governmental bureaucracy filed each of us through the door, shuffled through papers, and decided our fate.

Would we qualify for help or would we not? Mostly, this job was in the hands of minorities who were employed by the system and controlled it. They, themselves, probably knew firsthand the plight each of us was going through, having perhaps been in the same situation, either raised by parents or someone who also needed help, and doubtlessly experiencing prejudice too, making matters even more difficult. They knew only too well who we were.

It was the most humbling—as well as enlightening—experience of my life to become one of them. That they could feel compassion for others, after being shunned and even scorned by society, was a marvel in itself. This was a lesson in true forgiveness and humility. I never again would pass a person on the street that I recognized as one of these and not bless them or offer some monetary help. They were the no-name people, the shadows, but they were created in love the same as I. They were me and all of us—no discrimination or difference in the eyes of God. I blessed them because I thanked them for awakening me. They had shown me the way to gratitude.

I learned to bless the unpleasant and the struggle because they were forcing my soul to grow. I learned faith in God, too. When there was no one or anything else, I experienced that God was always there. It was only a matter of prayer, and there it was, as close as my heartbeat. It was my heartbeat; it was my soul.

Once, when I was literally down to my last 50 cents and quite hungry because I had little money in my pocket for food, I stopped at a street vendor who sold fresh fruit and vegetables and bought a banana for a quarter. A homeless person darted up to me and asked for the quarter I had left, and I gave it to him. Now he had more money than I did, but I knew that God would take care of me—and the homeless person, too. I managed to eat for a few days with the food I had in my refrigerator, and then, out of the blue, a check arrived. I recognized it as God at work, blessed it, and bought more food to see me through.

Recognizing that God was at work freed me to enjoy life. I stopped worrying about money and left the thinking to God. I did my part by learning to be thoughtful about money. This was what I began to call being a good steward of God's resources. God supplied, and I did my part by doing the work that was required, and God took care of the rest. This became my no-worry philosophy.

I can't say that at first I didn't worry. When I'd get down to my last dime—and I mean not enough to even ride a subway—I'd panic and call Silent Unity in Unity Village, Missouri, and ask them to pray for me. They always did without question, and every time the challenge I was having would subside. Prayer then became my big healer of everything.

It wasn't always easy to yield to the fact that things would turn out all right, but the more I worked on it, the better I got at letting go and letting God. After all, when our head is chattering away with fear, anger, resentment, and lack of faith, God can't get through. We have to clear the circuits. I did this by remembering how many, many times God came through, even at the last minute, and nothing even remotely as bad as I was projecting ever happened—hard times, maybe, but never a catastrophe. I kidded that the worst thing that could happen was that I would die and then I wouldn't have to pay next month's rent. To me, there were worse things than death, and living in anguish paralyzed by fear was one of them. Not that any of us want to die or hurry it up, but that's the worst that could happen, and it never did.

And even if it had, was that really the worst? When I prayed for Mother before she died, I didn't ask that God save her, because God has his own ideas, but I prayed that his will be done and I would accept that. She died and I accepted it. Then I saw her in that dream looking young again, fit, trim, and walking Big Boy the dog, and I knew it was just fine. I never worried again. That was the kind of faith I had been developing ever since and would use the rest of my life.

In the Bible, God asks Solomon what he wants and Solomon answers that he wants an understanding heart. God grants him that and all the riches he didn't ask for, too. That was what I wanted: an understanding heart, because with that we can figure out all the rest. Worldly riches may follow, but understanding and compassion for others store up eternal treasures.

A friend suggested that I consider supplementing my government help with some work. I rarely had enough resources to see me through an entire month, and I was always down to the last of my food and many times unable to afford a subway. Since my industry had changed—and didn't want me anyhow—I began to look into smaller photographers who took headshots for aspiring actors. Several employed me, but even with that and help from the government, it was still not enough to really adequately sustain me. I wanted to sell one of my screenplays or the musical but that wasn't happening. Though I appreciated the learning experience of being poor, I didn't want to remain there. I believed that people remained poor because they accepted that was all they could get. That wasn't for me. I was certain that somehow I could do better.

One evening on the phone, I was complaining to a woman friend that I had tried everything to get my writing through the doors of people who could do something with it, but that nothing was working.

"Well, you haven't tried everything," she said in the authoritative tone that annoyed me the most about her.

"What haven't I tried? I worked like hell to get two production companies to do staged readings of my musical, I send out queries all the time about my screenplays and the musical, and nothing ever comes of any of it."

"Well, you still haven't tried everything," she restated with that superior edge in her voice.

"Well, I don't know what I haven't tried," I said, somewhat defeated, and feeling worse now that I had talked with her.

There was a pause, and then she said, "Why don't you write the story of your life?"

"Don't be ridiculous. Who'd buy that?"

"You're always telling stories about the celebrities you worked on, and everybody loves them."

"I wouldn't even know where to begin."

"Just go over to your computer and start: 'I was born in Glasgow, Kentucky...'"

How utterly stupid, I thought, and couldn't wait to get off the phone. Why had I consulted with her in the first place? She always knew more than anyone, and that was her most irritating characteristic. Besides, what did she know about writing or publishing or any of it? I went over to the computer, turned it on, and wrote: "I was born in Glasgow, Kentucky..."

When I had done a sizable amount of writing and was feeling confident and even enjoying the writing process, as well as what I had written, I bought *Writer's Market*, a telephone-book-size reference book that lists agents and publishers in all fields of writing, and sent a multitude of query letters to agents. Surprisingly, quite a few replied; one in California, who seemed particularly interesting, caught my eye, and I contacted her.

As it turned out, she was an agent from hell: a dictatorial, abrasive, abusive, controlling harpy if there ever was one, hell-bent on rewriting my story herself. I was working on an old second-hand Macintosh computer— circa somewhere in the '90s—that was nothing but a glorified typewriter. It certainly had no capacity to send or receive e-mails, nor the capacity to open any documents.

The screaming this woman did at me every time Kinko's or my copy shop sent her a document on my behalf that she couldn't open on her end was horrendous. And she herself was still working on an old Mac and had to send things to one of her writers who returned them to her in some format that she could open. The only capacity this woman had more than I had was the capacity to e-mail, and e-mail she did, totally capitalizing words she wanted to emphasize to scream her irritation with me about some matter.

She rewrote the first chapter of my story and edited my writing so severely that I didn't recognize my writing and my voice any longer. Not only was it boring and uninteresting even to me, I was sure it would appear the same to a publisher. Whenever I'd suggest a change, she'd rant at me via one of her famous e-mails until I desisted.

Determined to turn my book into a celebrity memoir—exactly the opposite of my intention—she submitted her writing of the book to publishers, and it wasn't accepted, though she had insisted throughout that she was a published writer, implying that she knew what she was doing and I didn't. Thankful to be out of this situation with this impossibly arrogant, dictatorial woman, I gladly took back my book and resumed doing what I had been doing: writing about a section of my life in which celebrities played a part but were not the entire focus. For me, they were just simply my day job.

In retrospect, I had jumped too fast into this relationship, grateful that someone wanted what I did, and hadn't bothered to check on her with other clients, which I eventually did and found that everyone had had difficulties with this woman. The lesson I learned was to wait until the right person came along, trust my instincts, and not accept that someone is an expert just because they say so. No one knows better about us than we do.

To be fair, she did give me ideas about how to form the book. I had begun it back in my hometown and she told me that no one gave a damn about that because they didn't know me. I was a new writer and needed to immediately get into what I had to say about the make-up and fashion business and the celebrities—good advice that I took. I resolved that with persistence I could eventually find the right agent or publisher for the book—and I did have a couple more agents, one worse than the other, but never as bad as the first—and then other factors played into it. At a church I had begun to attend I met a kind gentleman who had just had a book published by the publishers of this book. He recommended my book to them, they liked it, and this is the book you are now reading. Persistence is usually the key to success but, in this case, I believe it was divine guidance that got this book published—for whatever reason, but I am truly humbled and grateful for its publication.

As Mayor of New York, Guiliani had made it a far safer place than it had been in many years, and the tourists were returning. Bill Clinton was our president—sometimes good, sometimes bad, depending on whether his sexual proclivity was flaring up—and Reagan had announced his Alzheimer's, beginning his long, sad journey to his death in 2004.

In '97, when Helen Gurley Brown threw her party at the Pierre to celebrate Scavullo's newest book, *Scavullo: Photographs 50 Years*, it was as much a celebration for that as it was a farewell for everyone who attended. Brown was leaving *Cosmopolitan* magazine—with which Francesco was no longer affiliated, replaced by photographer Patrick Demarchelier—and the artists at the party, including myself, were over the hill and on their way out. Many would soon be dead, including Francesco in 2004, followed by my old combatant, Richard Avedon, nine months later the same year.

My life had so drastically changed, and I myself had so changed, that seeing this old tribe at the Pierre was like a bad trip back in time that no longer applied to me. Everyone there was simply no longer relevant or important to me. Writing had so completely replaced my make-up art—as make-up had once replaced my fashion illustration art—that I was disinterested in the splattering of fashion information from any of these people. Fashion—and frankly, the whole bunch—bored me, and it was a relief to get away from them and return home.

What had been my search—the fame and fortune bit—I'd had all along. It was deep inside me; all I had to do was be patient and one day it would spring forth, as it did. True, there wasn't so much fortune, or even fame, that emerged, but a deep feeling of well-being that I had always yearned for. It was this God-thing, a power deep inside that I had to uncover, learn about, and accept that was the real search. It had been like a trip down the yellow brick road, and as Dorothy in *The Wizard of Oz* discovered, "There's no place like home." I had to discover, like Dorothy, that I'd had it all along. I didn't even have to leave Glasgow, Kentucky; it was exactly where God had placed it when I was born.

"If I ever go looking for my heart's desire again," Dorothy says, "I won't look any farther than my own backyard, because if it isn't there, I never really lost it to begin with."

Like others in the country, when the Millennium came, I gathered with friends at another friend's apartment and celebrated. Unlike other New Year Eves I had known in the past, this one was different by one significant thing: we would no longer put 19 in front of the year. It felt odd, like the loss of an old friend. All of the catastrophes that had been predicted—like our bank balances disappearing, alarms going off, and a whole disruption of civilization—didn't happen. When the Millennium arrived, other than the roar from the crowd in Times Square—that wasn't far from the party—and a few fireworks, things remained pretty calm and orderly.

Before the party, a friend and I stopped by Unity and prayed with the more sedate group there before going onto the livelier gathering. I thanked

God that I had made it this far, and I blessed Mother and Michael who hadn't. I was sure that they could experience it, and the days to come, through my eyes.

In 2001, America had its most terrifying and destructive experience in its history when Al-Qaeda terrorists destroyed the 110-story twin towers of the World Trade Center in New York.

That morning, I was on the phone with a friend who had called to tell me that a plane had just hit one of the twin towers and it was on fire. My first reaction was that pilots couldn't maneuver their planes properly—like the Army Air Corps B-25 bomber that had ploughed into the Empire State Building in 1945, killing 14 people. As we watched on TV, another plane slammed into the other tower, and people began jumping from the windows until the cameras mercifully stopped showing it. Then the most horrific, unbelievable nightmare unfolded before our eyes when both towers came tumbling down like a child's Tinker Toys. With people screaming, pandemonium broke out as the TV crew and everyone ran for their lives as the thick, grey dust engulfed them and swallowed them up.

I stayed glued to the TV for days after that, shocked at the horror I had seen. It was inconceivable that once again humanity had chosen the mass murder of thousands of innocent people who had no involvement or say in governmental choices to solve its problems.

Had the Holocaust stopped the Jews from procreating? Had Hiroshima stopped Japan from once again becoming a great nation? What about Vietnam, or Germany? Had any of the killing stopped anything, aided anyone, other than perhaps rearranging some global monetary conditions? Everyone was still here, still doing what they'd always done, but what about the masses of innocent people who were denied their lives? Did killing any of them solve anything other than cause a lifetime of pain and sorrow for those left behind who had never done anything against the perpetrators of this cowardly act?

Was horror, grief, and destruction the reward for killing? It was as if the world had learned nothing—and where was God in all of this? The terrorists evoked the name of God to do this dastardly thing. Could they honestly believe that the God I knew, the God of love, could possibly condone this?

I was incensed—and worse: I was psychologically screwed up by the event. I had watched as planes destroyed a building in downtown Manhattan, the city where I lived. How dare they! I was angry, and I was afraid. Isn't that what they had wanted? How had Londoners survived with Germany pummeling their beloved city and country with bombs? They were more courageous than I.

I felt that everything I had written was absolute rubbish and had no purpose, that everything, really—compared to this event—had no meaning or purpose whatsoever. It had been hard enough struggling with the deaths in my life, my mental and financial conditions, struggling to get back on my feet, but now this. And my suffering was nothing compared to those who had lost loved ones in the catastrophe. If ever I felt like ending it all, it was then.

I briefly saw a psychologist—an ineffectual woman connected with my health plan—to try to get my head screwed on properly, but her unsympathetic, even bored nature told me to move on. I decided that I was strong enough on my own to handle whatever was bothering me. It was the effect of the tragedies in my life that was resurfacing, but it wasn't real. I'd had enough Al-Anon and spiritual understanding by this time to know what to do—certainly better than some lump sitting there looking at her watch until my time was up. I even had a momentary fantasy of taking over her job. I couldn't have done worse than she did. I would depend on God—as I always had—and that would be my answer.

Several weeks after the disaster, I went down to Ground Zero, as the destruction area in downtown Manhattan was now being referred to. It resembled a city of grey dust. Dust, inches thick, covered the buildings that were still standing, storefronts that weren't blown out, every inch of their insides, and all of the streets. It was a ghost town that advertised hamburgers, restaurants, clothing, and drugstore items with no customers. The windows were mostly blown out, and the buildings that were standing were vacant. No one wanted to live, work, or do business there. They couldn't with the stench of air so foul that we were advised to cover our mouths and noses.

Cops prodded the band of people shuffling with me along the sidewalk to keep moving, while vendors, intent on making a sale, sold American flags and other trinkets, made in Thailand and China, commemorating the event. I didn't blame them for trying to make money—I knew what it was to be poor and in need—but at a time like this, it was hard to take.

By going down one of the side streets as I was instructed to do, I caught a glimpse of the shells of buildings that were destroyed, which I'd seen on TV, standing on angles like ghostly sculptures with an indication of windows where there were no windows, testifying to the disaster. Downtown Manhattan resembled the war zone that it was, like photos of the ruins in Germany after massive bombing in the Second World War, and here it was in my hometown.

Coming back uptown, I passed Bloomingdale's, close to my neighborhood, and pictured the same scene up here as I had seen downtown. It was as if we were again entering a horrible time, as we had gone through in Vietnam, only that had been over there and this was here.

Everywhere, on fences, sides of buildings, lampposts, stop signs, anywhere that could contain them, were pictures of loved ones and desperate pleas to help locate them. They didn't exist; they had been mowed down by malicious killers selfishly thinking only of their cause.

I went back to Al-Anon, which I hadn't attended in a while, talked a bit, and got things straightened out for myself. I found that when things bothered me, it was best to say it, get it out, and somehow that put it in perspective. The worst was to let it stay bottled up inside where it could cause damage. The overwhelming feeling of hopelessness and despair finally went away and I was freed.

I continued my make-up work with smaller photographers whom I worked with regularly, but I still struggled. I took comfort in my writing, for which I now had three agents representing my book, screenplays, and the musical. Still, it was an anxious waiting game.

In 2002, I read that make-up artist Kevyn Aucoin had died. I knew only too well the pitfalls of fame and glamour in the fashion world. It was hard not to succumb to its trappings, and I was sorry that it had taken him. I knew what it was to be gifted and lost.

Then, in 2004, I saw on TV one evening that Francesco Scavullo had died. He was 82, but still it seemed too soon. I made sure to leave open the following evening to go to the Frank E. Campbell Funeral Chapel on Madison Avenue where he was—along with everyone else I knew who all seemed to want to end up there. What they did in there that made the place so good, I had no idea.

I wouldn't attend the funeral the next day because I'd had enough of funerals, but I wanted to say goodbye to an old acquaintance, probably more of a business acquaintance than a friend. After all, he had called "all the way from Florida" to give me my farewell of "Thank you for all your beautiful make-ups all these years." The least I could do was walk up Madison Avenue to the funeral home, which wasn't far from my apartment.

I called Francesco's old agent with whom I was still in contact, the one who had jump-started his career when it all began. She was the true source of his success, having rescued him from near obscurity in the '70s and gotten him started with *Vogue*, and he never even thanked her.

"Would you like to come with me tomorrow night?" I asked.

"Why?" was her response.

Francesco had not been kind to a lot of people; he had been insulting and even cruel to some. Hiding behind a camera all those years didn't really allow that many in, and few really knew him—if any. I had caught glimpses of the human inside that indicated there might be more, and that was why I was going. However, having been so unceremoniously tossed out a door that she had helped open didn't encourage this agent to feel much sympathy now.

"I understand," I said, and the invitation was dropped.

I arranged my schedule the following evening to arrive at the funeral chapel at a later time when I expected everyone to have long ago come to pay their respects and gone. Instead, I found the whole gang just coming out of the front of the chapel after an impromptu service where some stood up and put in a good word for the deceased in case he needed one to get him on his way. As much as I was grateful to have avoided that, I was still annoyed that I had to once again face this bunch that I couldn't seem to shake from my life.

The hairdresser that had once told me I'd never be as big as the make-up artist Way Bandy when I got Gilda Radner's booze from the photographer's refrigerator came tumbling out the door first. Actually, he was right about me not being as big as Way Bandy, or Kevyn Aucoin either, but what he failed to note was that it was my choice, that I had found something better, something that brought me joy, while that work never did—nor did these people.

"I stood up in there," relived the hairdresser, "and said 'my name is so-and-so and I am an alcoholic.' No, just kidding."

"Well, that was your first lie," I replied, and had a good chuckle.

As he was protesting my remark, the hairdresser who had done Elizabeth Taylor's hair when I did her make-up for the *Good Housekeeping* cover broke in to inquire where they should eat. A female make-up artist whom I had met before—that I was told had always admired my work—was introduced to me again. I admired her work too, said hello, and abruptly broke away without a suggestion about where they might eat, though I knew the area well.

In the chapel hallway entrance, I passed the grey-haired model with the pristinely sculpted hair—a bit disarranged at the moment—whom I had seen at Helen Gurley Brown's fête for Francesco at the Pierre. She was announcing her grief so loudly to someone on her cell phone that it appeared she intended to be perceived as the most aggrieved person there.

Inside the rather fussy, formal main chapel room on the first floor, with architecture obviously lifted from a church auditorium, people were still buzzing about, perhaps relieved now that an earthly evaluation of the deceased had been sent up. At the front of the room was a closed casket laden with white lilies, perhaps Francesco's favorite flower, or the flower one lays on a casket.

Crammed inside a small vestibule off from the main room was a horde of people surrounding Sean Byrnes, Francesco's partner and studio manager whom he had met on Fire Island in the '70s. Super Chick from my old Arthur disco days—now known as Ann—who had gone on to represent Francesco for a time, greeted me and suggested we get together with as much sincerity as the smile I returned in response. Sean, looking pale, gaunt, much older than I remembered, and strangely like Francesco, saw me in the group and pulled me over.

"I always loved your make-ups," he complimented. "Call me sometime."

I smiled that smile again, having no intention of acknowledging any of these invitations, offered a kind word, and went to the casket. As I stood there looking down on the closed box, thoughts of everyone's mortality roamed my head.

"This is the way the world ends," I heard T.S. Eliot say, as I'd heard it when my friend Valerie died in '86. "Not with a bang but a whimper."

"The mass of men lead lives of quiet desperation," I heard Henry David Thoreau echo.

It was true. Most of us live our lives in desperation, fearful much of the time, alone most of the time, and we die that way. Perhaps it was especially true for Francesco, fighting his demons aggravated by his tortuous mood swings, eventually diagnosed as a bipolar disorder. And in the end, what was it about for all of us? Why had we come? What was the purpose of any of it? Fame? Fortune? I thought that was what it was about for me, but I now knew that was a childish illusion.

I stood there for a moment observing the whiteness and purity of the lilies that covered Francesco's casket, inhaling their aroma.

"Consider the lilies of the field," the Bible said. "Solomon in all his glory was never arrayed like one of these."

We had all considered ourselves important, Francesco and all of us who worked on his photographs, but were any of us as important or the work ever as beautiful as even one of these lilies? And would the fashion world skip even one beat now that most of us were gone?

"Thank you for all your beautiful photographs of my make-ups all these years," I quietly paraphrased Francesco's goodbye to me.

With people still trickling in—while none of the rich and famous that he had photographed throughout his career showed up—I left the group inside chattering in muffled tones, passing in the hallway a woman I had made up for Francesco's '76 book, *Scavullo on Beauty*, and the grey-haired model still on the sidewalk on her cell phone prominently displaying her grief for everyone going and coming.

I don't know what my life would have been had I not ventured onto that yellow brick road. I doubt I would have written a book; I wouldn't have had much to write about. But like Dorothy in *The Wizard of Oz*, I, too, discovered there's no place like home. Home is where the heart is, and I developed a heart along the way like the Tin Man; and like the Lion, I needed a bit of courage to venture out; and I learned a bit of wisdom doing it, like the Scarecrow. Discovering all of these was an inside job. And when I dug down deep inside, there was a Wizard, whom I chose to call God, who was there all the time waiting for me to reach out and ask Him to guide me through the scary forests and witches of life.

On my way back to my apartment, I pondered what my life might have been had I not had an alcoholic father; had he participated in my life instead of yielding to Mother. And the girl I went with at Pratt ... what if I had married her as she'd wanted and Mother hadn't interfered? I broke it off, but we continued our sexual relationship, even after she had married, until we both found the courage to end it. My roommate at Pratt came to my bed to supposedly comfort me from my grief over the girl, and that began my first homosexual affair. I finally told him to leave, which he did, but would I have turned out the way I was had it not been for that? Probably.

I got sick with pneumonia after that affair at Pratt and called Mother from the hospital to tell her about it. I relayed that I was depressed, leaving out most of the details why.

"Well, dear," she had said, "you still have me."

"Yes, Mother ... I still have you."

And so it was through most of it all. She had said when I was born there was a massive fire in town that had burned down an entire block. She said she could see from her hospital bed the orange-red reflection from the fire in the night sky.

"I knew then," she said, "that you were destined for something."

Well, I certainly tried, but it didn't work out as we both had planned. Now I didn't even have her anymore, or Michael, or my career—oh, my fabulous, important career—but I did have me. That was cause for celebration because there was a time when I didn't even have that. The composite of it all had made me what I was, as it makes all of us. Maybe that was inadequate sometimes and even unacceptable, but I did the best I knew how to do. Whatever I was or would be was all I would have in this lifetime, and I blessed it all.

The future?

Well, it will be like all futures—in the future, and I will embrace it, and when it's over, I just want to hear God, or someone, say, "Well done." That's important, I think. Just "well done." No fanfare, fireworks, or drum rolls— just "well done." Maybe that's the most any of us can expect from our lives— not the fame and fortune the child in me once searched for.

Reflecting again on the poem by Henry Wadsworth Longfellow that Mother had suggested for me to say to my graduating class so many years ago:

> Lives of great men all remind us
> We can make our lives sublime,
> And, departing, leave behind us
> Footprints on the sands of time....
>
> Let us, then, be up and doing,
> With a heart for any fate;
> Still achieving, still pursuing,
> Learn to labor and to wait.

My young mind could never have comprehended how long that would take, or the struggle required, leaving even one tiny imprint anywhere; and I was doing it for me anyhow. I learned that life wasn't about me but about my connection with a spiritual power, a higher purpose that I call God. And it wasn't about the achievement but the trip along the way. I did it kicking and screaming at times but life was always patient, waiting for me to calm down before continuing on with the work I had been given.

Since this book was mostly written, I have had heart surgery—a grueling experience, both the surgery and the recovery—and I taught make-up for two years in the Fashion Department at Pratt Institute, my old art school, where it all began. Going back seeing the old buildings, the expansion of new buildings, and the bright, young faces that I taught was like a déjà vu. I had come 360 degrees with all of it. From the bright, young face that I used to be, I had learned to forgive and lighten the baggage that I carried in life. We all did as best as we understood things at the time, and I forgave myself, and others that I had held hostage. I learned that whatever hand we've been dealt in life, whomever and whatever I might want to blame for this or that, it is still my responsibility to play the game—and I stopped my whining. And I now know that if we could contribute even one significant imprint, positively influence even one bright, young mind ... that would be sufficient reason to have come here.

And when we leave?

Some time after my dream about Mother with the dog Big Boy, I had another dream where she came to me while I was asleep and said, "It's time to get up," as she did many times when I had to catch a flight back to New York.

"Oh, Mother," I said, "I'm so sorry if I hurt you."

She ignored this because it didn't matter anymore.

"It's time to go," she said. "Get up."

I did, and I followed her to the door where a great light beamed like a swirling mass of energy. She stopped and turned back to me.

"Not yet," she smiled and kissed me, and disappeared into the mass of light.

I knew the next time she came I would follow her into the light and never look back.

Index